Our Sixties

Our Sixties

An Activist's History

Paul Lauter

UNIVERSITY OF ROCHESTER PRESS

For Doris
"In the Morning, In the Evening, Ain't We Got Fun"
(Ray Egan and Gus Kahn, 1921)

TABLE OF CONTENTS

ACKNOWLEDGMENTS

Many, many friends and colleagues have contributed to this book, so I want to start with the most important: my compañera Doris Friedensohn. Not a single paragraph in this book, indeed not a single sentence, has remained unimproved by her charmed editorial pencil. And that doesn't begin to say anything about her support and encouragement over the many years I've plugged away at this project. Dedicating *Our Sixties* to her is only a tiny gesture of thanks.

The members of my two writing groups have heard or read versions of most of my chapters. They have helped me to refine what I was trying to get at and to revise the prose I placed before them. Thank you to Erica Burleigh, Bettina Carbonell, Susan Harris, and the late Chris Suggs for their intensive reading. And to Marc Bernstein, Joseph Chuman, and Patricia Lefevere for hearing me out on numerous occasions.

Diana Hume George, my sometime buddy at union meetings, edited much of the text and considerably improved it. Alice Kessler-Harris helped me turn what I was doing toward credible social and cultural history, and Rachel Brownstein made the connection for me with the University of Rochester Press—their confidence in what I was doing helped me move forward. Louis Kampf, as he always does, corrected and argued with me about many parts of this story, especially those events on which we had worked together. Tris Farnsworth read and most usefully commented on early chapters, as did Judith Coburn and Trudy Johnson-Lenz. Ellen Schrecker gave me the wisdom of a historian, as we both tried to clarify the story of the New University Conference. Erika Gottfried wonderfully supplemented my own archive and provided very helpful comments. Howard Levy steered me back on course when I went off into rhetoric and, with James Lewes, helped me more fully understand the GI antiwar movement. As a frequent comrade, Claudia Piper helped me to see what our activism aspired to and accomplished. Caryl Ratner shared her knowledge of film in most helpful ways. And Sandy Zagarell, as ever, challenged and improved what I was trying to say.

Trinity College has supported this project both academically and financially, and I am indebted to the college for all its help. My wonderful colleagues in the English Department have assisted and sustained me over the many years it took to complete this work; thank you in particular Chloe Wheatley, Chris Hager, Cindy Butos, David Rosen, Francisco Goldman, Lucy Ferriss, Margaret Grasso, Milla Riggio, Sheila Fisher.

Archivists at Smith, Amherst, the University of Massachusetts/ Amherst, and particularly Trinity helped me a lot. I want to thank Nanci Young and Alex Asal, Blake Spitz and James Kelly, and Rick Ring, Henry Arneth, and others at the Watkinson Library at Trinity College, where my own archive is located.

Dick and Mickey Flacks gave me a model for my own work in their terrific memoir, *Making History / Making Blintzes*. They have also provided much help along the way for me, not to speak of vital friendship and encouragement.

Sonia Kane, the editorial director of the University of Rochester Press, the people she selected to read my manuscript, and her intern, Samantha Vaccaro, have been most supportive; this book is much the better for their criticisms and counsel.

෬   ෬   ෬

Our Sixties was completed, set in type, indexed, and ready to go just before the lethal events of 2020 began. It preceded COVID-19 and its millions of victims; the police murder of George Floyd and the powerful Black Lives Matter demonstrations that have followed; also my personal struggle against the return of lung cancer. Had such events come first, this might have been a different book, one reflecting a world more dramatically fractured than the one I write about here. In the Sixties, we did not perceive our world as irreparably broken. We believed—certainly I did—that we could redirect our society to end white supremacy, militarism, imperial aggression, male dominion, and other forms of illegitimate authority. My fundamental acknowledgment remains to my comrades in the Movement, with whom I worked, from whom I learned, and to whom I owe such virtues as this book may possess.

Chapter One

THE MOVEMENT AND ME

During the 2016 presidential campaign, Americans discovered that one of the major candidates called himself a "socialist." A "democratic socialist," to be sure, but a socialist nonetheless. For many—not all of them on the far Right—the word evoked the Enemy, the Other, Satan, even Stalin. Good grief. How could we have a socialist running for president of capitalist America?

As we entered the 2018 political campaign, many more candidates were calling themselves socialists. And some got elected, too, generally as Democrats.[1] Polls suggest that a majority of Americans no longer pledge allegiance to capitalism. Membership in the Democratic Socialists of America climbs daily. The stars in the Democratic Party firmament, like defeated Congressman Joe Crowley, sink in the east—and in the west, too. Hillary Clinton has disappeared from the screen, displaced by Alexandria Ocasio-Cortez. Even the *New York Times* ran a story on the first page of the *Sunday Review* by Corey Robin explaining how socialist values—he cites "freedom"—differ from capitalism's dominative culture.[2] Bob Dylan's lyrics have once again become relevant: "Something is happening here," Mr. Jones, "but you don't know what it is."[3]

Fifty-some years ago change was also afoot. And Mr. Jones didn't know what was happening then either. Then, we didn't speak of "socialism" but of the "movement." Capacious terms, both could be interpreted differently by different individuals and groups. But always, both spoke change. In the 1960s change meant ending segregation and white supremacy, terminating the war on Vietnam, and eventually combatting sexism, homophobia, and other forms of inequality and conflict.

Today, the push for change takes different names: Black Lives Matter, #MeToo, Coalition to Stop Gun Violence, Red for Ed, Green New

Deal. Speaking change does not require socialist or even identifiably progressive names or programs; indeed, by the time you read this, the name "socialism" might have once again been pushed to the margins of American political discourse. I think not, because what's at stake are the values, like freedom and equality, and the goals—like supporting public schools, ending gerrymandering and other threats to voting rights, and seriously addressing climate change and inequality—for which "socialist" or "progressive" have come to stand. Bernie Sanders, again a candidate for president in 2020, defined "democratic socialism" as "the right to quality health care, the right to as much education as one needs to succeed in our society, the right to a good job that pays a living wage, the right to affordable housing, the right to a secure retirement, and the right to live in a clean environment."[4] That sounds different from the characterization by Eugene Victor Debs—five times the Socialist Party candidate for president—of socialism as "the collective ownership and control of industry and its democratic management in the interest of all the people."

Perhaps this political tendency will be renamed "new socialism." Many prefer "progressive." In any case, today's change agents, whether they call themselves "socialists" or "progressives," are already deeply engaged in transforming America, especially at the local level.[5] Their challenge to the dominant forms of American politics, like that of the social movements of half a century ago, starts from the margins, expressing the hopes and demands of an initially small but dedicated minority. Fifty years back, we movement activists were few; but as our numbers grew and we became many, we brought change into the center of the American social and political world.

That's not an unusual American story. The American Revolution, some have argued, began with a protest carried out by a few score of activists, many dressed as Mohawk people, who tossed 342 chests of tea into the Boston harbor. "No taxation without representation," they proclaimed. The militant effort to end slavery, which flowered as abolitionism, began when activist blacks were joined by radical whites, like William Lloyd Garrison, in demanding immediate and unconditional emancipation. This familiar American story helps explain how a few dozen women and fewer men at a Seneca Falls church in 1848 slowly, over many decades, generated a movement that changed the culture and the laws that kept women subordinate—without the vote in a democracy and without control over their property or children in marriage. None of these revolutions has been completed, needless to say, except the separation of the United States from Britain. But all have involved related processes of change: a marginalized but dedicated minority producing a social and political difference in a divided and often enraged nation. So it was in the sixties and so it is, I want to argue, with today's spreading involvement in a new progressive movement.

The movements of half a century ago, like today's drive for social change, swept up people of many ages and backgrounds, from many walks of life, and many political aspirations. They transformed lives.

Mine included.

I come from an ordinary, middle-class Jewish family, which left Vilna in Lithuania and Sambor in Ukraine late in the nineteenth century, establishing a foothold in New York City's Lower East Side, then in Harlem on 113th street, and later up in the Bronx. The men of the immigrant generation, tailors both, saw their children through high school and into comfortable jobs. They also lost children: my father's brother to an elevator accident and my mother's sister to early cancer. On the other hand, my father's other brother became a billionaire. And the one boy among my mother's siblings always seemed to have two things in mind: chasing women and union jobs in theatrical lighting for himself, his kids, and his nephews—which he obtained. But nothing in my family's history suggested an unusual future for me as a movement activist or a nascent socialist. Indeed, no one in my family attended political meetings of any sort, much less worked for a political party. A neighbor down the hall in our apartment building, a New York judge and weighty Democrat, courted my mother after my father's early death, but that was about as close as we got to politics in any form.

In junior high school, my contribution to a science fair was demonstrating a table-top flame thrower, but I didn't go on to create explosives from fertilizer. Soon after, I had my first exposure to socialism: hearing Norman Thomas argue persuasively against the draft. Like Henry Kissinger, I grew up in Washington Heights, but I did not become a war criminal. Instead, I spent the better part of two decades at or near the epicenter of a social and political movement that shook these United States: I dedicated myself to the drive to terminate our country's war policies. As a child, I thought a black man's color would come off when we shook hands. As an adult, I got busted for helping to rewrite my nation's racial script. Like most boys, I hated dishwashing, bed-making, peeling potatoes, and other "women's work." But in the sixties and seventies I was often the only man at feminist meetings. When I first started working for the Quakers in 1963, I modeled the frustration and self-pity of a glum student of great poetry, exclusively by white men of course, except for Emily Dickinson. By the end of the decade I had shed my academic skin and emerged, a little scratched up, as a movement activist and regular contributor to the period's most interesting journal, the *New York Review of Books*. And the texts I was reading led me far beyond my literary education or my vague liberalism.

How did these changes—social and personal—come about? This book attempts to answer that question, and in the process provide insights into how movements, "revolutionary" or otherwise, happen. I also will propose a few things today's activists might adapt from earlier feats and fiascos. The following pages track the processes, vital once again today, by which ordinary people—including a somewhat repressed, raw, and immature fellow like me—found not God or the secret of financial success, but power and rebirth in the sixties movements. I learned, as today's activists are learning, to be effective. In the process, I emerged from the closets in which I tried to hide from desire, from poetry, and from the electricity that animated them.

In these pages, I want to challenge the notion that "the sixties" were an unfortunate aberration, remembered, if at all, for the invention of sex. That's a view widely held by those who slept through the years between Dwight Eisenhower and Gerald Ford, and also by other unfortunates who weren't born until the circus had packed up and moved away. The sixties, I'm going to argue, were good for the country and healthy for people, cats, and other slightly domesticated species. Also, we learned a lot. History doesn't repeat itself either as tragedy or as farce. But when a society has been led into a darkening cave, wisdom lies in taking advantage of such flashes of light as the past offers to us. My life hasn't been extraordinary. But it does provide some illumination for those committed today to changing circumstances we can no longer abide.

A very long time ago, when I first thought of writing this book, two titles suggested themselves: *My Life in the Movement,* and *The Movement in My Life*. Either, or both, seemed suitable because I felt I had not begun to live until I first became involved in "the movement." But what was this movement? I participated in the 1964 Mississippi freedom schools, got arrested in Montgomery during the march from Selma, worked full-time for a number of peace and antiwar organizations, sat in on the terrace of the Pentagon, joined my students in street actions as well as in starting a chapter of Students for a Democratic Society, ran a community school in Washington, helped organize a call urging men to resist the draft, co-founded The Feminist Press, and became statewide vice-president of my teachers' union.

But what, if anything, connected these events, apart from the fact that I and others like me were involved in them? The movement was—like today's progressive activity remains—much more than a catalogue of policies we opposed: racism, war, patriarchy, exploitation, huge disparities of wealth, unrestrained climate change, and the like. It is not a recipe for utopia. Nor is it the sum total of goals we embraced: peace, equality of opportunity, universal health care and housing, one person one vote, government "of the people, by the people, for the people." The movement had to do with people working together, often outside established social and political frameworks, to improve—indeed, transform—the world they found. Like the idea of socialism today, the movement, based on radical principles of equality and people before profits, was a way of implementing fundamental change in that world.

That's all very abstract. And it doesn't explain why someone like James Meredith would march down a highway from Memphis to Jackson all alone as a demonstration against fear. Why someone like Captain Howard Levy would take on years in prison by disobeying military orders to teach Green Berets elementary dermatology—because, he insisted, what little he could show them would be used not to provide real medical care but to recruit villagers in Vietnam to support the American war.[6] Why Fannie Lou Hamer would face firing, eviction, and beating for encouraging neighbors to register to vote. Why others without now-familiar names would leave cushy jobs to work at less-than-minimum wages (or no salary) in some poverty-stricken community rife with addiction. Or camp out for weeks in a city park or refuse food to call out the unjust power of the 1 percent. Or risk their careers by illegally striking in an effort to return adequate funding for children's classrooms. Or fight back against thugs or cops sent to break up a picket line or protest, or to shut down a place where you could peacefully embrace your friend, like Stonewall. People working together. For change.

Movement people played many different roles. Some organized voters to demand that their congressmen cease supporting the Vietnam War. Some assaulted the sensibilities of the bourgeoisie with signs and whistles and chants, as Act Up more recently did in the 1990s.

Others risked their bodies at lunch counters, on interstate busses, on the railroad tracks of troop trains. Others still drew together hundreds, then thousands, then hundreds of thousands of people from all over these states into marches on Washington, or San Francisco, or New York, or the Chicago Democratic National Convention. My own efforts to build organizations that challenged things as they were succeeded sporadically. The New University Conference (NUC), like Students for a Democratic Society (SDS), arose and then sank. But organizations like Resist, The Feminist Press, *Radical Teacher* magazine, and the *Heath Anthology of American Literature*, which I had much to do with starting, persist. In the second decade of the twenty-first century, they still do useful, sometimes transformative work.

Of course, not everyone involved in the movement cared about organizations. I once chaired a fundraiser for *Liberation* magazine focused on various theories about the assassination of John F. Kennedy. When I came to take up the collection, I talked about the importance of sustaining organizations like the magazine. Someone from the audience called out, "we don't want no fuckin' organizations." So it was. Despite my anarchist comrade's disdain for organizations, I maintained my commitment to them. I became a movement administrator, even—hateful word—a bureaucrat. I learned that there are no simple rules for the care and feeding of organizations. Like tropical plants, with too little water, organizations dry up and blow away; with too much water and nourishment, they rot. Organizations do not themselves bring about revolutions, but revolutions do not occur without them. While the sixties movements did not revolutionize the United States, they produced valuable organizations and lasting changes, of which we are properly proud. I will examine them in this book in the hope that the discussion might be useful to those acting for change today.

Looking back on my first three decades, from the last days of Herbert Hoover in 1932 to the first years of JFK in 1961 and 1962, I remember a perfectly ordinary upbringing in the Bronx and Washington Heights, among middle-class, FDR-supporting Jews. I remember as a child actually seeing Franklin D. Roosevelt in the back of a big open car, part of some procession driving down the Grand Concourse in the Bronx. When he died, I was playing outside our apartment house. A terrible silence enveloped the neighborhood like some salty fog.

My parents were distinctive among their middle-class friends, perhaps because my mother worked outside the household through much of the 1930s, mainly at an art and antiques dealer, Leo Elwin and Co. As a result, we had a rounded, drop-leaf eighteenth-century table in the dining room, as well as seven (one missing) early nineteenth-century chairs to go with it. Both my parents wrote shorthand, my mother Pitman and my father, a court stenographer by profession, Gregg. They attended outdoor classical music concerts at Lewisohn Stadium on the nearby campus of City College of New York and had many 78 RPM records with Arturo Toscanini conducting Brahms and Beethoven. Summers they rented a house in Long Beach or more often at some bungalow colony in the Catskills, where I met my first wife, Tris. From the liberal Book Find Club they bought many selections, such as Arthur Miller's *Focus,* Lillian Smith's *Strange Fruit,* and Norman Mailer's *The Naked and the Dead.* A neighbor and colleague of my father's, Joseph Van Gelder, subscribed to the then progressive *New Republic* and shared copies with us after he'd finished reading them. The witty takedowns of politicians in the magazine's "TRB" columns written by Richard Strout shaped my own politics,[7] just as, perhaps, Paul Krugman's columns might form the thinking of liberal young people today.

Reading TRB columns did not underwrite activism in my family, neither in our workplaces nor at school. Occasionally, in displays of rebelliousness, I liked to argue against social studies teachers who criticized socialists and communists, whoever they might have been. The Soviet Union was an ally against Hitler, right? And therefore among the good guys, weren't they? Wasn't FDR meeting with Stalin? What could be wrong about that? As for communists, so far as I knew they were as scarce on the Grand Concourse and 170th Street as Republicans.

The closest I got to political action was shaking my blue-and-white can for the Jewish National Fund at the 171st Street subway entrance. We turned in the cans at the afternoon Hebrew classes, which gave me some doubts. After all, Hebrew classes were a farce: we learned to sound out the letters and words in order to be Bar Mitzvahed, but we never found out what the words meant. Not that the words, even when I later stumbled on an occasional translation, meant anything at all to me. What was I to King David or he to me? Who or what was this god who regularly brought down his wrath on the stiff-necked Hebrews, not to speak of goyim? What relation had these words, in an obscure language that read backward, to the Jews who were my neighbors and relatives? Bar Mitzvah seemed some inevitable ritual, promoted by my father's father. Hebrew school, I complained, left me so little time I would have to stop piano lessons. OK, I'd sacrifice music—a stupidly rebellious decision. Being a Jew mostly remained mysterious. I knew it meant taunts from the scrubby Irish kids at the end of the block and an occasional scuffle. It could have meant death camps had we been living in Europe. Jews ate different foods, I knew, like the little, yellow unfertilized eggs in my grandmother's chicken soup. But what did Jewish identity really mean, I continued to ask well into my career as a teacher and writer?[8] I suffered from occasional outbreaks of this question, but it gave me even less anxiety than my social studies teacher's worry about persuading us to be good anti-communists.

During the war we moved to Manhattan's Washington Heights neighborhood from the Bronx. My father hoped to gain appointment to a remunerative position as a court stenographer in the New York County (Manhattan) Surrogates Court. He'd finished first in the exam for that job, but some rat informed the authorities that he'd been living in the Bronx when he'd taken the test. Though he never said anything to us kids, we came to realize that not getting the appointment became a bitter disappointment in his quiet life. Perhaps his frustration also kept him from talking with me about setting life goals—I never had any and generally took opportunities as they came upon me, or didn't. I think he viewed ambition as an embarrassing motive; certainly I did. He was most deeply committed to my mother's happiness, not to material success. He turned down opportunities to go into business and stayed with court stenography rather than attending law school, though he knew more about the law than most lawyers. My father played an unorthodox though good game of tennis, always beating me and most of his peers. I don't recall any instruction in tennis, nor indeed in any other athletic activity. I became a powerful, though slow swimmer who, in later years, could free dive to sixty feet. But for the most part, I had to find my own way.

My mother, a vivid, active woman who lived to 106, was a terrific dancer—a paradigm of the Charleston. She tried, with only small success, to instruct me. I developed my own style, and too often my own steps, but she was always able to follow my lead, however weird. I came to love dancing, even in my own odd way, though I seldom found as responsive a partner as my mother. In the late 1930s, she was also a fine amateur actress, and turned down an invitation for a screen test because, she apparently thought, taking that road might be troublesome for my father.

Our move to Manhattan—or at least its upper fringe on 186th Street, down the block from Yeshiva University—was precipitated by the family's need for another bedroom to accommodate my two sisters, newly arrived on the scene two years apart. My parents' Bronx bedroom, with its two single beds and his and hers mahogany dressers, could not house a second child's cradle. And it clearly wouldn't do, would it, for an adolescent boy to share a bedroom with two girls.

Subsequently, I commuted to one of New York's great specialized schools, Bronx High School of Science. My own class, January 1949, was the first to be integrated—that is, with girls. I fooled around sexually with boys of my acquaintance, sometimes in the back row at the Hayden Planetarium, and later with a few girls. Math appealed to me; I had even taught my junior high class a couple of times when the sub floundered. At Bronx Science, I began thinking I'd become a physicist, and so went away freshman year to the University of Rochester. I wasn't sufficiently confident to challenge the Jewish quota at Columbia, though I was admitted to the expensive University of Chicago. Nor was I one of those top-drawer A-plus students; I always saw myself, for better and often for worse, as an unassertive A-minus. Rochester possessed a big Navy-funded cyclotron as well as an older machine in the basement of the Physics building. The graduate student I worked for in rebuilding the old cyclotron was interested in radioisotopes for medicine, not Los Alamos for bombs. At Rochester, I was altogether an overweight social misfit: when boys from the main River Campus took the bus in for a mixer at the women's college, I managed to get off at the Eastman School of Music. It never occurred to me that some fraternities were not interested in recruiting guys from New York, much less Jews. I hosted a program on the campus radio station but all I remember about it was mispronouncing Goethe's name. I also tried playing football with guys who had been recruited from WASP high schools and who, a couple of years later, would anchor an undefeated team. Wisely, since I'd never participated in tackle football except in daydreams, the coach didn't give me much playing time. Returning to New York as a sophomore, I finished my undergraduate degree at what we then called NYJew, now better known as NYU. I toyed with majoring in radio and learned to intercut Tchaikovsky's symphonic music into drama. Instead, I did the honors program in English, completing a thesis on the poet E. E. Cummings, which included a bibliography and index to first lines—not the last time I would feel the pull of a library.

Tris and I were to be married, young as we were. In fact, I was so young, still twenty, that *both* of my parents had to appear with me to obtain a license. A girl of eighteen needed only one parent. Tris was an undergraduate at Brooklyn College, and we had a number of friends there, among them a very nice guy named Edward M. Cohen. Eddie was, as I recall, editor of the student newspaper, the *Kingsman.* Only much later did I discover that this student paper had been brought into existence by the college president, the fiercely anti-communist Harry Gideonse. He had smashed the previous somewhat left-leaning student paper, the *Vanguard,*[9] basically for questioning one of his decisions to deny a promotion to a leftist professor. Eddie would go on to a long career in the US Foreign Service. It measures my political innocence that I didn't imagine that there might be connections between his work as editor of Gideonse's new paper and his acceptance in the State Department. Or that his impeccably Jewish name could also work to promote him professionally in Foggy Bottom, then interested in recruiting Jews of suitable politics.

Marriage, in the culture of the early 1950s, meant that I needed a source of income, so I took a teaching associate job at Indiana University. Transferring Tris's credits from Brooklyn to an out-of-town university would be no problem, and she enrolled as an undergraduate. Indiana was one of only two graduate schools foolish enough to give a teaching associate position to someone like me, without a master's degree and grammatically unenlightened. I arrived at the Indiana School of Letters just before my twenty-first birthday in June of 1953, wildly ignorant of the literature taken for granted by the faculty and most of my fellow students. Ironically, my unfamiliarity with what T. S. Eliot—still a looming presence in 1953 literary circles—called "the whole of the literature of Europe from Homer and within it the whole of the literature of his own country" (from the essay "Tradition and the Individual Talent") would ultimately prove advantageous. I had absorbed none of the conventional loyalty to "the tradition"—what was Tennyson to me or I to Tennyson?—so I could more easily, in time, transform myself into a man who helped to overthrow the prevailing literary canon.

The School of Letters was the most prominent institute for literary criticism in 1950s America. Every summer, half a dozen cutting-edge critics like John Crowe Ransom, Irving Howe, Alfred Kazin, Leslie Fiedler, R. P. Blackmur (aka, "Boston Blackie," according to Fiedler), Cleanth Brooks, and William Empson came to teach an intense six-week course and to deliver an influential lecture. I studied with Fiedler, Brooks, and Empson, though none of them supervised my long master's thesis, "Walt Whitman, Comrade and Lover." It was one of the first serious efforts to link Whitman's sexuality—especially as revealed in his manuscripts at the Library of Congress and at the New York Public Library's Berg Collection—and his poetry.[10] I learned close reading of poetry from the first four weeks of Mr. Brooks's course. The last two weeks, taught by the poet Delmore Schwartz, showed me how different it might be to approach a literary text through the politics of its time. Writing for Schwartz on Andrew Marvell's "The Mower Against Gardens," I learned more than I ever wanted to know about the differences between English and French garden styles—and also what I did need to know about what made working men like mowers hostile to gardens and their proprietors.[11]

At Indiana, I also took a course with the poet Robert Lowell entitled "Some French Poets and Rilke." We read Pernette du Guillet and Maurice Scève as well as Charles Baudelaire and Arthur Rimbaud. My paper for the course compared translations of Rimbaud's "Le bateau ivre"; I even ventured my own versions of a few stanzas. Lowell read French alexandrines as if he were chanting his own English blank verse. His eyes nervously jumped about, never seeming to settle on the text or person before him. When I showed him some of the poems I had been writing, he smiled and said "good efforts." I haven't written more than four or five stanzas since.

My wife, Tris, did so well as an undergraduate history major at Indiana that her mentor, Robert Ferrell, insisted she pursue a PhD at Yale, his doctoral university. Her fellowship helped open the way for me to also come to Yale, where I hurried through a year of graduate courses, and another fifteen months working on my dissertation on Emerson's rhetoric. The English Department at Dartmouth, where I got my first full-time job in 1957, was outfitted with an IBM Executive typewriter, complete with proportional spacing, on which I was able to produce a handsome text, with carbon copies, for what I thought would be the first third of my dissertation. My advisor, Charles Feidelson, responded to the 214 pages with a note congratulating me for having finished. "But I haven't," I wrote back, "that was only the first third; I intend to go on to Thoreau and my goal, Melville." "No," he responded, "we don't want any more of these two-volume, 700-page dissertations like Harold [Bloom]'s." Suddenly, I was no longer a student. I needed to make arrangements for my parents to come to New

Haven to see me off to adulthood. At my rainy commencement, they were relegated to the gym; I was among the doctoral candidates in Woolsey Hall who missed our cue, in Latin, to stand and receive our degrees. It didn't matter.

Meanwhile, in Hanover, New Hampshire, Tris rapidly completed her own dissertation on William C. Bullitt, the first American ambassador to the Soviet Union. While scholarly projects had become a norm in our household, Tris was also intent on becoming a mother. After her worrisome miscarriage, we systematically focused our efforts on conceiving kids; my role was to return from class or my Sanborn House office at whatever time her thermometer told her she might be fertile. Tris gave birth to our two sons, David and Daniel, eleven months apart at Mary Hitchcock Hospital. At the time, I didn't begin to appreciate how extraordinary it was for her to complete a dissertation and give birth twice within a period of two years. I did much of the cooking, and our second baby, Daniel, was generally my responsibility, especially when he was cranky in the wee hours. A few years later, Tris would publish the dissertation[12] and later go on to a career as a Russian historian[13] and a professor at Wells College. In the 1950s neither of us would have been familiar with the word *feminism*, but like others, we'd begun implementing a few of its practices.

Leaving Hanover, we moved to the University of Massachusetts, where I taught for one disastrous year, 1959–60. Then, after I'd been fired—maybe, as I would always suspect, for union and anti-ROTC activities—we continued on to Hobart and William Smith Colleges in Geneva, New York. Two things are worth noting about that time: "we" moved, but in fact, I moved and took with me Tris and the kids, David and Daniel, not to speak of Sir Andrew Aguecheek, our charming collie. "We" never considered the possibility—it was, after all, even before *The Feminine Mystique*—of Tris seeking a full-time position in a college history department, as she later did. What shape might our lives have taken had we entertained that possibility? Our conventional upbringing, one that the movement would later unsettle, made it all but impossible for us, or at least for me, to entertain such an idea. Besides, as Tris put it, she had a one-year-old and an infant to think about, not a new job. In fact, I had pulled her away from the community she had enjoyed in Hanover. She dumped me a few years later, so maybe such unilateral choices rankled . . . or maybe not, as she later asserted to me.

The choice to leave Dartmouth for the University of Massachusetts was partly the result of my discomfort—what a pusillanimous word—of being a New York Jew-boy in Hanover, New Hampshire, circa 1958. At Dartmouth, I helped my pacifist graduate-school buddy, Allan Brick, post flyers proposing that "men of draft age" might be interested in becoming conscientious objectors. Allan, as a conscientious objector during the Korean War, had spent two years of alternative service teaching in a girl's reformatory.[14] He was a large man, like a college football guard, and projected a well-developed sense of himself as empowered, authorized to press forward to bring about peaceful change, most of all in America's foreign policy. We also brought A. J. Muste, one of the most radical peace activists of the time, to speak to a largely hostile audience. In response to a rumor that some fraternity guys were coming armed with rotten fruit and vegetables, we seated wives and children in the first two rows of the small auditorium. Fortunately, Muste was more than capable of defanging his opponents. Here was this old guy, skinny as Gandhi, empathetic, analytic—a master teacher about the Cold War, the nuclear standoff, and our students' indistinct futures. Whatever the students made of his talk, I learned a lot.

The Korean War had started promptly on my eighteenth birthday. While the army portrayed by Norman Mailer and James Jones appalled and frightened me, I'd never heard of conscientious objectors before I met Allan, much less thought of applying to be one. I lacked the Methodist and Quaker grounding that informed his life decisions. In the draft, I'd come up IV-F (not suitable for service), probably because when I'd taken my physical in Indiana, among the many farm boys, I mentioned in the interview having sex with other guys back before high school. So much for me, the psychiatrist apparently concluded, and no loss. For Allan, as for Muste, nonviolence was a way of life; for me, it became an interesting aspiration, which would thread through my subsequent experience. My politics, such as they were, were mainly formed by rebelliousness.

I did display a defiant streak toward authority, like an occasionally flashing red light. Back in Junior High School 117, on the day I was to take the exam for Bronx Science, I had called the vice-principal a "Hitler," because he had, unfairly I thought, consigned our whole class to detention for some whispering during a class change. At Indiana, I started a fight with a guy in the dining hall who had made some anti-Semitic crack. I had a temper, I was told.

At UMass, during the one year I taught there, I tried directing these critical energies to useful ends. I joined the teachers' union, a small and youthful operation. It had been organized largely by Sid

Kaplan, whose essential work on African-American culture and history I then knew nothing about, and Jules Chametzky, an active lefty and a pioneer in the study of Jewish-American writers. Then in November my father died and I stayed in New York for three days to sit shiva. When I returned, the acting "head" of the department, a certain Vernon Helming, explained that my pay would be docked since I had accumulated only two days of leave. I vigorously protested up and down the halls of the administration building, especially because the amount they docked me[15]—more than a full day's pay—put our family in serious debt. Shortly thereafter, a group of students began a campaign to remove ROTC from the UMass campus. I wrote to the student newspaper, which had editorially supported them, suggesting mildly that two articles in the *Nation* by Allan Brick and Gene M. Lyons criticizing ROTC might be of interest.[16] I had already begun writing for journals of opinion—the *Nation*, the *New Republic*, and most of all, the *New Leader*—and a letter to the student paper editor seemed perfectly in keeping with such activity.

Then, early in 1960, when the local branch of the Committee for a Sane Nuclear Policy (SANE) leafleted Amherst's showings of the movie *On the Beach* (1959), I experienced for the first time the anxieties and pleasures of handing political tracts to friends and neighbors—and perhaps to one's bosses. SANE had been formed in 1957 by a number of prominent liberals worried by the increasing reliance of American military leaders on nuclear weapons. They characterized policies like "mutually assured destruction" as literally MAD, and organized to support treaties banning nuclear tests and reducing deployment of nuclear weapons, which threatened the future of human life on the planet. Leafleting at *On the Beach*, a movie about the end of civilization, constituted some sort of breakthrough for me—call it a political coming out, a transition from reading and talking with one's friends, or even signing some petition. Experienced activists often forget that moment of change, when the butterfly emerges from its cocoon, and one sees oneself reflected differently in the eyes of the unknown neighbor receiving the leaflet—"Dr. Spock Is Worried"—from your hand. No more hiding, no more temporizing, no more going back. You are now public and, if not transformed, certainly changed in ways that signify as much as holy water sprinkled on one's head, or the holy scroll carried in festive procession round the shul or synagogue.

It never occurred to me that these doings—leafleting, writing to the paper, angrily questioning administrators—were risky for a brash, untenured instructor. In any event, I was fired. Within a year I was on the move again, this time to upstate New York. Apart from my freshman year in Rochester, I knew about the area only Nicole's comments about Dick Diver's dreary final abode in F. Scott Fitzgerald's *Tender Is the Night*: "She looked up Geneva in an atlas and found it was in the heart of the Finger Lakes Section and considered a pleasant place."[17]

I was writing regularly for the *New Leader*, although I was not particularly interested in its liberal and anti-Stalinist politics. Strange as that may now sound, I was largely unaware of the journal's political history, featuring skirmishes among Schachtmanites, Lovestoneites, Cannonites, and the like. What I wanted was an outlet for writing about books, such as Vladimir Nabokov's *Lolita* (I wrote one of the first reviews), Christiane Rochefort's *Warrior's Rest*, E. E. Cummings, as well as Emily Dickinson and Henry David Thoreau, and Jewish authors like Karl Shapiro and Isaac Bashevis Singer. I was not a red-diaper baby and I knew very little about domestic Cold War conflicts and the varieties of sectarian left and liberal political positions. I found all that dreary. A year or two later I would write a nasty review of M. Stanton Evans's silly right-wing book about campus "unrest," a then largely imaginary creature, but mostly I stuck to literature that occasionally edged over into my still conventional politics.

One of my few encounters with serious political matters had occurred when I was a green freshman at Rochester sometime in 1950 or '51. I had gone to hear Ted Poston, a black reporter for the then progressive *New York Post*, speak about the "Little Scottsboro" case, an unbelievably gross assault on the rights and lives of four young black men in Groveland, Florida.[18] I went, despite having no black friends or even acquaintances, and knowing no black writers and nothing about African-American history. Black music, especially Bop—Bird, Dizzy, Monk—I *loved*; when I lived at home with my parents, I listened to Symphony Sid, New York's main jazz DJ, under the covers of my bed. I went to clubs like the Royal Roost and Birdland. Later, I would wear my one-button lounge, knee-length blue jacket and yellow angle-zippered shirt to the opening of Bop City in New York. But that world, for me, ironically remained separate from "politics."

Poston was a terrific narrator who moved and angered many in that largely white audience. A few, myself included, joined the NAACP on the spot. Later, I told my parents what I had done. While they were hardly unsympathetic to the NAACP's work on the case, my mother worried that by joining such an organization I might have jeopardized my father's job as a stenographer in the NY State Supreme Court. At the time, her reaction seemed exaggerated; it did not make any deep impact on me. She later insisted that the Rosenbergs lived down the street from us, which may or may not have been the case. But such was the paranoia and anxiety on which Cold War culture fed. One never knew. Only later, when one of my teachers at New York University, Edwin Berry Burgum, was fired for being a communist, did I begin to appreciate the dangerous Cold War shoals that my mother had perceived. Even so, I signed many of the dozens of petitions supporting the effort to reinstate Burgum. Later, at Indiana, I played a tiny role in the Green Feather Movement, which had been organized to protest efforts by a member of the Indiana school textbook commission to ban "subversive" writings like *Robin Hood*. We passed out what were said to be asbestos bookmarks with the message "They're your books; don't let them burn them." Despite these gestures, politics was a footnote on my agenda in those early years of my career.

I might have gone along with the program, stayed at Hobart, worked to elect Johnson and Humphrey just as I had worked for Kennedy, and become an upstanding professor of English. But I was lucky: my wife dumped me. It was no fun at the time, of course. She was engaged in an affair with a guy in the History Department; rejected, I was shattered. I remember her going off one afternoon, not very far away: I sat in a comfortable chair in our living room contemplating a handful of sleeping pills. Then I swallowed them. My next recollection, in a hospital, was my own strange-sounding voice saying politely but insistently to a nurse, "Please let me die." Clearly, I had to get out of that small town. At that point Allan Brick, who had moved on to Goucher College, proposed that I become the director of peace studies at the American Friends Service Committee (AFSC) in Philadelphia. I knew hardly anything about the AFSC, and even less about how they defined "peace studies," except that they published and distributed a series of pamphlets called "Beyond Deterrence." What else might emerge remained to be seen. And here, I think, my movement story begins.

But leaving it at that suggests that "the movement" of the sixties, which I was joining there in Philadelphia in 1963, should be seen primarily as an autobiographical phenomenon, related to my personal growth. It was that, to be sure, and this book participates in the conventions of a personal chronicle. But more to the point, the movement would come to transform my understanding of education and work, and therefore of politics. Of course, education develops and transmits important skills. But the real issue, I began to see, was how such skills and the experiences from which they derived help us transform the institutions of our society: to bring about not a utopia, perhaps, but a "better world in birth," as a song I would soon learn had it. A world, that is, free from such terrors as the Holocaust, the atomic bombing of Hiroshima and Nagasaki, and events like those at Scottsboro, Alabama, and Groveland, Florida, not to mention those arriving every day in the twenty-first century. My experience of the movement was not about me as an individual but about how I became part of a collective effort to bring about a just and peaceful world.

Such words as "just," "peaceful," and even "collective" always make me nervous. They evoke for me Ernest Hemingway's famous remark in *A Farewell to Arms* about how abstractions are "obscene" beside "the concrete names of villages" and the numbers of roads and regiments. Yet, we need such words and the goals that they evoke. In a just and peaceful world—let's say a new socialist, progressive world—a few dozen men would not be able to hoard wealth equal to that possessed by some 80 percent of the globe's population. Rich and powerful regimes could not use bombs and drones to impose their will on others. Opportunity would depend not on the color of one's skin, the configuration of one's genitals, or even the accident of one's birthplace but, as Dr. Martin Luther King Jr. put it, on the content of one's character. Education would provide not opportunities for profit but a primary path to an individual's and a society's future. Citing the work of Patricia Robinson, Patricia Haden, and Donna Middleton, Robin D. G. Kelley writes that these women "saw education as a vehicle for collective transformation and an incubator of knowledge, not a path to upward mobility and material wealth."[19]

Kelley's words capture how I came to think about my work as a teacher. From the American Friends Service Committee in Philadelphia, and then most powerfully from the Mississippi freedom schools of summer 1964, I learned very different lessons about education from the ones I'd been taught quite well at NYU, Indiana, and Yale. My years at those universities did, happily, set me on the road to material well-being. But the education I will chronicle here endeavored, in the words of Aeschylus, to "tame the savageness of man and make gentle the life of this world." While those goals elude us in the America of

2020, *la lucha continua*. Today's renewed interest in socialism as a democratic aspiration encourages me.

Still, a fundamental anomaly has always shaped my experience of the movement. An atheist Jew, I worked at the American Friends Service Committee for people whose activities expressed deep religious values. For the Student Nonviolent Coordinating Committee (SNCC), I was a white guy committed to assisting black activism. When I joined Students for a Democratic Society (SDS), I was already a professor. At meetings of early women's groups like The Feminist Press, I was often the only man. I ran the United States Servicemen's Fund though I'd never been in the army. Ironically, perhaps, again as a Jew, I found myself at home in academic organizations, however much they were WASP enclaves. My anomalous position in movement venues made me a bit shy about expressing my opinions too directly. Often it seemed best to keep my views to myself. In the movement it was always a question of who had the right to speak, much less to interrupt. The answer had generally to do with identity—how well you fit into the group. Too often, I didn't.

Besides, for a long time after I became active, I felt ignorant. And I was. So many comrades and friends seemed born into socialism, teethed at left-wing summer camps, confirmed by Pete Seeger; they now studied or taught politics, sociology, and tomorrow's history. What did I know? I read poetry. As my readers will see from my many quotations, poetry continued to be a central element of my political practice. I well remember a meeting of the New University Conference Steering Committee in 1969, at which I first realized I could analyze the politics of that moment as well as others in the group to whom, over years, I'd been particularly attentive. In a room which suddenly seemed bright and comfortable I could speak, not with great authority, perhaps, but not burdened by doubts. All the same, certainly in my own eyes, I never became a movement "heavy." Like Eliot's "Prufrock," I was not "Prince Hamlet, nor was meant to be": neither, however, was I an "easy tool" swelling "a progress." But I had come a long way from passing out SANE leaflets at *On the Beach* in Amherst. This is a report, then, of an ordinary participant learning to carry out the progressive values of the sixties movements for change.

Over the years, I've carried around a symbol of my changing life. One evening when we were together, a woman who was important to me gave me a present: a small, balsa wood model of the kind of hill that leaps up from the waters of Ha Long Bay in Vietnam or the coast of Iceland. Grey, like rock, this hill is filled with small crevices that, in a full-sized promontory, might serve as puffin nests. My hill is surprisingly light, about five inches high and six or eight around the base. A white-and-black gull perches on top, a very plain gull, wings outspread in flight. Mary didn't need to explain the symbolism of her gift. Over the years, as I've carried my balsa hill from place to place, I've added a couple of smaller birds. It now resides atop a small bookcase dedicated to critical works about the changing features of "American literature." It continues to speak to me about flying.

About this book: first, almost everything in it derives from my direct experience or observation. I've read many accounts of the sixties—histories, memoirs, biographies, statistical analyses. There's more I did not look at or don't know about, enough to occupy me for what remains of my waking life. Writing for the *New York Review of Books*, I learned from Bob Silvers not to clutter my text with obsessive references to others' work, as we scholars tend to do. On the other hand, he instructed me to substantiate my conclusions with comprehensive notes. That's what I've done here.

Also, I've tried to avoid powdering over the flaws easily observable in the person I was in the fifties and sixties. I shared, if precariously, the attitudes of Cold War America and of my male friends: anti-communist, chauvinist, racially uninformed. But this book is about change—in the society and culture and, of course, in the narrator. The person who emerged from the sixties differs from the fellow who stumbled into them. And that's my point. It provides me with a reason for adding to the colossal library about the sixties. Besides, as an academic as well as an American activist, I was encouraged by Benjamin Franklin's justification for writing:

> Hereby, too, I shall indulge the Inclination so natural in old Men, to be talking of themselves and their own past Actions, and I shall indulge it, without being troublesome to others who thro' respect to Age might think themselves oblig'd to give me a Hearing, since this may be read or not as any one pleases.[20]

I'll leave it at that.

Except: just in case you thought the title referred to my age, I must tell you that, as I write this revision, I am eighty-seven years, three months, three days, and some hours old. So.

Chapter Two

AMONG FRIENDS IN PHILLY

How does a budding professor turn into a blooming revolutionary? In late summer 1963, as a bedraggled thirty-something who had just lost his marriage and stepped out of his job, I moved from a town in upstate New York, Geneva, to the big city, or a big city, anyway: Philadelphia. The following summer, I played a small part in one of the most influential projects the civil rights movement carried out, Mississippi Summer. This chapter concerns the beginnings of my conversion from academic to activist. Conversions don't generally resemble the apostle Paul's, struck by the hand of God on the road to Damascus. Rather, they happen slowly, provoked by small revelations, fresh insights, and friendly guidance; inspired by new pleasures, some of the body, some of the eyes and ears, others of the heart and mind. Or so I found it to be.

One evening that fall of 1963, I maneuvered my car into its alleyway garage and returned to my tiny Center City, Philadelphia, apartment from a late date. I knew I'd find a few people from Students for a Democratic Society camped out in my apartment. I'd been in the front row at the Academy of Music with a new friend, Helen Vendler, who was teaching at Swarthmore, to hear Eugene Ormandy conduct Brahms's smiling Second Symphony. Helen and I would both begin teaching at Smith College the following fall, and someone there had suggested that we might want to meet. An inspired proposal. One of the cleverest people I'd ever met, Helen loved conversation, better even than I had come to love Bassetts ice cream. Divorced from her former husband, Zeno, a philosopher, she lived with her child in suburban Philadelphia. She was certainly lonesome and welcomed talk and play. She had had an intense but, I thought, narrow education at Emmanuel, a Catholic women's college in Boston. Poetry was the food of her intellect; music existed only at the fringes. I recall some time later when I took her to a concert in Amherst being surprised that she had never heard my favorite, Mendelssohn's Octet. I'm sure I amused her with my fragmentary pacifism. She doubtless found it peculiar when I appeared for a date one evening announcing that, for some forgotten purpose, I was fasting that day. She wondered how that would affect her dinner or any other evening adventure. "Not at all," I reassured her.

Helen threw off inventive ideas about poetry like sparks in any conversation—about food, teaching, desire, raising a child, living in suburban Philly. I thought she was already, in her young career, a peer of the intellectuals with whom I had studied at the Indiana School of Letters. In time, she became one of our most notable literary critics. But I was launched there in Philadelphia, and even more so the following year in Northampton, on a trajectory that would carry me quite far from her world of literary criticism. A decade and more later, when I returned to the study of writers and books, armed with urgencies and skills from the movement, I had become determined to challenge the standards of literary history and the received accounts of what our culture told us about what we ought to value, teach, and learn. In brief, that is the personal story recounted in this book: how a naive and floundering fellow in a tiny Spruce Street apartment in Center City, Philadelphia, came, through the agency of the sixties movement, to take leadership in reconstructing the great house of American literary study.

Two small rooms constituted my second-floor apartment. The one in the rear contained a single bed and a small wooden dresser; the other, in front, held a couple of folding chairs and my grandmother's square, red, metal-topped table, which I set against the wall adjacent to a pullman-style stove and fridge. Somewhere, perhaps atop the dresser, I'd placed a record player. I remember it not at all, but I know that I bought *The Freewheelin' Bob Dylan* and listened often to "Don't Think Twice, It's All Right":

> An' it ain't no use in turnin' on your light, babe
> I'm on the dark side of the road.

The song captured how I usually felt, alone and gloomy in my apartment. Such song lyrics as I knew—not exactly popular ones, like those of Tom Lehrer—shared a kind of fifties mirth:

Since I still appreciate you,
Let's find love while we may.
Because I know I'll hate you
When you are old and gray.

But I wasn't finding much to be amused about those first months in Philly, so Dylan felt more suitable to my lonely sulks.

The back window of my apartment overlooked a modest yard, with a pear tree from which I would derive much consolation, especially when it blossomed in the spring. I had rented the place only after the real estate agent, exasperated by my hesitancy over the dozen flats I'd seen, asked, "Do you really want an apartment?" This one had the advantage of a garage in a nearby alleyway where I could stash my Corvair convertible, white with red leather seats. "Lost a wife, got a convertible," as my shrink had put it.

I had come to work as the director of "peace studies" for the American Friends Service Committee (AFSC). Mostly, we published and distributed a series of pamphlets called "Beyond Deterrence," well-written if somewhat academic efforts to propose new directions for US foreign policy in general and the problems presented by nuclear weapons in particular. To run this program I'd moved to Quaker Philadelphia. On this November 1963 evening, when I tiptoed in from my late date with Helen, I found a dozen people tucked into sleeping bags distributed across the floor. They had come to Philadelphia to attend a meeting of SDS, Students for a Democratic Society. I had learned about SDS only a few weeks before when I visited three of its founders, Dick and Mickey (Miriam) Flacks and Tom Hayden, in Ann Arbor. They hoped I would publish the SDS founding statement, adopted at a meeting in Port Huron, Michigan, and named after that place. Perhaps it could be part of my AFSC series, or distributed as a separate pamphlet, as we had done with A. J. Muste's influential "Speak Truth to Power."

Dick and Mickey have remained close friends over these fifty-some years, through much travel, my three wives, and many, many jobs. Their joint memoir, *Making History / Making Blintzes*, helped inspire my efforts here.[1] Hayden, with his prominent nose, struck me as oddly homely in the way of some Irish politicians. But many women have told me over the years that he seemed to them quite sexy; certainly he had relationships with some of the most beautiful women I'd ever met, Sandra Cason and Jane Fonda, for example. Clearly, I was missing something. I wasn't missing his rhetorical skill: he could persuade a

fire hydrant to change places with a telephone pole. Hayden's beau-
tifully shaped arguments often began quietly, without flash, without
calling attention to the speaker himself, and in language that his audience actually spoke. You were persuaded before you noticed how he
had moved you from F to V. The "Port Huron Statement," for which
Hayden wrote the initial draft, offered a cogent and far-reaching analysis of American society, though not one particularly well-suited to the
framework of my "Beyond Deterrence" series. It drew together questions of racism, poverty, foreign affairs, education, and other policy
issues which, at that moment, pundits generally held to be *separate* concerns. "Beyond Deterrence" wasn't calculated to examine how nuclear
bombs, Jim Crow, and universities might be related, much less how to
organize a radical challenge to established power. But the "Port Huron
Statement" did provide such an analysis, together with ideas about
shaping a program for change.

The same pundits today, or rather their spiritual heirs, would likewise argue for the separation of politically charged questions: what has
Black Lives Matter to do with #MeToo, much less with the rights of
Palestinians? A major part of Hayden's genius was to draw together the
issues that troubled young people in particular in the early sixties. That
helped account for the appeal of the "Port Huron Statement." Defend-
ers of the status quo seldom seem to see how the operations of what, in
1967, we came to call "illegitimate authority" in one political domain
engage opposition in what seem to them quite different realms. The
common threads are power and its corruptions. For example, black
activists in Mississippi in 1965, confronted with pervasive racism, would
come to question the racist roots of American policy in Vietnam.
Attempts today by billionaires to impose ill-grounded "reforms" on
American schoolchildren lead students, teachers, and parents to question the legitimacy of moneyed power itself—a key element of socialist
thought. To question what overweening policemen do with guns readily leads into questioning what arrogant nations do with drones and
jets. Power corrupts—yes. Great power corrupts greatly—yes. Learning
to question the corruptions of power is learning to combat all forms of
"illegitimate authority."

Hayden believed that some complex interaction of radical action,
such as Mississippi Summer in 1964 or the demonstrations at the 1968
Democratic National Convention in Chicago, and possible changes
fostered within the Democratic Party itself could transform American politics. Direct action on campuses across the nation, in local

communities, or in the streets of Chicago would pressure those with decision-making authority—deans, senators, mayors, presidents—to bend policy toward progressive goals. Perhaps. Like most Americans, up until this point in my life, I had figured that politics mostly consisted of presidential campaigns every four years; I had been half of Citizens for Kennedy in Geneva, New York, in the 1960 election, and I was proud that we had won the city for the Democratic nominee for the first time in almost thirty years. But in 1963, I had not begun to think through the political issues addressed in the "Port Huron Statement."

During the Cuban missile crisis, I had spent many hours curled up on a daybed in the vestibule of our Geneva bedroom—in despair. The military base across Seneca Lake was said to be a depot of nukes and therefore an immediate target. At any moment, I expected to be vaporized in a nuclear attack.

> We will all go together when we go.
> All suffuse with an incandescent glow.
>   (Tom Lehrer, "We Will All Go Together When We Go")

Only the trauma of being discarded by my wife, which had precipitated me out of my academic appointment and into the AFSC job and my Spruce Street apartment in Philly, forced me to begin reconsidering what "politics" might mean.

I knew, or thought I knew, why "Doctor Spock is Worried," to quote the famous Committee for a Sane Nuclear Policy ad of that time; that was, after all, my job. SANE was a secular organization, its rationale rooted not in a moral peace "testimony" like AFSC, but in the understanding, expressed in its name, that American nuclear war policy was *in*sane. By no means politically radical, SANE tried to present itself as a rational adult speaking to difficult but extremely powerful children. Dr. Benjamin Spock, famous for his *Common Sense Book of Baby and Child Care,* had told parents that they were well-enough informed to make sane decisions about their children's upbringing. Calming an angry or needy two-year-old was as hard as changing the ideas of those committed to "mutually assured destruction," MAD, as American nuclear policy was designated. Like most parents, I could understand where people in SANE were coming from.

But JFK and his administration eluded me. Like many of my students at Hobart, I had felt engaged by Kennedy's vision of a Peace Corps and appreciated his liberal mandate, "ask not what your country can do for you, but what you can do for your country." But then, why had he brought the world to the doorstep of nuclear holocaust? Why had he failed to protect civil rights demonstrators against "Bull" Connor, Birmingham's chief of "public safety"? Why was he getting the country bogged down in Vietnam, a faraway and unknown place that surely was no threat to us? More and more it occurred to me that what I could do for my country was to oppose his policies. Why then had I actually campaigned for Kennedy? What had the politics of opposition to do with the traditions of humane letters and the analysis of literary texts I had been teaching? I had many, too many, questions, echoed back to me in the lyrics of Bob Dylan's popular song:

> Yes, 'n' how many times must the cannonballs fly
> Before they're forever banned?
> > (Bob Dylan, "Blowin' in the Wind")

I was pretty confused.

The SDS people like Tom Hayden and the Flackses seemed confident that they could develop answers to such dilemmas. Their socialist orientation would in any event provide them with the ability to formulate coherent questions. In practice, few activists of the sixties consistently pursued so hopeful a program both within and outside of the Democratic Party as Hayden. I always wished him well, but I could not join in either his romance with or his rage at the Democrats. Nationally, they came to seem like a machine for producing disillusion, which is what I mostly felt in the aftermath of my Citizens for Kennedy experience.

What I thought about SDS was initially shaped by my gratitude that no one among the group scattered across the floor of my Philadelphia apartment had preempted my bed. I learned very little more about SDS that weekend. The leaders, many of whom were camped out in my place, were engaged in an absorbing internal debate. Some wanted to build on-campus chapters that would mobilize students around issues of war, the draft, disarmament, segregation, and the general campus detachment from politics. The university, as presented in the "Port Huron Statement," was a site where young people, who would create the future, could "see the political, social and economic sources of their private troubles and organize to change society."

Others in SDS were just beginning to implement a program called Economic Research and Action Project (ERAP), designed to place college students in poor communities like those in Newark, Baltimore, Cleveland, and Chicago.[2] Their goals: organize residents to press for local changes—everything from traffic lights to opposing police brutality—as well as more fundamental reforms like a guaranteed annual income. These strategies for change differed—that was obvious enough. But the implications of these differing ideas, in terms of politics or personal activity, remained quite murky to me. By 1964, after months of movement participation, I became active in Students for a Democratic Society, though I had gotten my PhD in 1958 and clearly no longer qualified as a "student." Then again, I had begun studying what I had never learned in school: how the American system worked, in politics, economics, and society. But for now, in Philadelphia, fall 1963, I busily tried to figure out what I was supposed to do as director of peace studies, apart from finding venues for selling our AFSC pamphlets and listening gloomily to "Hard Rain."

My assistant director at the AFSC was Martin Oppenheimer, a sociologist. His intellectual and political work prepared him more fully than mine to implement peace studies.[3] Marty's immediate family had managed to get out of Nazi Germany with him just in time; most of his other relatives were murdered in the Holocaust. He had been active in the Socialist Party, as well as in a number of left political sects, and also in the Congress of Racial Equality (CORE). Thin and restless of manner, he brought real experience in organizing and in direct, nonviolent action to our program. With George Lakey he would shortly publish a book, *A Manual for Direct Action*,[4] which explained how to implement nonviolent political campaigns. My credentials, such as they were, consisted of a PhD in English from a fancy university and full-time teaching jobs at three reputable colleges.

Early on, at Hobart, I had also organized what might have been the first academic conference on nonviolence at an American college. The process of putting the conference together certainly tested my commitment to nonviolence. I had invited a sociologist, Irving Louis Horowitz, to work with me on developing the program and, presumably, the book that might emerge from the meeting. In Horowitz I encountered for the first time an academic whose act was that of a hoodlum. What was his take on nonviolence? I could imagine him baiting the participants just for kicks. I had been given a budget and naively struggled to stay within it. Horowitz had a different view. Hobart, he decided, could well afford whatever we needed to spend to bring off a conference on a topic made urgent by the ongoing sit-ins and freedom rides of the southern civil rights movement. So he spent lavishly and left it to me to explain our mounting expenses to the administration. Fortunately, I had already made most of the initial contacts with possible speakers, activists like David McReynolds, academics like political scientist Mulford Q. Sibley, and those who did both, like Staughton Lynd. We all knew about nonviolence as activism; at the conference many of us learned for the first time about its long history, its connections to earlier movements for change like abolitionism, and its built-in philosophical conflicts. A book emerged from the contributions to the panels, which I co-edited with James Crouthamel (a historian at Hobart), but it was never published.[5] In the larger scheme of things, organizing the conference prepared me for whatever the AFSC might have had in mind for peace studies, especially because it enabled me to think about the social and intellectual space where activism and higher education intersected. This was the terrain I was learning to occupy.

It took some time after I had settled into my Philadelphia apartment to define a program involving pacifism and the academy. Marty came to work every day full of ideas about what we might do. But I remained perplexed. Then one morning as I was shaving, I asked myself: What does he think about while *he* shaves? I knew what constituted my nagging thoughts: What had I done wrong to precipitate my wife into an affair and out of our marriage? How could I correct what had happened? Did I really want to? Wouldn't it be better, I asked myself, to abandon that miserable subject and focus on what we needed to do that day and that week in the peace studies program? In time I learned how to center my thinking on what was to be done. How interesting shaving came to be.

How could we activate peace studies on campuses and in academic professional associations so that students studied peace and not just war? My predecessor in the position of director, Gordon Christianson, was a professor of chemistry at Connecticut College, then still a women's institution. He had been involved with the Committee for Non-Violent Action (CNVA), which regularly confronted, peacefully of course, the nuclear submarine base at Groton, down the Thames River a bit from the college. The closest I'd ever come to direct action was passing out leaflets in Amherst. Besides, in a way I did not yet understand, I was deeply committed to the academic world. Bringing A. J. Muste to Dartmouth, for example, represented a small step in the right direction. But the larger question was how to make Muste's values a significant part of the educational program at Dartmouth and at other

American colleges and universities. How could studying peace and justice help transform higher education? For such was our modest goal.

Marty and I began looking for opportunities to recruit academics from a variety of backgrounds to this project. The Society of Friends provided a rich terrain. Kenneth and Elise Boulding, for example, had long been working in the field; in fact, Kenneth Boulding had published a book in 1945 called *The Economics of Peace,* and even before that, in 1942, *A Peace Study Outline.* The Bouldings were also instrumental in starting the *Journal of Conflict Resolution* and a Center for Conflict Resolution at the University of Michigan. I went out to visit the center (which is also when I met with the SDS leaders) and to talk about how peace studies might be pursued within the American Economic Association. The chairman of the AFSC National Peace Committee, Gilbert White, a well-known geographer, facilitated a newly formed peace research group within the Association of American Geographers. We helped start a Committee on Peace Research in History within the American Historical Association.[6] I talked with colleagues in a variety of other fields about developing such committees in their professional associations. We also helped foster a National Association for Peace Research. Some of these groups continue to this day, others morphed into left political organizations within particular academic societies. They assisted in laying the groundwork for the later teach-ins and the establishment some years after of the New University Conference.

My trip to Ann Arbor in 1963—when I first met Hayden and the Flackses—provided the impetus for organizing peace studies, generated new thoughts about politics and academic work, and established a relationship with this previously unknown group, SDS. But the trip also set me loose. I had been on a plane only twice before: coming home from Rochester at Thanksgiving my freshman year at college and flying to Chicago the morning after my marriage. Now for the first time I was living on my own, neither in my parents' apartment nor attached to my immediate family. I traveled as part of my AFSC job. I took to flying, despite feeling that any plane with me on it was likely to crash . . . and so what? Before the 1963–64 year was out, I had visited Seattle, San Francisco, Pasadena, Los Angeles, Houston, New Orleans, Atlanta.

It was all work . . . to be sure: finding out what AFSC outposts did with "Beyond Deterrence," and running some workshops focused on one or another of the pamphlets. But also, in those early days, I entered the emerging debate over the place of activism in the academy. Our pamphlets were all very well in a Quaker book display, other academics said, but did they belong on a college syllabus? What role might Mulford Q. Sibley on "Unilateral Initiatives and Disarmament" or Sidney Lens on "Revolution and Cold War" serve in a properly balanced, impartial educational curriculum? One of my roles, I came to understand, would be to engage colleagues for whom "academic" presumed "objectivity," balance, detachment. But was that so? Did honest engagement with the issues of that day, or this—Cold War, segregation, military power, sexual tyranny, immigration—require intellectuals and teachers to remain somehow neutral? And if not ourselves exactly, at least our syllabi, our classrooms? Was college education in fact neutral, balanced, objective? Should it be? Or was the answer "blowin' in the wind"?

At Hobart a year or two before, I had complained about the subtitle of the required Western civilization course: The Origins of Christian Civilization. Was that implicit equation of "Western" and "Christian" what we wanted our students—Jewish, atheist, Unitarian—to accept? Likewise, when we presented the myths and symbols then central to American studies, were we implicitly supporting a belief in American "exceptionalism"? Were we acknowledging the righteousness of "our" policies and action, as in Cuba or the Dominican Republic or coming, coming, coming Vietnam? Was this "objectivity"? What did that word mean? Was it the academy's false god, one we would need to pull down?

Gradually, I realized that my work editing and distributing our neat pamphlets hid a tossing sea of not merely academic controversy. My job, I began to see, involved issues that would become increasingly conflicted as students brought back to campuses commitments to justice and peace learned at the segregated lunch counters of the South or discovered in the operations of American military power in remote venues overseas. In time—for example, at Columbia in 1968—the issues of racism and militarism on campus would break into the headlines. But not yet.

These concerns occupied me particularly when, in Seattle, I was able to be with a woman I'd happily encountered at a small meeting at Pendle Hill, an important center near Philadelphia for seminars on the issues we were trying to address at the AFSC. At Pendle Hill, Sue Gottfried represented the AFSC peace program in the Northwest. She had a way of posing awkward questions in her unique accent: "But why," she would ask, turning "why" into a two-and-a-half syllable word, "why do you think that would be useful?" "I know I talk funny," she said, explaining her Galveston twang. I knew smart academic women; I was still technically married to one. But I'd never come across a woman so capable of engaging men as political equals. I was smitten. In Seattle, a city configured for lovers, she took me around, including to a fair at which I bought two sumi drawings, my first purchase of art. We made a date for a couple of weeks later to explore the beach at Malibu as well as each other.

I'd never been in love. I knew about attraction, and even a little about sex, which I was avidly pursuing now that, at thirty-one, I was free to do so. But the jolt of wanting only to talk and touch and hold, press my face between her breasts, think of nothing but the small woman warm within my arms—this I knew nothing about. Nothing in my life had prepared me to be so lost, then mysteriously found. The many sonnets rattling around in my head gave me language, but no idea of what the words signified. Meaning, I was discovering, emerged from a magic-seeming process involving talk, touching, sex, and breathing together in rhythm to the ocean outside. These connections transformed how we felt about each other, and so ourselves. I felt created anew, washed freshly onto the foggy Malibu beach. I began to discover a person I could like, myself, because the woman I admired so intensely loved me. Her look and her touch, the way her voice caressed me allowed me to believe I was worthy of care. She seemed likewise calmed and increasingly secure in herself, gaining confidence as we gained love.

We talked about the work on which we were embarked. In 1963, a peace "movement" barely existed. Nonviolence, to which she was viscerally dedicated, remained a concern of engaged southern blacks, yet was barely meaningful as a philosophy for political work among most antiwar activists. It was all too easy, given the weight of indifference, the clatter of scorn, to lose touch with the inner guide nonviolence could provide. And thus, too, to lose track of the confidence to move forward "then most when the whole cry of voices is on the other side" (Ralph Waldo Emerson's "Self-Reliance"). Emerson, about whom I had recently been writing,[7] was not a subject of our conversations. His cadences would have seemed too high-flown for the occasion: "And we are now men, and must accept in the highest mind the same transcendent destiny; and not minors and invalids in a protected corner, not cowards fleeing before a revolution, but guides, redeemers, and benefactors, obeying the Almighty effort, and advancing on Chaos and the Dark" ("Self-Reliance").[8] Although we might have giggled to think of ourselves "advancing on Chaos and the Dark," there on the deserted beach, we were doing just that. The love we had begun to share braced us for the struggles to come—against the darkness of the growing war and the chaotic tyrannies of racism. In 1964, we could not have imagined a mainstream historian writing more than fifty years later that "American youth culture" of the late 1960s, "overwhelmingly favored nonviolence, even while embracing ever-stronger tactics of civil disobedience and resistance to end racial injustice and to stop the carnage in Indochina."[9] The nonviolence of King and Muste and the Quakers for and with whom we—Jewish radicals—worked seemed aspirational, hopeful. But nonviolence was not yet, at least for me, a clearly known political strategy.

It was as if, there in California, I seemed to have entered a country previously unknown to me, a bit uncanny, even happily contradictory, like our magical passion at the cold Malibu beach. I was learning to tolerate changeable, perverse weather. On a warm Sunday in San Francisco I took the bus to a concert at the Legion of Honor. When I emerged, the fog had rolled in and the temperature had dropped twenty-five degrees; by the time the bus arrived to take me to where I was staying, I was shaking in my short-sleeved shirt. What might Emerson have said about such inconsistency? A week later, in Pasadena, I stepped out of my motel in the morning, looked to the left, and saw a large hill that had not been there the day before. My heart started pounding: Had I been transported during the night, or suddenly awakened from a Rip Van Winkle sleep? No, my AFSC escort explained: the smog has lifted enough to see the terrain. I was still learning the elementary geography of this brilliant world to which, with Sue, I had happily gained entrance.

In early spring, I traveled to Houston and, of course, nearby Galveston to see where Sue had come from. My flight from New Orleans was delayed for a couple of hours by "weather." Near the Houston airport, we encountered deep fog, which seemed to permeate the plane and silence all talk. As the plane settled downward, passengers drew themselves up and stared toward the cockpit as if to urge the pilot onward through the forbidding whiteness outside the windows. When we finally emerged from the fog at a few hundred feet and saw ground lights, a great exhaling broke the silence. People resumed suspended conversations. I, too, had been scared, I realized, not indifferent, as I had been on all flights before. My calculus of meaning had shifted: love and movement work were making my life worthwhile.

In New Orleans I met with Richard P. Adams, an American literature scholar I'd encountered at Modern Language Association meetings and a gentleman of the profession. He took me for dinner to
Antoine's, an almost mythical restaurant in the French Quarter and a
culinary wonder to someone for whom a pastrami on rye had seemed
the ultimate delicacy. Adams was writing a book on William Faulkner,
but he was also active with the American Civil Liberties Union, backing
the civil rights movement's push for change in the Deep South. He
revealed to me how a person quietly devoted to his profession could
also become active in seemingly unrelated social causes. New Orleans
itself provided R&R for movement militants from rural Louisiana, Mississippi, and Alabama, as I would find out in a few months. But as the
responses to Hurricane Katrina many years later demonstrated, the
city was hardly immune from the long-standing effects of racism. All
that seemed very distant from the red-paneled walls of Antoine's or the
dowdy splendor of the old Hotel Monteleone. I saw in Adams living
connections between literary interpretation and political activity.

From New Orleans, I took the train north toward Philadelphia,
watching the spring unscroll backward as I traveled north. I stopped in
Atlanta to meet with Staughton Lynd, whom I knew from my nonviolence conference, and Howard Zinn; both were then teaching at Spelman College. They told me about the plans for Mississippi Summer
and urged me to participate in the freedom schools. I soon began to
figure out what I might usefully do. Howard was ten years older than
me, tall and straight, and witty. A working-class Brooklyn intellectual,
steeled against war by his experiences as a B-17 bombardier,[10] Howard
possessed an unfailing sense of hope. When I stayed with him and Roz,
his wife, at their place in Newton, they always buoyed me for the frustrating organizational work of peace activism. Knowledgeable about
sometimes obscure but telling events in America's story, he deployed
them in books like *A People's History of the United States* and *The Indispensable Zinn*.[11] These works helped reset our understanding of American
policies and practices, from slavery to the Cold War, from segregation
to Hiroshima.

Over the years, as we wrote on some of the same subjects, I came
to appreciate his straightforward, often wry style as well as his insistence on—to borrow one of his titles—disobedience and democracy.
Democracy required distrust of official pronouncements, especially
those voiced by presidents, like Lyndon Johnson or Richard Nixon, or
university presidents like John Silber, who tried to practice autocracy

at Boston University, where Howard later taught. Howard's careful research and analysis led to confirmations of dishonesty, such as Johnson's promotion of the Gulf of Tonkin "incident" to provide him with a rationale for escalating attacks on Vietnam. Verification of such deceit led Howard not only to express doubt in hundreds of talks and articles but also to disobey, civilly of course, practices underwritten by official lies. Too often, he would find himself in paddy wagons with others who actively rejected segregation, war, and despotism.[12]

Staughton, three years older than me, had that forceful, slightly withheld, and puzzling demeanor of Quaker elders whom I had encountered in Philadelphia. Set on a path, he would continue through the heaviest flak. A picture of him, his face and white shirt splattered with mud (or red paint or blood?) but moving forward at the 1965 Assembly of Unrepresented People, remains vivid in my mind. He and Howard were historians by trade, but they brought to the practice of teaching and writing about history a perspective informed by the movement, in particular civil rights activism, in which both they and their students were deeply involved. They provided me with a model of academic engagement that would help define my work when I returned to teaching after my year with the AFSC.

I wondered: How did such activism transform the academic work they carried forward? How would new relationships with activist-scholars like Howard Zinn and Staughton Lynd change me as an academic and an intellectual? How might my work and travel for AFSC likewise transform the literary and cultural labor I had been doing before I'd moved to Philadelphia and had continued during that year? Answering such questions remains central to my work, even now, fifty-five years later, and it has returned to the agenda ever more forcefully since 2016.

In June 1964, I organized the conference Teaching About Peace Issues, held at NYU's Bronx campus, now Bronx Community College of the City University of New York (CUNY). Harold Taylor, the former president of Sarah Lawrence College, and founder and chair of the Committee of Peace Research, delivered the keynote address. Taylor was a major academic bulwark against the onslaughts of McCarthyism during the Cold War. He had organized legal counsel and community organizations to support Sarah Lawrence faculty who had in 1953 been subpoenaed by the Senate Internal Security Subcommittee; for a liberal intellectual like me he was an academic hero. In organizing the conference, I wanted to make peace research and teaching about peace kosher on campuses still anxious from the impacts of Cold War McCarthyism. Taylor was the perfect spokesperson for that goal, both intellectually and in terms of his impeccably turned-out appearance— no scruffy peacenik he.

Sharing information, especially about how to teach peace studies, constituted one practical objective of the conference.[13] In preparation for the meeting I had pulled together a "kit" of materials. Most of it consisted of syllabi and bibliographies for peace studies courses being taught across the country, primarily but not exclusively in colleges and universities. The titles of the courses themselves reveal the orientation of peace studies at the time.[14] Such courses asked why people might choose violence or, occasionally, nonviolence. They examined assumptions about the existence, not to say characteristics, of "human nature": Were people "naturally" violent and societies inevitably conflicted? Ways of resolving conflict—mediation, conciliation, adjudication— were often important to curricula. Peace studies used techniques like statistical analysis, survey research, projections from sample populations, and modeling—for example, designing alternative forms of government, like world law, to control or limit violence. In short, peace studies courses were and probably still remain concerned with the priorities of activist social scientists: how to shape and, if possible, alter behavior and institutions.[15]

Such curricula, it seemed to me, did not make for a thrill a minute in the classroom. But then again, surveys and statistics reflected more than the everyday methods of social scientists. They also derived from the need of peace studies practitioners to establish their professional credibility. The intellectual terrain of the early sixties was politically conflicted, to say the least. Supposedly hard-headed realists—the "masters of war" like Robert McNamara and Walt Whitman Rostow, who brought us Vietnam—characterized those who spoke of disarmament, peace, or even conflict resolution as fuzzy-minded liberals, "snowflakes" today. People like Norman Cousins debated with people like Henry Kissinger, and if the former had a larger and more friendly readership, the latter affected more directly—even before he joined the government—policy initiatives and political practices. These last were the primary goals of peace studies. The audience to which peace studies academics spoke, the implicit "reader" of their work, was most often the decision-maker, the lobbyist, the government official, and even the few politicians who read. Indeed, the connections between the academic disciplines of history and political science and government are . . . well, notorious, as names like those of Woodrow Wilson, Arthur M. Schlesinger Jr., Kissinger, or Samuel Huntington remind us.

The Teaching About Peace Issues conference did *not* constitute a political breakthrough like the teach-in movement of the following year. That may partly have had to do with the orientation of peace studies toward decision-makers, rather than toward the mobilization of an activist movement. All the same, the conference did illustrate two vital points about the growing movement of the time. First, pacifism remained central to the development of action for change. Others have written about the importance of the Fellowship of Reconciliation (FOR), for example, and its small but influential cadre of militants to the emergence of a nonviolent but activist civil rights movement.[16] But pacifist activity constituted a significant seedbed for many other kinds of work for change, especially during periods like the 1950s, when an organized left was quiescent or largely repressed. Pacifist organizations like the FOR, the AFSC, the War Resisters League, and, today, Christian Peacemakers may seem marginal to some. They don't run candidates for president, or even the Congress; they seldom organize huge demonstrations against whatever is the current war or call attention to themselves. Working within such an organization, I learned the meaning of a passage with which I had been familiar in Thoreau's "Civil Disobedience":

> Action from principle, the perception and the performance of right, changes things and relations; it is essentially revolutionary, and does not consist wholly with anything which was. It not only divides States and churches, it divides families; ay, it divides the individual, separating the diabolical in him from the divine.[17]

I think, for example, of one member of my committee at the AFSC, William Davidon, a physics professor at Haverford College and later a board member of the draft-resistance support organization Resist (which I will describe in chapter 8). It rapidly became clear to me from meetings of the committee that Davidon would never be easily governed by the accommodationist logic of an academic profession, or even by the gradualism of developing good work like peace studies. He acted from principle. I learned some years later—no surprise—that he was the primary organizer of the 1971 break-in at the FBI office in Media, Pennsylvania, which not only helped undermine the credibility of the FBI but also revealed its illegal COINTELPRO (counterintelligence program) to destabilize civil rights, antiwar, and feminist organizations.[18]

The Teaching About Peace Issues conference also helped in its small way to lay the groundwork for more powerful campus actions to come. That is, it enabled many of us to set aside older notions about the supposed disinterestedness of academic study and research. Of course, we were not about to imitate pro-war activities like the Michigan State program to train and support the tyrannical police of South Vietnam or Columbia's backing of the Institute for Defense Analysis. But it did help us to understand that research and teaching, however they might claim to be "impartial," inevitably had a politics. Not of the "vote for me" or even "which side are you on?" kind. But of the kind that asked "what are the political implications of the choices we make about what to study and what to teach?" The conference challenged us to ask why the achievement of peace had little of the material support provided to the pursuit of war. And, central to the teach-ins of 1965, it made clear why learning about the history and society of Vietnam was not a marginal academic enterprise, but absolutely central to the point of higher education in the mid-twentieth century.

In my own field, that insight came to be called "the question of the canon." It molded our ideas about the writers, stories, and poems to which we devoted our criticism, and to which we chose to introduce our students. Did it matter whether, teaching modernism, we restricted ourselves to T. S. Eliot, Ernest Hemingway, and Wallace Stevens and omitted Langston Hughes, Zora Neale Hurston, and Amy Lowell? Well, yes. It mattered, though it sometimes remained hard to explain, especially to some of our traditionalist colleagues, why our choices engaged the critical questions of who and what in our society were important.

In arguing with associates, I often used the instance of Hobart's Western civilization course, also known as the Origins of Christian Civilization. The first year consisted of four units: the Hebrew Bible, Greek literature, Roman literature, the Christian Bible. It was really an excellent course, carefully organized with very useful briefings for the staff, well-informed lectures, and, of course, wonderful readings. But I became more and more restive. Why, for example, had we never looked at what was being written between the last of the Hebrew scriptures we read and those of the earliest Christians, which provided the climax to the course? There were many such writings I knew vaguely— the Book of Judith, the Dead Sea Scrolls—gathered under the heading of "intertestamental literature." Why not take up some of these? The initial reaction was one with which I would become all too familiar: "But" . . . piously, "are they any good?" That question led into a tangled aesthetic swamp, for which I, happy innocent, had no adequate road-map. "And even if they are pretty good," came the follow-up, "do they hold a candle to *Isaiah* or to *Oedipus*? We don't have time for every-thing, after all." And so it went over the sherry, so sweet, a product of the Great Western vineyard, just down the lakeshore from Geneva, New York.

But then, much to my colleagues' credit, the tone shifted. Per-haps we should have a closer look. Perhaps . . . well, let's think, per-haps someone should examine, no, re-examine those texts. Perhaps they are worth considering for a lecture. In fact, perhaps you, Paul, as the resident Jew (that, of course, was never said) might think of getting together such a lecture. And so, as "the-one-most-involved," I dug deeply into that massive field, largely unknown to me, and arrived at lecture time with two hours and more of notes, an instruction to the students to just listen and forget copying down what I said, and a machine-gun delivery that at least blew away the mistaken assump-tion about four hundred silent years that had defined the ground. So, yes, it mattered who and what we read, and, yes, it made sense to read Frederick Douglass as well as Benjamin Franklin, Zora Neale Hurston as well as Ernest Hemingway. And it was essential not only for "the-one-most-involved" to have read and come to admire those previously little-known texts, but also for all the colleagues and students to join in that crucial exploration.

That intellectual—and organizing—task would become the North Star of my professional life. During the 1963–64 year when I worked at the AFSC, I completed a volume I had begun earlier for Anchor Books, the major publisher of "quality" paperbacks, called *Theories of Comedy*. I think it's quite a good collection of classic and some contem-porary texts, and it even sold well. But within a couple of years I had launched into a book that eventually was called *The Conspiracy of the Young*.[19] It contained chapters on freedom schools, "channeling" and draft resistance, and free universities, among other things—quite a remove from traditional literary theories of comedy. So were the essays for the *New York Review of Books* that Florence Howe and I wrote on edu-cation, draft resistance, and the like. That radical change in my intel-lectual focus would soon lead to enterprises like The Feminist Press, the *Reconstructing American Literature* project and, growing out of that, the *Heath Anthology of American Literature,* not to speak of my own books like *Canons and Contexts* and *From Walden Pond to Jurassic Park.* The conference Teaching About Peace Issues enabled me to step away from earlier definitions of academic work and embrace a new movement-oriented understanding of intellectual labor.

In the meantime, stoked by my passion for Sue—so far off in Seattle, so close in her letters, so present in the AFSC work—I tried to learn what a commitment to nonviolence might entail day by day in Philadelphia or elsewhere. Editing the papers from the Hobart conference on nonviolence, as I did that year, seemed to me a worthy academic exercise. Engaging in nonviolence, with the powerful support of her love and her advocacy, provided a different challenge. Those passions could not be abstracted or turned toward the theoretical tasks on which academics thrive. Rather, I had to ask how I might respond to the urgent call of a growing and demanding movement. I would begin learning new answers, especially regarding race and education, in Mississippi that summer of 1964.[20]

My experiences during that year at the AFSC Race Street headquarters, my Center City apartment, and the other venues I occasionally occupied pointed me in many unanticipated directions. The most challenging, aroused by my relationship with Sue, concerned the interaction of sexual liberation and movement activity. Over time I would learn about women like Emma Goldman, Margaret Randall, and Dolores Huerta, whose lives and work demonstrated the power of that connection. Their lives enlightened me. I can hardly claim to have unraveled the intricacies of this dialectic, much less the contradictions I found in my own actions. But nothing in that Philadelphia (and Seattle) year so radically changed how I came to think about myself sexually and (thus?) as a movement activist.

Sexual intimacy, I began to realize, had quite different meanings in our society for most men and for most women. But the budding sexual "revolution" of the mid-sixties didn't provoke deep male thinking about such gender dissimilarities. On the contrary, these questions might inhibit a primary goal: pleasure. Why bother? It seemed to me, vaguely, that most women I encountered sought with the pleasure some sort of stability in and through intimacy. Men I knew, myself included, seldom did. We reached for pleasure and also for the masculine affirmation that sexual "success" (what a revealing word) seemed to confirm. Having been kicked out of a constraining marriage, I fucked when and wherever I could. So did most of the guys I knew in

Students for a Democratic Society and the Student Nonviolent Coordinating Committee. Most were better at the game than I, but no matter. If I wasn't exactly catching up, I was coming to understand through practice what "successful" men from time immemorial claimed to know and do. Or so we men liked to say to ourselves, mostly in signs and gestures to one another.

In that still innocent (or stupid) moment, open sexuality didn't seem contradictory to a primary, loving, if in my case, long-distance relationship. Desire was everywhere. Love, for me, was in Seattle.

Still, desire and activism could come together in quite unpredictable ways. "What would you think about driving me down to Chester tomorrow night?" A young black guy, my colleague Barbara said, had begun picketing downtown stores in that town, just outside Philadelphia, with a sign saying "Don't buy where you can't work." The sign referred to the refusal of these stores, whose clientele was mostly African American, to hire blacks as clerks and salespeople. Now, Barbara explained, "There are nightly marches from a church through the downtown." "Is it safe?" I wondered aloud, thinking that my little white Corvair convertible, of which I had become quite fond, wasn't the ideal car to drive to a demonstration in the middle of Chester. Barbara laughed, "Sure, what do you think could happen?" At that moment, in the afterglow of satisfied desire, my head cradled on her thigh, I wasn't thinking much at all.

Barbara sensed my anxiety. I'd heard of Chester, gone through it on the train. I'd never been *in* it, of course, and had no idea what I'd find there. I vaguely remembered that my friend Allan Brick had grown up there. More to the point, I'd spent very little time with black people. In the Bronx, if there were black students at P.S. 88, in Junior High School 117, or even at Bronx Science, I didn't know them. Rochester (despite my brief membership in the NAACP) and NYU hardly differed. Charles Davis, the NYU English Department's one black professor, taught the honors program in which I had enrolled, and I had fleetingly tutored the Indiana University athletic star, Milt Campbell, during my time in Bloomington. But the thought of marches and demonstrations in black Chester propelled me into an unknown domain. "You've never been on a march, huh?" Barbara asked. "No." "Good time to start. Besides, they're fun." I had definitely learned to respect her definition of "fun."

The demonstrations, as it turned out, had mainly to do with the continuing segregation of Chester's schools and the dreadful condition

of the mainly African American school buildings.[21] The young pick-
eter, Donald Brooks Jackson (by that time Muhammad Kenyatta, a
transition new to me) was not yet twenty and an ordained minister.
The singing at the church, the enthusiasm of the nightly march, Chester's police sweating mightily behind their clear plastic masks, the
sense that we could accomplish something—all felt liberating to me.
Making a serious commitment to civil rights activism seemed possible.
I would do so soon enough in Mississippi Summer, 1964.

Chapter Three

MISSISSIPPI SUMMER

A Quaker Vacation

A scene in the 2000 movie *Freedom Song*,[1] set fifty-some years before the movie was made, illuminates the dominant culture of Mississippi in the century leading up to 1964. A small black boy of about five, Owen, wanders into the "whites only" luncheonette at the bus terminal of "Quinlan," a fictional representation of McComb, Mississippi. His father, Will Walker (Danny Glover) has been talking for a few moments with the baggage handler, a friend and former customer at his gas station. The baggage handler, like others in the black community, has been warned away from patronizing Walker's store because he has questioned the system of racial segregation. You can't push against them, his friend warns Walker. Now he discovers that his son has literally stepped into the middle of that system, for Owen is being gently held by a grinning young white man in the luncheonette. In the ensuing scene, fraught with tension, the whites—still grinning—force Walker to spank his son right there, in public, to "teach him" his place, which is *never* in a "whites only" establishment. Of course, Will Walker is being taught *his* place, subordinate to the smirking white guys in the luncheonette.

The humiliation of Will Walker and his son might be a minor moment in the arrangements of segregation: no one is evicted, arrested, beaten, or murdered. No churches are burned, no homes bombed, no black men shot. However, looked at more closely, the scene dramatizes the daily operations of racial power. Will and Owen are unmanned and enraged by their very lack of control in this everyday incident. A never-stated, always-present threat of heavier violence underwrites segregation here. If Will doesn't agree to chastise his

son, the whites will cheerfully provide the lesson. The economic consequences of expressing even the slightest qualm about the system—
here threatening Will's customers—also helps maintain segregation.
In the film, which concerns the development of the freedom movement in southwestern Mississippi, the most repressive area of the state,
the scene quietly evokes the racist burden of the status quo.

I thought about that world in July 1964, riding a Trailways bus
from Baltimore to Jackson, Mississippi. On vacation from my AFSC
job, I had resolved to participate in Mississippi Summer, an effort by
the civil rights movement to use hundreds of volunteers to penetrate
the most intransigent bastion of southern segregation and lynch law,
Mississippi. Three civil rights workers, James Chaney, Andrew Goodman, and Mickey Schwerner, had been missing in Mississippi for
weeks. While their bodies have not yet been found, we all knew they
are dead. Frankly, I was scared. The presence of federal agents in the
state had not prevented daily incidents of violence, intimidation, and
arrest. We—my friend and I on the bus—are heading into a strange,
violent world that we know, to the extent that we know it at all, only
from studying the gothic fictions of William Faulkner in college and
graduate school.

We had also been reading the press and other nonfictional
accounts of life in Mississippi before the freedom movement.[2] For
instance, in 1963, nine Mississippi counties have *no* black people
registered to vote (eligible African American citizens in these counties ranged from 1,071 to 5,172); in sixteen counties, the number was
under ten.[3] In Amite County, one black person was registered. A cotton gin in Amite was the site of the murder, before a dozen witnesses,
of Herbert Lee. Lee, who had been supporting efforts to register black
voters, was shot by E. H. Hurst, a member of the Mississippi legisla-
ture. Hurst was never prosecuted. One of the witnesses, Louis Allen,
later told the FBI that he had been forced to give false testimony exon-
erating Hurst to a hastily assembled grand jury. After he talked with
the FBI, Allen was also murdered. Voter suppression, emerging again
in 2016,[4] has a long history. Schools, libraries, pools, water fountains,
jails, and restaurants were strictly segregated—when, jails apart, they
were even available to black people.

In fact, the schools, separate and altogether unequal in facili-
ties, textbooks, and class size, taught segregation. A journalist, Jerry
DeMuth, reproduced excerpts from a reader prepared by the powerful
White Citizens' Councils for third and fourth graders:

The Negro has his own part of town to live in. This is called our Southern Way of Life. Do you know that some people want the Negroes to live with white people? These people want us to be unhappy. They say we must go to school together. They say we must swim together and use the bathroom together. God has made us different. And God knows best. Did you know that our country will grow weak if we mix the races? White men worked hard to build our country. We want to keep it strong and free.[5]

Tom Brady, a member of the Mississippi Supreme Court, wrote in *Black Monday*, a kind of handbook for the Citizens' Councils:

You can dress a chimpanzee, housebreak him, and teach him to use a knife and a fork, but it will take countless generations of evolutionary development, if ever, before you can convince him that a caterpillar or a cockroach is not a delicacy. Likewise the social, political, economic and religious preferences of the Negro remain close to the caterpillar and the cockroach.[6]

A shocking level of violence—surpassing that even of police toward black men in 2019 America—underwrote such racist sentiments. They were widely expressed in the press, by public officials, and others in power. Searchers for the bodies of the three murdered civil rights workers during the summer of 1964 discovered the corpses of five black men in Mississippi rivers. During that summer, the Council of Federated Organizations (COFO), an umbrella organization that encompassed many of the groups fighting for change in Mississippi, assembled a thick pamphlet listing hundreds of arrests, beatings, burnings, and other violent incidents directed against both Mississippi African Americans and Freedom Summer volunteers. The pamphlet included the many bombings of black homes, churches, and businesses in McComb, later called the bombing capital of the world. While nine Klansmen ultimately confessed to planting the bombs, a local judge let them off with suspended sentences; they had been "unduly provoked" by civil rights activists, he explained. Activists themselves were much more likely to face beatings, jail, and reform school.[7] The 1964 summer project expected to change such conditions.

Certainly, we were overly optimistic, and perhaps naive. It had taken a war to end slavery. Now, a century later, would it take yet another war to end segregation? The sides were drawn up and had been engaged in overt struggle for over a decade. White Mississippi deployed the White Citizens' Councils, the local sheriffs and courts, the terrorist Ku Klux Klan, and the weight of segregated institutions, from schools and libraries to swimming pools and housing. At least in public, racists monopolized the instruments of violence, right up to the Jackson Police Department's wartime tank. What resources could the freedom movement deploy? First and foremost, the determination of the black community to bring change in the face of hate and violence, and the courage of activists old and young who had been confronting Mississippi terrorism. Now, too, the commitments to equality of the daughters and sons of liberal America. In addition, the movement tapped the significant resources of teachers', auto workers' and packinghouse unions, the northern press, and many churches and synagogues; also, at a considerable distance, of the more progressive elements in the political establishment outside the South. The movement would erect nonviolence as an aspiration and as a shield. But a significant number, mainly of black Mississippians, saw and practiced armed self-defense against the depredations of white supremacists.[8] Few doubted that there could be mayhem. But it was again time for Reconstruction.

As noted above, the push for change in Mississippi in summer 1964 was headed by the Council of Federated Organizations. This umbrella group incorporated, sometimes uncomfortably, SNCC (Student Nonviolent Coordinating Committee), the NAACP (National Association for the Advancement of Colored People), the SCLC (Southern Christian Leadership Conference), and CORE (Congress of Racial Equality). The complex interactions of these organizations, local and national, and the development of the movement over the preceding years have been addressed in detail by historians like John Dittmer (*Local People*), Charles M. Payne (*I've Got the Light of Freedom*), and Taylor Branch (*Pillar of Fire*).[9] My goal here is to add to the historical record the perspective of one somewhat older, white volunteer, to describe the powerful impact that Freedom Summer had on his life and particularly his work, and to examine the implications of what he learned for cultural and literary study.

My small "assignment" involved bringing films on nonviolence to projects, mainly freedom schools, across the state. I was also expected to teach Negro history—as it was then called—and Negro literature in freedom schools. A flyer from that summer explained that the freedom schools aimed "to create an educational experience for students which will make it possible for them to challenge the myths of our society, to perceive more clearly its realities, and to find alternatives—ultimately new directions for action."[10] Experienced teachers and civil rights activists had prepared an imaginative "citizenship" curriculum on topics like "the Negro in Mississippi," "myths about the Negro," "the power structure," "material things and soul things," "the movement," and the Holocaust.[11] But the unstated curriculum, as another report put it, required confronting the reality that students "live in Mississippi, and it is not comfortable. The Freedom School can perhaps develop a climate in which the people can explore reasons for and ways to change Mississippi."[12]

The freedom school curriculum posed three critical questions:

    1. What does the majority culture have that we want?
    2. What does the majority culture have that we <u>don't want?</u>
    3. What do we have that we want to keep?

To this list some students added a fourth question:

    4. What do we have that we don't want to keep?

I was struck then and I still marvel at the "open" character of these questions; it reveals more about the freedom schools, perhaps, than the particulars of African American culture and history, the power structure, or even the movement, however significant these were.

A connection between education and action for change defined the freedom school. The name of the enterprise—freedom school—infers that connection: school must help to create freedom. Schooling involves not only socializing kids and teaching skills like math, though math was in fact part of the freedom school curriculum. But also, and critically, schools should help students learn "to challenge . . . myths" and to perceive "realities" as bases for discovering "directions for action," ways of changing the society in which they lived. Freedom schools, that is, have a politics. All schools do, although they rarely become explicit. In recent years, for example, those favoring the privatization of the American educational system have tried to substitute the off-putting and negative phrase "government schools" for "public schools." "Public," as in you and me and our neighbors.

The big question concerns the kind of politics shaping school. In 1964, the freedom movement took on the segregationist politics of Mississippi. This political challenge remains with us and provides a compelling reason to look closely at freedom schools from half a century ago. I am not suggesting that in 2020 the politics of schools are shaped by terror and murder, as was true in Mississippi. No one would assert that legislation like No Child Left Behind—with its regime of high-stakes testing, "teacher-proof curricula," schools as centers for private profit—was calculated to maintain segregation or would help to produce a "school to prison pipeline." Yet it helped do both. The question remains: will schools, especially schools of poverty, continue to perpetuate an abysmal status quo, or can they pursue the task of "educating for insurgency"?[13]

The freedom schools were, of course, only one part of the explicit program of the Mississippi Summer Project. Voter registration (or, as some called it, "voter restoration") constituted the highest priority, together with enrolling potential voters in the Mississippi Freedom Democratic Party (MFDP). To that end, the movement had for some years sponsored classes to prepare adults to register to vote—a frustrating, dangerous, and usually fruitless endeavor. The MFDP, toward the end of the summer, challenged the seating of the "regular" segregationist delegation to the Democratic National Convention in Atlantic City. The summer program also helped set up many community centers; it fostered "white folks" projects to try building bridges across the racial divide; it pushed for federal farm programs to support the needs of black farmers. It also lobbied the Johnson administration and even the FBI, as it had earlier lobbied the Kennedys, to protect project staff and volunteers. The struggle against segregation occurred on many overt fronts.

But also, there was an implicit program. The younger white volunteers from the North, unlike me, usually knew a few black kids. But they knew little about their actual lives, about how segregation played out daily in New York and Philadelphia, as well as in Charleston and Biloxi. They were ignorant about the poverty and terror, along with the cultural values, that mattered in black lives, especially in the Deep South. The boys might have played basketball with black athletes, and the girls might have known black women who cleaned their houses and their schools. They might have listened to R&B but had little sense of the Detroit world from which it emerged. In 1964—and in 2019?—it required uncommon imagination to penetrate the color line that has continued to mark American society. The parents of volunteers were, if anything, even less aware of life across the border. Whatever else it wanted to do, the Mississippi Summer Project would penetrate those boundaries and hope to mobilize newly awakened, mostly middle-class northerners to act for change. That might take sacrifice—the sacrifice, as it did, of young lives. But black lives had been martyred for four hundred years in America. Now, organizers thought, a significant cadre of activists, mostly youthful, would learn the values and experiences of their peers across the color line; now they would think about the actions suggested by that knowledge. Traveling on that Trailways bus into deepest Mississippi represented one small instance.

Of course, my own ignorance worried me. Yes, I held a PhD in English from Yale, had been a college professor for some six years, and was the AFSC's director of peace studies. But I knew virtually nothing about African American history or literature. On the bus, I overcame anxiety and sleeplessness by reading Saunders Redding's *The Lonesome Road* (1958), about Africans in America.[14] It brought me a good deal further than my grammar school accounts of George Washington Carver and Booker T. Washington. In 1964 literary criticism and American literature constituted my expertise. There, at least, I *did* know Negro novelists—all *three* of them: Richard Wright, James Baldwin, and Ralph Ellison. Of course, I hadn't studied them or taught any of their books. It would be almost a year before I did that in a college classroom. But I had read *Native Son* and *Go Tell It On the Mountain* and had copies of both books in my suitcase. Still, my ignorance as a credentialed academic a dozen years older than most of the other volunteers and the Student Nonviolent Coordinating Committee (SNCC) staff embarrassed me. How could I teach what I'd only begun to learn?

These concerns vanished when we arrived at the bus terminal in Jackson. Practical matters are the first real challenge: How do we make our way to the COFO (Council of Federated Organizations) office? What if we got into the "wrong" taxi in this sharply segregated system? Who knows where we'd end up? We needn't have worried: my denim work shirt and my friend's denim skirt—movement uniforms—identified us. A black cabbie rapidly took us in hand.

Since she will play an active role in this narrative, I should here introduce my companion in this Mississippi journey, Florence Howe; we would become partners for much of the next eighteen years. Most people have at least one distinguishing physical feature, noticeable to any observer. I have a large bump on the right side of my forehead: my "residual horn," some friends say. Florence, whose hair was quite black, had from an early age a white streak in the midst of the black, somewhat like Susan Sontag. Some described her streak uncharitably, and others found it foxy. Committed and adventurous, Florence had joined her students at Goucher College in challenging segregation in and around Baltimore and on the Eastern Shore of Maryland, no playground. She had been close with reporter and activist William Worthy, who by that time, as Phil Ochs's ballad put it, "isn't worthy" of a US passport according to the State Department.[15] In Mississippi, she would start a COFO freedom school at the Blair Street African Methodist Episcopal (AME) church in Jackson.

COFO had its office at 1017 Lynch Street (I couldn't make up this street name). The taxi drops us at a long, dim storefront. Inside, we find a hive of telephones, radios, mimeograph machines, beat-up furniture, piles of legal briefs, and freedom school curriculum materials. Everywhere staff and volunteers, old and young, black and white, exchange the latest information; they wise-crack and glance occasionally at the new group of volunteers, of which we are a part, spilling into a front corner of the office. As they busy themselves, we watch worriedly the slow passing of police cars outside the office windows, which open on the daily pulse of Jackson's black community. Eventually we are transported to Tougaloo College, a historically black institution, for three concentrated days of nonviolence training. We are not preparing for sit-ins or freedom rides, so our training does not consist of what to do when some overexcited high school racist pours ketchup on our heads. But we do learn how to protect our vitals from kicks, and how to use our bodies to cover a comrade being assaulted.

Our training is primarily intellectual and cultural. Meetings begin with song: "Ain't gonna let nobody turn me roun'," "I love everybody, / I love everybody, / I love everybody in my heart," "Oh, freedom, / Oh, freedom, / Oh freedom over me, / And before I be a slave, / I be buried in my grave, / And go home to my lord and be free." Or, sometimes, "And I'll fight for my right, / To be free." Most of us, whites especially but also blacks, are northern and academically educated. We're ignorant of the ways of racist Mississippi—and also of southern black churches, southern black kids, of the movement itself. Gradually at Tougaloo, we begin to learn about our students. Later, I would be fascinated by their interest in the hair on my arms, the strangeness of our bodies. Later still, some girls in the town of Harmony[16] get over initial shyness and begin to teach a klutzy dancer like me their endlessly inventive steps. Much later still, I realize that the music, the songs and the dancing, are our introduction to the beautiful and to us barely known culture of black Mississippi.[17] We begin to learn what Bernice Reagon meant in saying that "songs are only a vehicle to get to the singing," because "singing is an organizing experience."[18] We learn singing; we also learn that our challenge has less to do with opening the students to our lessons than opening ourselves to them—to their interests, concerns, and songs as black kids in early sixties Mississippi.

At Tougaloo, we discuss the larger purposes of the Mississippi Summer Project, what we might be teaching and also learning. Gradually we adjust to a new and vibrant educational domain. But not a utopian one. Our orientation begins with a tape from the similar session at Oxford, Ohio, where the initial group of volunteers, a month earlier, had been introduced to Mississippi Summer. The taped voice of Professor Vincent Harding expresses his gratitude for our participation: "not as a Negro, but because as a human being you help me to know that there are human beings who live for something else than being cool and dispassionate." Quickly he plunges into a fundamental tension of the project: that we must come to Mississippi knowing that Negroes may "hate your guts . . . . Even though you may have the qualifications to be in charge, they do not want you in charge. They will not let you be in charge."

Harding's candor about conflict, even within this movement for equality, leads to a discussion of antagonism between the races. It may take "the form of aggressiveness toward white women by black male activists," one staff member stresses, and hostility from black women who feel marginalized when they observe black men pursuing white women volunteers. This painfully honest discussion opens me to truths about which I had not given much thought: how sexuality can serve as a stand-in for power, but differently for the powerless and for the powerful; how "appreciation" and even love can be compromised by racial hostility; how the desire of activists to "prove they're in a new age" can evoke rage among those, white or black, who observe what they see as our "loose" behavior. These #MeToo lessons lie outside the scope of the freedom school curriculum. But they are critical to the psychological and political dynamics of the summer project, as well as to our own continuing education.

Security procedures loom large. Mindful of the trio of lost comrades, we pay close attention. First, use the long-distance WATS (wide area telephone service) line to phone ahead to the project to which you are headed, ask for yourself, tell them you will call back at the hour you intend to arrive. Second, when you arrive, check in and phone back, same procedure, to where you came from. If you don't, there will be searchers out for you within the hour. Third, report all suspicious cars (what cars aren't?); keep a low profile (can we walk the streets?); remember that your safety lies in the community, so don't endanger it unnecessarily (are *we* unnecessary danger?). In the exhilarating work of these days I feel my anxiety fade into a hardly apprehended ground tone.

Hiroshima day, August 6, in Indianola, Mississippi: a kid asks, "Why we drop the A-bomb on the Japs and not them Nazis?" "Why do you think?" "Hey, ain't it simple?" he responds. Another student: "What you think that man in your movie, the skinny one . . ." "Gandhi." "Yeah, him. What he do 'bout the Ku Klux?" The kids' questions, often so different from those my northern students would have posed, keep me vigilant. One day, later in the summer at the Blair Street AME church in Jackson, I'm asked to teach *Native Son* to a freedom school class. About a dozen kids, ages maybe eleven to eighteen, mostly girls, sit in a loose circle. None had, so far as I could tell, ever read a novel before, maybe not even a whole book. This one they devour almost overnight. They do so after they had spent the afternoon, as they did every afternoon, canvassing their neighborhood to find people daring enough to try to register to vote, or at least to participate in the simulated election held by the Mississippi Freedom Democratic Party for delegates to the national Democratic Party Convention coming later that summer in Atlantic City. The discussion, intense and jumbled, soon enough focuses on Bigger Thomas— what was it he wanted? They struggle with that bitter question. "He want to be a man," a sixteen-year-old guy maintains as all opposition fades into silence. Assent? Wonder? Rage? No one turns to me for an answer. What, in any case, would my answer mean for these black Mississippi kids, even could I provide one, as they file out for their afternoon of canvassing?

I am thinking: Why have I never had one class in the four colleges where I've taught as fervent and driven as this one in a hot Jackson church basement? It's years before most North American teachers discover the work of Paulo Freire or fully understand the role of desire and need in learning. I am also thinking: If *Native Son* is such a powerful work, yet one I never studied or taught, what else have I missed? That's what I ask a SNCC staff worker the next day. "Who else should I be reading?" "Why not try Paule Marshall? She's got a book out, *Brown Girl, Brownstones*." Out since 1959, I later discover. It will be almost another decade before we at The Feminist Press bring that book back into print.

Two primary lessons emerged for me in freedom school, my compass marks still as an intellectual and a teacher in the fifty-five years since that summer. One concerns the dynamic of learning: How could we—I—bring into classrooms the passion and involvement of that freedom school moment? The second raises what would later be called "the question of the canon": What is important to read and to teach? Underlying that question of the canon, another lesson, hidden in plain sight all these years, has come into view from events at Ferguson, Missouri, Staten Island, New York, Baltimore, Maryland, and elsewhere: "Black Lives Matter." Explicit in the mandate of the freedom schools is the lesson that schooling and empowerment are connected. The movement perspective I learned in Mississippi thus redefined for me the fundamental objectives of teaching and learning. How we study and what we learn express what and who our society sees as important, essential to know, and thus to respect; the curriculum defines not just what matters but who "matters."

Traveling from project to project during Mississippi Summer, I had many opportunities to observe other volunteer-teachers in action. They were young, dedicated, and generally knowledgeable about black history, the power structure, and even analogies between Mississippi racism and Nazi terror. Yet and still, they often did not connect to their students. For, or so it seemed to me, these freedom school teachers, in their enthusiasm to transmit what they themselves had been learning, were (like too many Teach for America kids today) reproducing the authoritarian structure of their own academic education. As they were instructed, freedom school teachers seated the kids in circles rather than rows. But as I wrote at the time, "many teachers could not grasp the fact that one cannot pour in facts, even about something presumably as important as the history of the students' own people."

The challenge of freedom schools was not *providing* facts and information but turning them into "knowledge ready for use." That did happen, but only when students brought to the makeshift classrooms their genuine need to understand their *own* experience, including that of the classroom, not some tradition, however certified as significant. During Mississippi Summer we volunteers began to appreciate education as a matter of life and death and not a pleasant luxury or some job preparation. Education was not just the materials studied but what studying them revealed about students and their lives. I wrote:

... in the freedom schools the real lives of students and their real experience in the classroom became central to their study. You asked questions about what might happen to, and *how* power would operate on, a student's father in Greenwood if he tried to register to vote, or if the student himself attended a freedom school, as in fact he was doing. You asked, how does what we do in freedom school here in Laurel differ from what happens in regular school, and why do these differences occur, and how does the difference make you feel? By thus concentrating on events as they actually occurred and feelings as they actually came out, the freedom schools did one of their main jobs: helped the students to recognize that the lives *they* actually led, the thoughts and feelings *they* actually had, had validity and importance, were worth studying and trying to understand.[19]

As Dan Perlstein and I wrote in our introduction to the *Radical Teacher* (volume 40, 1991) issue on the freedom school curriculum, "The freedom school idea was *not* to explain the social structure of segregation through the lens offered by students' undigested experiences, including their efforts to change their society. Rather, students were encouraged to see learning as inseparable from the uses made of it, knowledge and the struggle for freedom as synonymous." Ideally, freedom school teaching would begin from students' real experience and it would transform the students' understanding of that experience by clarifying what they saw as their "place in the world" and thus how they perceived and valued themselves.

For this kind of education to take place, both the students and the freedom school teachers had to be—this isn't an exaggeration—transformed. Yes, many freedom school teachers were, like me, radically changed by the experience. As teachers, we could not continue to function primarily as repositories of knowledge, however much that idea was embedded in our training. The students knew, in ways we could not, the details of their daily reality: why "white" gas stations were run by Klansmen, how the students' barber shop down the block provided them with magazines not otherwise available in the South, who could produce some sorely needed fried chicken and collards, why their school principal seemed to listen so intently to that white man in a blue suit. Local knowledge, they saw, was linked to the broader struggle represented by our presence and COFO. They began to experience learning not merely as a transmission of data, certified as significant by virtue of the texts from which it came and the tests to which it led. Rather, they began to take what they were studying—say, the American "Declaration of Independence"—and, as they did at the Freedom School Convention, use it as the basis for their own statement of goals.

> In this course of human events, it has become necessary for the Negro people to break away from the customs which have made it very difficult for the Negro to get his God-given rights. We, as citizens of Mississippi, do hereby state that all people should have the right to petition, to assemble, and to use public places. We also have the right to life, liberty and to seek happiness.[20]

Learning in this fashion, we hoped, might empower students to formulate changes they desired, to see them in historical context, and to engage in the work necessary to diminish oppression and enlarge their freedom in an altered world.

Teachers know that we need to meet students "where they are." But we don't always acknowledge that. Students, no matter how young, possess many kinds of knowledge and experience. These, in my view, need to come into the teaching and learning process. A very different theory characterizes today's "high stress" schools—often charters—in which students sit silently following the teacher alone with their eyes and minds. "One, two, three, eyes on me," as a KIPP-trained charter school teacher would put it. Only the teacher's knowledge and experiences count in such classrooms.[21] Students are expected to wipe from the slate their experiences and knowledge and "bank" what teacher provides. In this "banking theory of knowledge," as Freire called it,[22] what is not in the teacher's head is irrelevant—not only to the tests to come, but to the very idea of understanding.

My freedom school experience teaches that this authoritarian epistemology is nonsense. Further, the cultural dynamics that play out within classrooms independent of the ostensible subject matter—what Jules Henry called the "noise"[23]—produces much of the learning. Silenced children "learn" that what they know is of no consequence, that *they* are of no consequence; they come to see themselves as failures and think of schools as spaces of oppression. Upper-level classrooms of little learning and the harsh streets of American cities reveal every day the destructive results of such pedagogy. The freedom schools offered a very different model.

The second lesson I derived from freedom schools had no name in 1964; indeed, it would be well into the seventies before I ever heard the term "literary canon" much less "the question of the canon." In Mississippi, that seemed an abstruse phrase for something apparently simple: Why did we read and value what we read and valued? Did it matter if we read Faulkner or Wright, Hemingway or Baldwin, Eliot or Countee Cullen? Well, yes. Florence and I had success teaching E. E. Cummings, William Carlos Williams, and Langston Hughes that Freedom Summer. Students certainly had fun playing with Williams's good-tasting plums and Cummings's "goat-footed / balloonMan." And they wrote some striking take-offs.[24] Here is some of Sandra Ann Harris's, age seventeen, "Why Did I My Don'ts:

> why did I my don'ts
> why did I my dids
> what's my didn'ts purpose
> is it to fulfill my dids
>
> what isn'ts have I proclaimed
> what ises have I pronounced
> why can't I do my doings
> my couldn'ts do renounce . . . .[25]

Alice Jackson, also seventeen, wrote in a more explicitly political if also conventional (until the last lines) manner:

> I want to walk the streets of a town,
> Turn into any restaurant and sit down,
> And be served the food of my choice,
> And not be met by a hostile voice.
> I want to live in the best hotel for a week,
> Or go for a swim at a public beach,
> I want to go to the best University
> And not be met with violence or uncertainty.
> I want the things my ancestors
> Thought we'd never have.
> They are mine as a Negro, an American;
> I shall have them or be dead.[26]

The student poem by Lillie Mae Powell, aged eleven, from Pilgrim's Rest, forced me to think most about my own work as a critic and teacher. I know nothing more about her—and even the title appended to her poem, "A Negro Condition," may not have been of her own choosing.[27]

One day while I was visiting a certain
City this is what I saw. A Negro
Soldier with a broken arm who
Was wounded in the war.

The wind was blowing from the
North; there was a drizzle of
Rain. He was looking from the
Last place; his arm was in a sling.

The Negro soldier didn't go
Home. He was looking to the east
And to the west. His broken arm
Was in a sling.

A few years after Mississippi Summer, standing on an El platform in Chicago, I tried to remember Lillie Mae Powell's poem. As an experiment, I borrowed a page from Benjamin Franklin and wrote from memory the poem as I recalled it in order to compare it with the original. When I did so, I found that I had corrupted the poem in small but telling ways; in particular, I largely missed its wonderful use of enjambment (the continuation of a sentence without a pause beyond the end of a line, couplet, or stanza), though I had more or less maintained its vivid symbolism. The logic of its composition departed from many of the stylistic values I had learned in my classes at the School of Letters, Yale, and elsewhere. What else did I have to relearn about form and style to think usefully about writers like Lillie Mae Powell, or Paule Marshall, or, as I would later write, Countee Cullen's "Incident," or Sterling Brown's "Ma Rainey"? Indeed, about the many other African American writers with whom we are now familiar but who, in 1964, were as distant from the classrooms of our universities or the pages of professional journals like *American Literature*[28] as Jackson's Lynch Street seemed from New York's Fifth Avenue.

What was at stake in our choices of texts? Merely "cultural capital" as some critics have, I think, mistakenly theorized?[29] Relevance? A few works like Hughes's "Harlem"—"What happens to a dream deferred?"—seemed to speak more or less directly to our freedom school students' experiences. But was such "relevance" finally the determining criterion of value, or even of usefulness? Were our students' dreams really deferred or yet to be formulated? Should the curriculum change depending on the students one taught? What then became of culture, tradition, the "best that had been thought and said," what we later learned to call the canon? What became of our own hard-won PhDs?

Pushed by the experiences in Mississippi, Florence and I and others in our cohort began our own reeducation, filling in the omissions from our courses of study. We didn't have a lot of what came to be called "theory," but after Mississippi Summer we started reading Phillis Wheatley and W. E. B. DuBois, Zora Neale Hurston, Claude McKay, and Nella Larsen. These names, familiar to most students of literature today, were absent then from all PhD reading lists I knew about. They were largely absent, too, from anthologies, encyclopedias, critical texts, much of literary history, and from the curricula and magazines of white—that is, most—US institutions. Gradually, DuBois, Hurston, and others began to appear thanks to publishers like Mnemosyne, Third Press, and even Arno Press, which was purchased by the *New York Times*. The flourishing of the Black Arts movement of the mid-1960s and the advent of black power in the political world made a difference.[30] Within a few years, we would begin to change the canon that shaped the study of literature at all educational levels.

We would also change how we understood significance in literary study and other areas of the humanities. For example, were complexity and contradiction, an elaborate fabric of allusion, an edge of irony always and exclusively necessary to significance, as in "The Love Song of J. Alfred Prufrock"? Or, thinking of Lillie Mae Powell's soldier in "A Negro Condition" and Countee Cullen's "Incident," did we have to relearn the alphabet through which we expressed our ideas of cultural value? Could we comprehend the dynamics of historical change or psychological development if we saw events only through the eyes of white men? Or from the perspective offered by "the whole of the literature of Europe from Homer and within it the whole of the literature of . . . [a writer's] own country" (T. S. Eliot, "Tradition and the Individual Talent")? What was the meaning of "democracy" and whose lives did that term embrace, especially in a one-party state like Mississippi?

A practical answer to that last question emerged as the summer project of 1964 wound down. While most freedom school teachers packed up to return home, others headed to the Democratic National Convention in Atlantic City. There, a long struggle went on to seat the Mississippi Freedom Democratic Party delegates in place of the racist gang of white "regular" Democrats, who had been elected largely by excluding blacks from the polls. The MFDP seemed to be winning within the Credentials Committee, but gradually that majority was worn away by pressure from President Johnson, vice-president-to-be Hubert Humphrey, and other "friendly" delegates. Ultimately, a "compromise" was proposed to seat two representatives of the Mississippi Freedom Democratic Party as delegates at large and to acknowledge the remainder of the delegation as "honored guests" of the convention. The MFDP delegates and the COFO staff debated that proposal over many painful hours. Despite being pressed by close allies to accept it, MFDP and COFO finally rejected it as not a "compromise" at all but a persistent form of tokenism. Charles Sherrod, a veteran SNCC field secretary, wrote persuasively about that decision:

> ... the problem of "race" in this country cannot be solved without political adjustment. We must consider the masters of political power at this point and acknowledge that the blacks are not trusted with this kind of power for this is real power. This is how our meat making and money making and dress making and love making is regulated. A readjustment must be made. . . . The real question is whether America is willing to pay its dues. We are not only demanding meat and bread and a job but we are also demanding power, a share in power! Will we share power in this country together in reconciliation or, out of frustration, take a share of power and show it, or the need for it, in rioting and blood?[31]

To most of us, the case against seating the MFDP as the Mississippi delegation seemed unconvincing: it was clear that Johnson would thrash Barry Goldwater, even if Mississippi and much of the white South abandoned the Democrats, as they would do soon enough. Why placate those who were not with you in the first place?

But more fundamentally, why perpetuate the politics that helped sustain, even legitimate, American racism? To be sure, Lyndon Johnson was unusually successful in pushing for civil rights legislation, like the Civil Rights Act of 1964, just passed, and the Voting Rights Act to come in 1965. Such legislation certainly made a difference, as the number of black legislators in Mississippi, Baltimore, Maryland, and elsewhere would come to testify. Still, the results of the Democratic National Convention left more hostility and suspicion than hope in the hearts of Mississippi activists. Many had risked their lives to enter that convention hall; they had lost their jobs, their homes, and too often their friends. Why then were those who claimed to speak for liberal white America forgoing a critical opportunity to bring the democratic and anti-racist values of the movement into the Democratic Party and thus into the American mainstream? Tokenism was not meaningful "political adjustment," to use Sherrod's most restrained phrase.

There were reasons, good and bad, of course. Politics always finds its reasons: having allies for future legislation, trying to sustain Democratic hegemony in the "solid South," not to speak of the gravitational pull of white solidarity. Wondering what might have been, had the MFDP been seated, takes us out into an airy realm of speculation. To accomplish such a "political adjustment" required a radical cultural change, the kind of cultural change the freedom schools were designed to create. That kind of transformation still seems, thirteen national conventions later, to elude American law-enforcement systems and our political establishment. I say this despite the election of an African American president and hundreds of black people to office across the South, as well as in cities like Baltimore. The cultural change that existed at the edges of the Atlantic City convention did not produce a clear call to a different future. Perhaps such a call could never have emerged into a politics dominated by markets, the desires of old boys, and by the machines of war in the hands of spurious warriors.

But that is speculation. What is not speculation is the problem that conventional liberals, whose habitat is mainly the Democratic Party, have in seeing or even looking "left." They seem conditioned, as if they were born in Great Britain, to look to the right for oncoming traffic. Never left. Though what's coming from the left might indeed strengthen them or save them from defeat . . . or, perhaps worse, victory. The Democratic meeting at Atlantic City in 1964 provides a striking instance of this right-looking habit of mind. As need hardly be said, it remains a serious factor as we approach the election of 2020 and, as I write this, the contest for the Democratic nomination.

The visit of Vice President Hubert Horatio Humphrey to the Morgan Community School in 1967 offers a much smaller but vivid example. The word was out that something akin to the 1964 freedom schools was underway at Morgan in Washington, DC, and the vice president decided to check it out. But before he arrived to meet the teachers and engage the students, the FBI showed up. They arrested one of our Antioch master's degree interns at the school, in front of his class full of young students. The teacher, it seemed, was a draft resister! Dangerous! When I found out about his arrest, and the circumstances of it, I came racing down the corridor to confront Humphrey. Today, I'd probably have been shot. But then, I simply said, "Your FBI just arrested one of our teachers in front of his class. Why did they do that, frightening the children?" I asked. "He's just a draft resister, not in hiding or anything." "Well," said Humphrey, swelling to the occasion, "he'll have a fair trial." Obviously, he missed the point. We were trying to establish the school as a site of safety and support for children whose lives were already too crowded with police, arrests, and the daily fear of breathing while black. But the vice president and his handlers could not "see" that. Nor could they "see" the commitment of our intern to an alternative to the escalating war, which was rapidly undermining Lyndon Johnson's unfortunately named "war on poverty."

Like the Mississippi Freedom Democratic Party in 1964, our intern brought what was actually a gift to a politician who simply could not see it as such. I could imagine Humphrey in that very classroom, with the teacher present, explaining to his students that their teacher had violated a law and would be fairly tried. That from the nation's vice president might have been a powerful lesson. But it would have entailed risk, and was never considered. Instead, we, the children of the school, and the MFDP were told to squeeze ourselves into the hurtful constraints of a damaged party, rather than the party seizing in time the gift of change and hope. I always wanted to ask Tom Hayden about 1964 but somehow never did.

Mississippi was not transformed by the freedom schools, nor even by newly enfranchised black voters. But it was significantly changed. And those schools had an extraordinary impact on a generation of young and, like me, not so young activists. While I cannot speak for the Mississippi kids who participated,[32] I know about the changes wrought in me, and I know how these changes have played out in the work I have done for the past half century. Many Freedom Summer participants continued working in other movement venues: Kathie Amatniak, who became Kathie Sarahchild, helped—with other Mississippi activists like Sandra Cason (Casey Hayden) and Mary King—translate freedom school pedagogical practices into the fundamental learning strategies of feminist conscious-raising groups. Mario Savio organized for voting rights in McComb before returning to Berkeley and playing a central role in the free speech movement and the New Left. Heather Tobis Booth became a founder of the Midwest Academy and a key figure in voting rights campaigns. The brief narratives about the volunteers' post-1964 work at the end of *Letters from Mississippi* speak volumes about who came to Freedom Summer and where they went from there.[33] Just as a whaling ship may have been the Harvard for

Melville's Ishmael, the experiences of those hot church basements of Mississippi 1964 moved many of us far beyond our narrow educations at the Harvards and Yales.

At the end of Mississippi Summer, I returned to Philadelphia on the Trailways bus. Reclaiming my car, I put the top down and loaded it with my bed, my dresser, my grandmother's red-metal topped table, and a few books and records. Then I drove to Northampton, where I would begin teaching at Smith College. I arrived just in time for a staff meeting for the first-year course I was scheduled to teach. The people in the room all seemed to be strangers. Only later did I even recognize among them Helen Vendler, whom I had happily dated during the previous year. My mind during that meeting and after was still in Mississippi. That world, still so compelling, made my Smith colleagues, students, and classes seem as flat and peculiar to me as I, in my jeans and work shirt, might have seemed to them. Did I ever fully return to academe?

Chapter Four

PROFESSING AT SMITH AND SELMA

Bliss was it in that dawn to be alive,
But to be young was very heaven!

Wordsworth, not a poet with whom I ordinarily connect, conveys
the wonder of that time and place. This is a book about the transformation of minds, my own and many others'. In 1964 the dawn of change
cast splendor and excitement over all it touched, however rough or
silly a cooler eye might have pronounced our acts of desire, protest,
and expectation.

Not favoured spots alone, but the whole earth,
The beauty wore of promise . . . .
(The Prelude, XI, 108–9, 117–18)

Smith College, where I taught in 1964–65, had arranged a brilliant
schedule for faculty: we had classes on three consecutive days, Monday
to Wednesday for me, and then did whatever we did on the other four.
I began speaking, fundraising, and carrying out a variety of tasks for
Friends of SNCC, in New York, Washington, Poughkeepsie, and many
places in between. I learned how to use a mimeograph machine and to
write leaflets people could actually read. I joined others at Smith in cir-
culating a statement proclaiming resistance to the Vietnam War, and
in organizing a teach-in on that subject. I helped establish and sustain
a Smith-Amherst SDS chapter. I traveled to Montgomery with a couple
of my students during the Selma-Montgomery march and got arrested.
In short, for a wonderful academic year, I experienced many of the
pleasures of an undergraduate education at a fancy liberal arts college.

And this, too: as a single man of thirty-two, I was set loose among
exceptionally smart and attractive young women at a moment when having a fling with one's professor was becoming part of the educational
program. It would take a few years for the just-stirring feminist revolution
to challenge that perfidious mentality. Smith actually had a reputation

for hiring gay men—a number from Yale—presumably because they
offered no threat to its young women. That practice had come to a
disastrous end in 1960 when the Northampton Post Office had opened
a packet of what they designated gay "pornography" addressed to Professor Newton Arvin. In fact, the material was what we might today call
"beefcake" photography—scantily-clothed muscled guys—hardly sexual
in content, much less pornographic. But it led to Arvin's forced retirement, deep depression, and, too soon, cancer—and to Smith firing two
other English faculty members, Joel Dorius and Ned Spofford. The college's role in this affair was . . . well, scandalous. Not until 2002 did Smith
recognize Arvin's extensive contributions to American literary study and
his admirable teaching at the college by establishing an undergraduate
prize in his name. It did so only after Mt. Holyoke College, down the
road, had held a successful symposium on Arvin in 2001. The scandal
was not a part of polite discussion when I was teaching in Northampton.
I may have been the first single man hired into the English Department
after these events of the early 1960s.

At Smith, residential houses were encouraged to invite faculty
members to become affiliates—"mascots" was my loose term—and on
occasion to join the young women at dinner. Another charming privilege. I chose a house not too far from my small second-floor apartment
down a side street. Its real appeal was a stunning young woman who
might, to my still New York Jewish eyes, have arrived from a different
New England Protestant planet. Busily involved in the movement, I
worshipped from afar, though at some point I offered her a ride to
New York, where she disappeared into her obscure world. I cannot say
what she made of me and my little Corvair convertible, with which a
few days later I picked her up in the immense courtyard of 1185 Park
Avenue to return to Northampton. Years later I would fall in love with
and marry a Mt. Holyoke graduate of very similar personal and physical dimensions: a tall, blonde skier, at home in any and all social situations, and simultaneously at the cutting edge of feminist action for
change. I had taught at Dartmouth before, and had served as a teaching assistant at Yale, so I knew something of Ivied privilege. But Smith
presented a wholly new educational calculus. My Smith friend, like
my Mt. Holyoke wife-to-be, seemed to float in a cloud of entitlement:
objects of desire—a clever blouse, a coral pendant, a trip to Antarc-
tica—appeared with effortless magic. For me, and the Jewish women I
would mostly court, fulfilling expectations depended on our quickness
and the edgy work we carried forward. I taught goyim, and in time

would marry one, but even after Smith and marriage, I would never quite grasp the dynamics of such privilege.

At the same time, Smith also carried me a further step in the process of personal self-discovery, partly as a result of the tremendous power of the movement in that young and hopeful moment. I came to respect and indeed like what I found in the mirror. Even when I failed sexually, as sometimes happened, I didn't lose my hard-won sense of authority and even pride.

Helen Vendler and I had, the year before, both committed to taking positions in Northampton starting in the fall of 1964. We were each assigned to a basic first-year literature course that included texts such as Shakespeare's sonnets, John Milton's *Samson Agonistes*, James Joyce's *Portrait of the Artist as a Young Man*, and probably William Wordsworth, among other works entirely by and about white men. The point of the course, we thought, seemed obscure, if not deliberately provocative to its female constituency. At that point, neither Helen nor I would likely have described ourselves as "feminists," but we felt moved to mention our concerns to the director of the course. He intoned, "You will understand it, once you have taught it." Not true. The Smith course was, for me, the first collegiate instance of the problem of "the canon" that I had begun to be aware of in the Mississippi freedom schools and that I would pursue over the next half century.

The first instance of my other freedom school interest—moving toward a more interactive and student-centered education—occurred the following spring. I taught a big American literature survey, usually offered by Daniel Aaron, one of the fathers of American Studies, who was on leave. I made a few changes in the assigned texts, but I remained largely baffled by the lecture format. I enjoyed lecturing and was pretty good doing it, but I had not figured out how to turn this class of over a hundred students in a large auditorium into an active learning opportunity. Most of the seniors knitted, while the juniors manically took notes. Two-thirds of the way through the course, Liz Fusco, a Smith graduate who had become director of the ongoing Mississippi freedom schools, visited me. We had just begun reading Ralph Ellison's *Invisible Man*. Liz proposed that we ask the students to turn in their seats and talk with their neighbors about invisibility, theirs from each other and from us, and us for them. Some students made the effort. A third of the class walked out. After a while, with the remaining students, we began a heated discussion of the text, our approach to it, and the implications of our method.

A number of students wrote to me, some remained to talk after the next day's class, and others came to the office. A couple of seniors commented, economically on a half sheet of paper, "Since each hour of instruction costs Smith students $3.00, we estimate that your American lit class pays $600 for each of your lectures. In view of this fact would you justify yesterday's wasted hour?" Another wrote about how "Ellison did become visible to me, and more so through association with my own invisibility. It is the easiest way out to read the book, come to lecture, take notes and forget the whole thing. That is not a learning experience." A senior wrote at some length about the following day's class, at which we talked through the initial day on Ellison: "I think the intensity of the ill-feeling about Tuesday's class lies in the fact that most white American citizens have a deep-seated guilt feeling about the Negro problem in the United States and, in most cases, about their failure to take a stand and do something constructive about ameliorating it."

I appreciated the students' passionate responses to the class and their willingness to question what we had accomplished. But for a long time the usefulness of that small experiment eluded me. Some thirty years later, however, while speaking at a high school in Tolland, a Connecticut town near Hartford, the issue resurfaced. After the talk, one of the teachers came up to me. "I owe you an apology," she said, much to my puzzlement. "In fact, I've owed you an apology for thirty years. I was one of your students at Smith who walked out of your American lit class." She went on to tell me that she had taught *Invisible Man* and taught it well, thanks to that class. And not only that novel, she said. While I was charmed by her story, it proved nothing definitive about the experiment that Liz and I had tried. Still, that moment at Smith had broken for me the tyranny of the lecture format. While I never entirely abandoned lecturing, I no longer felt compelled to hold forth at the front of the room. More important, I came to question that image of "the professor" as a proper representation of the meaning of teaching.

Through the 1964–65 school year, politics were heating up at Smith, as they were on campuses across the country. Early in the fall, a student, Trudy Johnson, and I had circulated a flyer inviting people to a "Forum on the New Left" to discuss and perhaps act upon "social, economic, and political problems from a perspective outside the usual liberal-conservative framework."[1]

We were influenced by the suggestions of a recent Smith graduate who had become active in Students for a Democratic Society (SDS). Perhaps as a result of the forum a group of students at Smith and Amherst started an SDS chapter that spring, in which I became active.

A group of five Smith faculty and two students also issued a strong statement of resistance to the war. We wrote:

> If any remnant of decency is to be salvaged out of the barbarities of the Vietnamese war, a line must somewhere be drawn.
>
> We draw it now. "<u>We hereby declare</u> our conscientious refusal to cooperate with the United States government in the prosecution of the war in Vietnam.
>
> "We encourage those who can conscientiously do so to refuse to serve in the armed forces and to ask for discharge if they are already in.
>
> "Those of us who are subject to the draft ourselves declare our own intention to refuse to serve.
>
> "We urge others to refuse and refuse ourselves to take part in the manufacture or transportation of military equipment, or to work in the fields of military research and weapons development.
>
> "We shall encourage the development of other nonviolent acts, including acts which involve civil disobedience, in order to stop the flow of American soldiers and munitions to Vietnam."

The statement, which we debated over many months, was finally published March 2, 1965, in the *Sophian*, the student newspaper.[2] It sparked considerable controversy. I think of it now as an early instance of the effort to transform "protest" into what people wanted to call "resistance."

The SDS chapter, after considerable discussion, decided that some of us should join in the Selma-Montgomery march, scheduled for March 21–25. I agreed to drive to Selma with two students, Judith Coburn and Susan Herman, in my white Corvair convertible. One other Smith student, Posy Lombard, and a few from Amherst had gone on ahead. Stopping in New York, we joined a SDS-sponsored picket of the Chase Manhattan Bank, protesting its support for the apartheid government of South Africa. Some fifty students were arrested for blocking the back door of the bank, but we continued south. In Virginia my car broke down and had to be repaired. A local policeman approached me as I hung out in the garage. "Oh, oh," I thought to myself, "he's on to where we're headed, and wants to make trouble." In fact, the cops suspected that I was taking the young women, whom they had observed having coffee in a diner, across state lines for immoral purposes. They insisted on contacting Judy's parents back in St. Louis to make sure that she was traveling with their permission. She wasn't, of course. But her father, although furious, had little choice but to let her go on. Susan finessed by claiming her parents were in South America. So we continued deeper and deeper south, past a sign in Georgia marked "Trash Barrel." "Trash Barrel, Georgia," became a meme for us, relieving the mounting tension of the drive.

When we arrived in Selma, SNCC staff people told us that there were plenty of marchers. We would be more useful, they said, in Montgomery, picketing George Wallace's state capitol to publicize our slogan, "one man, one vote," and the refusal of Alabama to respond to that imperative. That effort, they added, might get us arrested. A number of pickets and demonstrations in the vicinity of the state capitol had produced much confusion about what would be allowed by the state or local police; we learned of several attacks on demonstrators by a horseback "posse" of local men not in uniform but armed with clubs and whips.[3] Susan, we decided, would not picket and not risk being jailed so she could, if it became necessary, raise bail money for us and others from colleges in the Northampton area. Judy and I, along with Marshall Bloom from Amherst, joined a small contingent outside the capitol. We found the sidewalk blocked off by police cars parked nose to tail. To climb over them was to invite a cop's night stick breaking your head. Plan B was to try picketing in the street, which we did. The troopers were on us in a minute for "blocking" the nonexistent traffic. Not a reporter in sight. We were promptly carted off to a police facility, fingerprinted, and moved along to Kilby State Prison on the outskirts of the city.

With three or four other white guys, I was brought into an enormous room like a school gym, in which forty or fifty men, arrested earlier, were already stashed. Our jailer told us to find a mattress and to stay quiet. Finding no free mattresses, we began to raise a fuss, yelling for the guards. Eventually, a guard led us down the hall to a space where the black men were held. "Bring some mattresses, boys," he told them, which they did. "Take a mattress," the guard said to us. We each picked one up and followed the guard back to the "white room." Why didn't I just plump down on the mattress in the "black area" and stay there? Sure, I would have been forcibly removed. But why should that have mattered? Weren't we in Alabama to fight segregation? Besides, the black guys were obviously having much more fun, singing, wrestling, gambling, dancing, feuding, meeting, as Junius Williams was later to report.[4]

What a vivid lesson! We whites of middle-class station were so well trained, so obedient to guards and teachers, texts and courses, figures of authority. It never occurred to us to use this chance to break the code of segregation. Soon enough, I learned a major movement lesson: question norms and expectations, power and ferocity. And thus my homage to Wordsworth.

I had placed my mattress down next to students from Amherst whom I knew from the SDS chapter. An error. They launched on-again-off-again arguments that lasted well into the night and picked up early the next morning. Questions about the march had been raised during our SDS discussion back in Massachusetts; new ones emerged from the local actions: What was the point of the march itself? Of getting arrested outside the statehouse? What good were we doing locked up in this gym? Weren't we feeding George Wallace's treasury? Shouldn't we be bugging the guards, at least by singing? The questions made sense and reflected some of my own doubts. But I needed to sleep after the long, tedious drive.

Susan, meanwhile, raised the necessary money, and most of us were sprung in time to join the dinner on the march's muddy last night and the final walk into Montgomery. But others, especially young blacks from the Montgomery area, were stuck in jail, as we learned after our release. Our group, now enlarged by the Amherst students and some local black kids, decided that we would raise their bail along the march route in Montgomery. We rounded up some boxes and hats, made a few signs, and as we marched called out to bystanders to contribute to a bail fund. They responded generously, not just with dollar bills and an occasional fiver, but also with countless pennies, nickels, and dimes. Kids, who had no money and for whom even nickel contributions were a strain, wanted to "join" the movement. Their responses helped me to see what a "movement" might be. It swept you up, in spirit, in song, and in marching feet. It made you reach into your pockets. I had seen it in smaller ways in Chester. Here, it was like a growing wave that would, we hoped, carry away Governor Wallace and the segregation he tried to uphold. Intimidation was being drained away, though discrimination, exploitation, and violence would not simply evaporate.

At the conclusion of the march, Posy asked whether she might borrow my car to drive people from Selma back down that highway

to home. There weren't enough places in Montgomery for everyone
to sleep and some had to be back for work. Important, I thought, but
still *not* a good idea. Bright white, seemingly fancy, with foreign (Maryland) plates, my car was a sitting target, and we had already had one
run-in on a back street with local racist guys trying to stop us. We had
two local black women with us in the back, and I had given the boys
the finger when they yelled "nigger lovers" at us and threw beer. They
had tried to block the street with their opened car door. I'd aimed
my car directly at two of the guys trying to stop us, narrowly missing
them, and raced back to the black community, horn blaring. My stupid
for treating the movement like a teen challenge. So I said no to Posy
about using the car; in fact, I discouraged her from making such a run.
Not without reason, as it turned out. That night Viola Liuzzo, a white
woman from Detroit, was driving a volunteer back to Selma when she
was shot to death along Highway 80 by Klansmen driving a car that also
contained FBI informant Gary Rowe. Another lesson: assume that the
worst can and often will happen in racist America, especially when you
challenge power and privilege.

Meanwhile, President Johnson's government was escalating the
war; it would move away from anything that might be called "liberalism" to continued escalation and, as many came to feel, hopeless
intransigence.

> How might we believe
> That wisdom could, in any shape, come near
> Men clinging to delusions so insane?
> (Wordsworth, *The Prelude*, XI, 44–46)

To stop the escalating war, we developed ever more innovative tactics to try making a war policy too costly, too divisive, too hopeless to
pursue. The idea was to convert the antiwar movement "from protest
to resistance," as the phrase of the time had it. What resistance might
mean remained to be seen.

Returning to Northampton, we learned that a new development
in antiwar activity had emerged at the University of Michigan in Ann
Arbor: an all-night "teach-in" on Vietnam. The first was held during
the last days of the Selma-Montgomery march. Very soon, teach-ins
were organized at Chicago, Columbia, and many other institutions.
Only a few students and faculty knew anything about Vietnam, including the history of its struggle against Chinese, French, Japanese, and

now American invaders. What better way to enlighten them—and ourselves—than to hold lectures, distribute literature, and create panels to debate questions of American policy and the escalating war?

Teach-ins were presented as primarily informative, and they were. But in my view their effect was less detached study than promoting activism. They seemed to me a logical extension into higher education of freedom school learning. At the very beginning of April 1965, some three dozen teach-ins nationwide helped promote the first large demonstration against the war, which was being organized by SDS in Washington, DC, for April 17. More important, perhaps, as Dick Flacks pointed out, the teach-ins represented not only an important antiwar activity in themselves but also a "pedagogical breakthrough." They provided an opportunity for faculty and students to generate a "learning experience" that brought together "the knowledge and expertise of academic scholars" and students to affect "democratic social action."[5] Their form registered as strongly with me as their content.

In the Pioneer Valley, we quickly organized our own teach-in, held in Mahar Auditorium at the University of Massachusetts, April 7–8. The planning group consisted of a newly minted four-college chapter of a faculty-based Universities Committee on the Problems of Peace and War, combined with the primarily student-comprised SDS chapters at the University of Massachusetts, Smith, and Amherst.

One feature of the first teach-ins involved a confrontation between speakers representing the State Department or the American military and academics questioning the war policy. Most government speakers were not well informed. Those who were, and who were involved in determining policy, preferred not to risk embarrassment on a campus from some smart-assed professor—or worse, a student. Thus, while teach-ins spread rapidly across the academy in the spring of 1965, they quickly became arguments among resident faculty and students working out different positions on the issues. Our substitute for a State Department spokesperson was a professor who had taken part in government service and who continued to support US involvement in Southeast Asia.

Well-known Amherst professor Henry Steele Commager, the initial attraction of our teach-in, helped to fill an auditorium of five hundred. "We have stumbled into the position of an aggressor," he said, contradicting the claims of American policy-makers, "while we would not tolerate conduct such as ours by other countries of this hemisphere." Commager put his finger on the central ideological basis of American policy, the assumption that "we are a people apart and providence watches our destiny." Poet and statesman Archibald MacLeish followed. He stressed standing up for one's values. Between them, Commager and MacLeish posed the central arguments of demonstrators and other antiwar activists: questioning "American exceptionalism" and insisting on the need to declare opposition to immoral government policies. Other students and faculty spoke out through the night, read poetry, commented on films, debated US policy. At 6 a.m., there were still some 250 people in the auditorium.

Suddenly, there were quarrels about Vietnam everywhere. We knew very little about Southeast Asia or about the American war there. The government was not forthcoming and the mainstream media of little help. To become better informed and to hold our own in the arguments, we read Robert Scheer,[6] Malcolm Browne, Wilfred Burchett, Bernard Fall, David Halberstam, Marguerite Higgins, Robert Scigliano, Võ Nguyên Giáp, and Ho Chi Minh; also, remarkable statements from Hanoi, Saigon, Washington, Beijing, and a variety of documents ultimately assembled into a collection by Marv Gettleman.[7] In bookstores and libraries we found an enormous literature dedicated to a country most academics outside of Asian studies had not even heard about a few short years back. But was learning about Vietnam enough?

A week later, we were again on the road, this time to the Students for a Democratic Society event in Washington. Two busses carried students from the four-college area; I drove my car, planning to stay with Allan and Peggy Brick in Baltimore. That demonstration, a first, was also notable for two things: the size of the turnout, some twenty-five thousand, which seemed to us in SDS enormous, and for its time was. The organization's president, Paul Potter, also called out American foreign policy in ways that had not been commonplace, even among those in SDS. He began by giving a wider meaning to the war: "The incredible war in Vietnam has provided the razor, the terrifying sharp cutting edge that has finally severed the last vestige of illusion that morality and democracy are the guiding principles of American foreign policy." Most people at the demonstration, he pointed out, had not been deeply engaged in antiwar activities; rather, they had come because of the systematic and increasing violation of human rights, of human beings in Vietnam by Americans. His analysis led to the memorable conclusion: "We must name that system. We must name it, describe it, analyze it, understand it and change it. For it is only when that system is changed and brought under control that there can be any hope for stopping the forces that create a war in Vietnam today or a murder in the South tomorrow or all the incalculable, innumerable more subtle atrocities that are worked on people all over all the time." Those gathered at the Washington Monument responded to Potter's call by crying out "name the system, name the system." "Name the system" became a watchword within SDS, as did Potter's insistence that the way forward led not through protests here and there but by building the movement:

> If the people of this country are to end the war in Vietnam, and to change the institutions which create it, then the people of this country must create a massive social movement, and if that can be built around the issue of Vietnam then that is what we must do. By a social movement I mean more than petitions or letters of protest, or tacit support of dissident Congressmen; I mean people who are willing to change their lives, who are willing to challenge the system, to take the problem of change seriously. By a social movement I mean an effort that is powerful enough to make the country understand that our problems are not in Vietnam, or China or Brazil or outer space or at the bottom of the ocean, but are here in the United States.[8]

Potter articulated powerfully something that I and many others in and out of SDS had been struggling with: how a movement differed from discrete actions to confront a racist incident or a wartime atrocity. Potter seemed to underline Thoreau's vision of "action from principle, the perception and the performance of right." Was that progression, I wondered, the point of my work as a professor at Smith, or anywhere else?

I was very conflicted about my work at Smith. Of course, I loved teaching these smart and expressive young women. Helen Vendler and I had done a joint class about modern American poetry in my big American literature lecture course a couple of weeks after the Washington march. The students hugely enjoyed it—they applauded—and so did we. I learned from Helen and was inspired by her. We'd responded to an invitation from the department's curriculum committee to propose a first-year course focused on learning about literature by writing it, knowing poetry by creating it. Our suggestions, we learned, were dismissed out of hand, with much sarcastic comment. I was regarded as something of a kook in the Smith department. Unfair, I thought. Both Helen and I were writing and publishing; we were recognized off campus for our intellectual work. Why weren't we seen that way locally?

I was not alone, of course, in being deeply enmeshed in the problems of student-centered teaching. An increasingly uneasy problem in sixties education, it was being taken up by many of the best young faculty everywhere. More and more, teachers in many fields sought ways to make their work in the classroom consonant with their values and politics. What, for example, we would later ask, did it mean to teach as a feminist, or as a socialist? New institutions were being created in which such questions were on the agenda: SUNY College at Old Westbury, where I would later teach, UC Santa Cruz, Evergreen, Hampshire, Ramapo, Richmond, Kirkland, Governors State, to name a few. In addition, many "free universities" came into being, often briefly, across the country. The teach-ins forced the issue. Faculty asked: What are the optimal circumstances for learning to occur? How might these be created? What academic norms and traditions prevent teaching designed to empower students? And, newly important, how were these educational concerns related to the larger issues of segregation, the ongoing war, patriarchy—the "system" that Potter had not named? I was dissatisfied with the standard course of study in American colleges: few women, fewer blacks, no Vietnam,[9] but *Samson Agonistes* and *Portrait of the Artist as a Young Man*. We understood that we had to educate *ourselves* if we were ever to achieve a just, fair, and peaceful nation. But how to go about that transformation?

These issues came to a head for me early in the summer of 1965 when I got a call from the American Friends Service Committee office in Chicago. Their peace education secretary, Jay Miller, was taking a job with the Chicago branch of the American Civil Liberties Union. They needed a replacement pronto. Would I be interested? Should I, I fretted, give up this attractive position at Smith with its engaging students to take up Potter's challenge of full-time movement work? Anyone familiar with today's academic job market and interested at all in college teaching, as I was, would be amused: Was there really a choice here? You hold on to the college job for dear life. But "that was in another country": the world of possibility it presupposed is now dead. In 1965 I didn't imagine that any choice I made could never be altered, as would now be true. Never. The problem, as I posed it to myself and others was: What kind of work should I be doing? Some form of teaching, perhaps different from what I had been engaged in at Smith? Like freedom schools or teach-ins? Or some form of teaching embodied in organizing for change?

I wrote two long letters to the chair of the English Department and to Dan Aaron, who was by virtue of our common literary interests something of a mentor. I tried to lay out why the kind of teaching I was doing at Smith did not lead to student learning but to entrapment. The idea, endorsed by the institution and by the students, and still by me, too, was for me to lay before them as effectively as I could the ideas already in my head. I would tell them what Emily Dickinson's "I started Early—took my Dog" might mean, how the connections between Benjamin Franklin and F. Scott Fitzgerald might be understood, what might be an appropriate approach for a young woman to James Joyce's *A Portrait of the Artist as a Young Man.* They would take notes, "bank" those ideas, and demonstrate they had done so by answering my questions on exams and in papers. Good banking got good grades.

But for me, education had to do with the discussions precipitated by the real concerns students brought to class in response to poems or stories that engaged them and spoke to their lives. Then we might discover how "I started Early" achieved its hold on them, if it did. Or whether, and why, it might be worthwhile to track the myriad historical and cultural references of Tillie Olsen's story "Tell Me a Riddle" or the cultural politics of Richard Wright's wonderful "Bright and Morning Star." Traditional literary concerns like form and allusion would emerge, that is, from students' engagement. Education, as I wrote in my letters, involved "freeing, or rather helping students free themselves, from stereotypes, limits, clichés, authority that imposes and constricts; helping them gain confidence in their own abilities, their own feelings; and helping them bring these abilities to bear on understanding those feelings."

Such an education might enable them to make up their own minds about what their countrymen were doing in and to Vietnam. And take up the responsibility, as Judy Coburn would do, for telling Americans what as an investigative journalist she saw happening in Vietnam. Or, as Posy Lombard did, after she decided what she might accomplish by confronting racism in Natchez and elsewhere in the South and teaching children there. Or as Merble Harrington would do, founding an organization to educate and support poor women of color in search of jobs and a future.

Unclear, I decided I needed a bit of a retreat to puzzle it out. I drove to the Cape, top down, stopped to get the key from the landlady, Mrs. Daisy, and drop my bag. I proceeded to Provincetown to pick up supplies at the market, and parked outside the cottage in the warm early-June sun. I awoke a few hours later when the dew began to fall. Perhaps, I thought, I was overdoing it—teaching, speaking wherever I could, making love, doing movement office work. But then again, I was getting a brilliant education at much less cost than, and having as much fun as, my Smithie students. All the same, and reluctantly, I decided to leave the place where I'd first encountered these admirable young women and devote myself full-time to movement work in Chicago.

Chapter Five

RETURN TO MISSISSIPPI (GODDAM)

In politics, success can bring as many problems as failures. During the 1964–65 school year, and just before, the movement leapt forward. Mississippi Summer broadened a primarily southern civil rights movement to involve large numbers of young northerners, primarily white; often, it caught up as well their parents, schoolmates, friends, and even their congressional representatives. The following spring, events in Selma, Alabama, and the march to Montgomery stamped the issue of voting rights on the national consciousness. Protest played loudly in schools, churches, and television stations throughout America. The US Congress, increasingly responsive to movement pressure, passed the Civil Rights Act of 1964, banning segregation (at least in theory). In 1965, in direct response to the Selma-Montgomery march, it approved a historic Voting Rights Act. In April of that same year, SDS organized the first mass demonstration in Washington against the Vietnam War—shortly after the initial US Marine Corps combat force had landed on the beach near Da Nang. On campuses across the nation, teachers and students reacted with excitement and uncertainty: What would changes in race relations and the new student activism mean for the organization of campus life, as well as for curricula and classroom dynamics? We were increasingly contesting the very definition of "education."

The assassination of Malcolm X in February 1965 also defined these months, along with the uprising against unemployment, crumbling housing, inadequate schools, and police brutality of the black community of Watts in Los Angeles. Change involved more than peace and roses. In fact, it proved hard to know what the next steps in our "revolution" might be. Everywhere movement activists gathered, we debated that question—in meetings of our new SDS chapter, in the Friends of SNCC office in Washington, in jail during the Selma-Montgomery march. Nothing seemed fixed—not what we did in our classrooms, in the streets, in our lobbying, even in our movement organizations. "We've come this far to freedom, / And we won't turn back," we sang. Yes. But just where were we headed? And with whom?

The SDS national office was moving from New York to Chicago. And so was I. A fortunate conjunction. I had been elected to the National Interim Committee (NIC). While my duties as peace education secretary of the Chicago region AFSC would absorb much of my time and political energy, I hoped to expand what I did in SDS, which I knew was an explosively growing political force. But first, I had committed to a number of movement activities for the summer: minimally, a Baltimore institute for inner-city teachers, and another series of workshops for volunteers in Mississippi. Both turned out to display in bold letters questions about direction and comradeship that were agitating the movement.

On the first day of my seminar I asked the teachers to help me place the chairs in a circle, which was not yet a commonplace of such events. It was spring of 1965, and we were at a National Defense Education Act (NDEA) institute for inner-city teachers in Baltimore held at Goucher College.[1] Once we were settled, I said, "It's your seminar. What do you want to talk about?" We sat in silence for the remainder of that hour. One of the men began drumming his fingers on the desk of his chair, then stopped, embarrassed by the noise he was making. Two women occasionally glanced at one another, wanting to *do* something, but unable to decide without speaking what that might be. Speaking appeared to violate some classroom protocol. We sat silently the next day too. Some of the teachers looked out the window, a few, longingly, toward the door. There was much shifting and shuffling, crossing and uncrossing of legs. One man, who periodically stared angrily at me, pulled the *Baltimore Sun* out of his bag. On the third day, a participant mumbled something angrily about this not being what he'd signed up for. One or two others hesitantly agreed. Why wasn't I teaching? I reminded the group that many of them had far more experience as teachers than I, and were also older. Finally, some ragged conversation ensued; we were started, more and less.

Was I being excessively aggressive toward the teachers? The institute staff had agreed upon a nondirective seminar. The report of the institute summarized: the "staff concluded that basic to the Institute day must be a group experience that proved that primary insights and actions must come not from the staff member, but from the participant himself."[2] Still, was I carrying my anti-authoritarian approach to a counterproductive extreme? Perhaps such shock treatment was necessary. Then again, American advisors in post–Soviet Russia talked of the necessity for "shock therapy," but used it to pursue their own political agendas. What was the proper balance between giving direction and waiting for student initiatives? Between content and method? Who knew? Clearly, we needed to move away from the stand-and-deliver model of teaching, which did not seem to be generating interest and involvement—aka, learning—among most students. But how to change things? More than half a century later, that dispute continues, though the contexts of the discourse—community control, small schools, No Child Left Behind, high-stakes testing, charter schools—keep changing.

Each morning, the members of my seminar observed Florence Howe teaching a literature class to a group of inner-city high school students. She used many poems, including "local" work like Countee Cullen's brilliant "Incident":

> I saw a Baltimorean
> Keep looking straight at me.
>
> Now I was eight and very small,
> And he was no whit bigger,
> And so I smiled, but he poked out
> His tongue, and called me, "Nigger."

And Williams Carlos Williams's "The Young Housewife":

> At ten A.M. the young housewife
> moves about in negligee behind
> the wooden walls of her husband's house.

Her students, half male, half female, predominantly African American, came from Baltimore city high schools. Allan Brick, the institute director, had worked hard to persuade school personnel to enroll "underachievers" with fair to good abilities; the schools did not like to acknowledge that they had such students. But we thought it important *not* to have a student group of conventionally successful kids. The purpose of the institute was unequivocal: "to broaden the teachers' awareness of student potential, their recognition that, while their students may be 'disadvantaged' when it comes to possessing certain skills and manifesting certain kinds of motivation, these students, sometimes actually *because of* their background, have talent and drive that make them highly educable."[3] We recognized the students as the "experts on themselves" and generally on their communities. Most of the students, we discovered, enjoyed talking about poems.

A young, white Appalachian woman, stringy of hair and thin of body, remains most vividly in my memory. I think it was she who explained to one of the teachers her dissatisfaction with regular school. The teacher wrote in her evaluation that the student complained: "'They don't teach us to think. All we get is subject matter. Who needs it?' Neither had I been taught to think," the teacher added, "much less to say what was on my mind."[4] Like most of the others, this student spoke readily in class, but in a heavy Appalachian brogue which could be difficult to follow. On other occasions we had heard her speak in Standard English. So we asked her why she didn't speak "normal" English in class, like us maybe. She stood looking at us for a while and then said, "I don't never want to *talk* like you, cause I don't never want to *be* like you." That put a whole new gloss on the "two language" problem, usually associated with southern African American dialect.

This student's complaint made it clear enough that teachers needed more engaging content, whether at the level of Dick and Jane or of Eliot and Pound. Her comment about "subject matter" also evoked for me the problem of the "canon," what is worth learning about. But "canon" was not the primary concern of this Goucher Institute. Rather, we were feeling our way toward a mode of teaching that did not depend on the authoritarian power of the teacher. Enough of "you're here to sit silently and acquire a bit of what's already in my head." Instead, we wanted a style of learning that could emerge from the knowledge, indeed the authority, of the student. Yes, the students were experts on themselves, on their families, neighborhoods, communities. How could we liberate such knowledge? How could we honor and make use of what students actually knew? How could we help them appreciate that knowledge, its sources, its extensions—and also what it left out? How might they best make use of it? That challenge, which we had faced in the 1964 Mississippi freedom schools, reappeared in this Goucher Institute.

Anti-authoritarian educational innovators like Paul Goodman, Paulo Freire, A. S. Neill, Abraham Maslow, and especially Carl Rogers heavily influenced the institute staff. Their writing prompted my initially silent seminar and formed the basis of a social "theory" class for the teachers led by Marty and Sara Oppenheimer. These ideas also animated the institute's approach to living arrangements on the Goucher campus, where all of the students and half the teachers resided. Mornings began with five unstructured roundtables, more or less based on T-group (encounter group) methodologies; four of them, dealing with everything from food and language to sex, involved both students and teachers. Role-playing sessions led by Samuel Burton helped to get both teachers and students out of themselves; they addressed tensions that might arise in classes or in the dorms and on campus.

The institute chalked up a number of successes. Most students read most of the assigned stories and poems. Class discussions, often complex, sometimes contentious, generally fun, involved observers and participants. The teachers—our primary audience—read widely, though we did not assign much. They found books and articles that engaged them, that they wanted their peers to read too so they could talk together—sometimes in my seminar—about what they were discovering.

Two external action projects emerged: the first, mainly for observation, involved a visit to a migrant labor camp on the Eastern Shore of Maryland, and a follow-up visit. The second had an action component: testing whether Baltimore-area real-estate dealers adhered to nondiscriminatory sales and rentals as the law required. The teachers designed teams to visit real estate offices to see whether black and white potential clients were treated alike. They practiced in the role-playing class. After their visits, they reported back to the group as a whole. I watched them become skilled at playing a real estate salesman maintaining the boundaries of segregation: "To be honest, you probably would not find that a friendly neighborhood." Or, "I have to find out if that apartment is still available—we just had someone else here who was interested in it." Then more piously, "Would you have sufficient income to persuade the bank that you would qualify for a mortgage in that area?" Discrimination in 1960s Baltimore, beginning much more than half a century ago, helped set up the segregated, impoverished city of today. Their findings also raised the big question of the relationship between excellence in schools and desegregation of neighborhoods. Did residential segregation lead to poor schools? Or did poor schools lead to segregated neighborhoods? Where, in what appeared a closed circle, could one intervene?

The teachers' projects challenged us as faculty leaders: would education, as we were conceiving it, necessarily lead to transformative action, as had been the case with most Mississippi freedom schools? Could—should—education and action for change be separated? This question has haunted American educational institutions. If you confront the crappy realities of your life in your classroom, as education at its best can and, in my view, should do, would you not want to try changing those realities? That is the doctrine proposed by Freire, pursued by Freedom Summer, implicit in our institute, and underlying the activity of our teachers. But how much action for change can be carried out by teachers or students from the public schools? Were we helping these teachers become more effective in the classroom? And/or better activists? Were teaching and activism as different as they appeared to be?[5] Would our strategies put the teachers' jobs at risk and lead not to better education but to unemployment?

I intended, when the institute ended, to return to Mississippi, this time with Sue Gottfried. We had corresponded extensively about a plan to staff workshops at the Mount Beulah Center in Edwards, Mississippi. We would lead discussion groups and show films to northerners volunteering in southern civil rights projects. The discussions would help them use these southern experiences back in their home schools or communities. The workshops had been planned by two long-term, dedicated white SNCC workers, Mary King and Dennis Sweeney. Later, Mary with Casey Hayden would be an initiator of women's liberation conscious-raising groups. Dennis, who had become a victim of movement PTSD and become sadly deranged, would later murder Allard Lowenstein.[6]

Most of what I had planned for Mississippi went up the flue. Sue, at the urging of the head of Seattle CORE, decided to remain there in Washington state, working on local issues of racial discrimination and segregation. Florence agreed to join me at the Mount Beulah workshops. She talked with the editor of the *New Yorker*, William Shawn, about writing a "Letter from Mississippi." He seemed interested. Shortly after the institute ended, we packed up her black English Ford and set out once again for the South. I should have known from the moment of our arrival that things were not working quite as expected: I introduced myself to the director, a white minister, who greeted me enthusiastically and, turning to Florence, said, "And this must be Sue."

Mississippi, we quickly discovered, had lost the attention of the national civil rights movement. Our image of Mississippi, like that of most people, whether or not affiliated with the movement, had been shaped in the exhilarating and often terrifying days of the previous summer of 1964. Almost everything had changed in a year: COFO had largely vanished, and with it most efforts at planning the activities of "freedom houses," groups like the Delta Ministry, and volunteers like us. Only one of our planned workshops was funded. Our workshop hosts at the Mount Beulah Center in Edwards were unprepared for the kind of project that had been scheduled. A cleric affiliated with the Delta Ministry expressed his frustration: "I'm willing to do what's needed," he said, "wash dishes, sweep floors, do anything that is useful." But he had been told by the white project director not to interfere with black people who were in charge of matters like the dining room. "Weren't there good reasons for that?" I asked. "But am I *not* supposed to tell Jake that if he leaves the mayonnaise jar out in the heat all day, we might be in for a case of botulism? Whites have expertise, but maybe it's not useful here and now." His wife chimed in: "A trained, mature, intelligent white volunteer might hew out his own role for a month. But unless he has these qualifications, and real perceptions, I'd say, stay home. Forget it." What functions might white volunteers, including us, usefully carry forward? Were we, practically speaking, a burden on rather than an assist to local people? A new form of white paternalism?

We encountered many such distressing moments. Arriving in McComb, a town that had been a focus of Ku Klux Klan terror and black resistance for many years, we discovered that the freedom house was a shambles. The sign on the sink, hanging by one small bolt from the wall, read "do NOT even breathe on this sink." A sea of used clothing, books, and trash filled the main room, twenty feet across—useless donations from northern supporters. The bookshelves sat empty. National organizations like CORE and even the NAACP sustained organizing from a distance, if at all. Increasingly, Florence and I focused on our writing, for the first time as coauthors. Heady work, reporting and assessing what was happening at that moment in Mississippi, summer 1965.

We had decided to visit Posy Lombard, one of my Smith students, who had just graduated. Posy was working in Natchez, known as one of the state's scarier, more violent places, canvassing for support of the Mississippi Freedom Democratic Party. Tall, rosy-cheeked, strong, Posy was adored by the children of the area where she lived. She introduced me to the flocks of children always clustering about her with the impressive title of "her own teacher." The chief priorities of the summer were twofold: encouraging black voter registration and the challenge of the Mississippi Freedom Democratic Party (MFDP) to the seating of the five white Mississippi congressmen. Mississippi members of the House of Representatives had been elected in significant measure because most blacks had been systematically disenfranchised; the MFDP decided to focus on this fact in order to raise the issue nationally. Most black people knew well enough the danger of trying to register, and while the very idea of voting retained its power, they often didn't see what might be accomplished through the ballot. So voter registration wasn't any easy task.

Posy also introduced us to the adults who lived on Wall Street near downtown Natchez. The wide main street of Natchez, with its impressive houses, echoed the plantation past. Behind those mansions ran narrow, rutted roads, like Wall Street, housing black people in small buildings divided into two cramped two- or three-room apartments. Natchez taught me a lesson about residential segregation and bussing: the black children living on Wall Street didn't walk to their neighborhood school. Instead, they were bussed (or walked two miles) to the edge of the town, where the segregated black schools were located. In ensuing years, when I heard northern whites complain about bussing, I would tell them about Natchez. When we asked people on Wall Street, particularly the women, about their issues, almost all spoke of ending segregation so their children could walk to the local school. We helped them draw up and circulate a petition to the school board to begin formulating a desegregation plan—an effort that ended in disaster.

Florence and I described that long, complex story in our "Letter from Mississippi," designed to be of interest to William Shawn. The "Letter" remains unpublished. We were not yet very practiced in this craft. Our concerns then were at the margins of *New Yorker* interests: sex, violence, and particularly resistance to the widening war. In the summer of 1965, who wanted to read the mainly dispiriting news from this particular US battlefront? Much of the nation, outside the South, had rallied to the civil rights cause during Mississippi Summer in 1964. But in 1965 the messages coming from Mississippi differed.

One major message, we discovered, was the increasing resistance to the Vietnam War among black people in Mississippi. In July of 1965, word arrived in McComb, Mississippi, that John D. Shaw, a young black draftee of twenty-three who had participated in 1961 civil rights demonstrations there, had been killed in action in Vietnam. A group of his classmates, with Joe Martin of McComb and Clint Hopson, a law student from New Jersey, wrote and passed out a leaflet titled "The War on Viet Nam." Here's what it said:

Here are five reasons why Negroes should not be in any War fighting for America:

1. No Mississippi Negroes should be fighting in Viet Nam for the White Mans freedom, until all the Negro People are free in Mississippi.
2. Negro boys should not honor the draft here in Mississippi. Mothers should encourage their sons not to go.
3. We will gain respect and dignity as a race only by forcing the United States Government and the Mississippi Government to come with guns, dogs and trucks to take our sons away to fight and be killed protecting Miss., Ala., Ga., and La.
4. No one has a right to ask us to risk our lives and kill other Colored People in Santo Domingo and Viet Nam, so that the White American can get richer. We will be looked upon as traitors by all the Colored People of the world if the Negro people continue to fight and die without a cause.
5. Last week a white soldier from New Jersey was discharged from the Army because he refused to fight in Viet Nam and went on a hunger strike. Negro boys can do the same thing. We can write and ask our sons if they know what they are fighting for. If he answers Freedom, tell him that's what we are fighting for here in Mississippi. And if he says Democracy tell him the truth—we don't know anything about Communism, Socialism, and all that, but we do know that Negroes have caught hell here under this American Democracy.[7]

The MFDP's *Newsletter* reprinted the leaflet, with a brief story about its distribution. It created a jingoistic storm. Every Mississippi newspaper and politicians across the South chimed in to deplore this supposedly "unpatriotic stand" by the organization—which had not endorsed the position taken by the leaflet, but simply reported on it. Many in the black community were unhappy with its circulation, if not necessarily with its substance.

The leaflet's contents reflected an increasingly widely held view among black southerners. We heard that antiwar sentiment on a raggedy porch in McComb, when we talked with Joe Martin's mother, who for no observable reason had been questioned by the FBI. We found it in New Orleans, as part of the response to a short Czech antiwar film, "The Magician," which I had shown to good results on numerous occasions in 1964. We encountered questions about the war among black people everywhere—for example, in a poem written by Mrs. Ida Lawrence, of Rosedale, a small Delta town near Greenville, Mississippi:

> We say we love our country
> We say other people love their country
> We said that all men are brothers.
> What would we call the war
> in Vietnam
>
> Would we call that brotherly love
> Does the word freedom have a meaning
> Why do the history books say
> America is the Land of Liberty a Free Country,
> Then why do all mens Negro and White fight
> the Vietnam and Korea why cant we be Americans
> as North and South regardless of color
> What does we have against
> the Vietnams?
> Why are we fighting them?
> Who are really the enemy?
> Are Vietnam the enemy or we
> Americans enemies to ourselves,
> If we are the same as Vietnams
> Why should we fight them?
> They are poor too.
> They wants freedom.
> They wants to redster [register] to vote.
> Maybe the people in the Vietnam
> Can't redster to vote
> Just like us.[8]

By the end of the summer, growing antiwar sentiment among black Americans had been summed up in one leaflet by the phrase "No Viet Cong never called me nigger."

But liberals who passionately sustained the civil rights movement had not yet turned against President Johnson's war policy. Indeed, most liberals saw the questions of civil rights and the war as separate. For example, earlier that summer, in June of 1965, I had been organizing a faculty committee to support the Mississippi Freedom Democratic Party (MFDP) challenge to the seating of the five "regular"—that is, segregationist—Democratic Mississippi congressmen. I wrote to a number of academics opposed to the increasing American involvement in the Vietnam War. Many joined the committee. But some saw the step as, at best, a diversion of resources and attention, or, at worst, an imposition of Old Left ideology upon a New Left movement. Indeed, a well-known practitioner of American studies, one of the founding fathers of the field, explained to me why he could not sign our statement. While he was on the whole opposed to US policy in Vietnam and in favor of the MFDP challenge, he wrote,

> the connection between the two implicit in this letter is forced and dubious; and it defeats the very aims of your program to have academics seeming to submit themselves to synthetic ideological arguments. By that I mean that only on the basis of a priori ideological assumptions could anyone possibly believe that the Negroes of Mississippi, if granted the vote, necessarily would be any more opposed to the U.S. policy in Vietnam than the rest of the electorate.[9]

Of course, that was not an argument we were making. But the real burden of his complaint came later in his letter: "As a veteran of the Thirties, when again and again I saw good causes dissipated by just this sort of imposition of ideology upon perfectly straight-forward political issues, I find this disheartening." In other words, we were repeating the mistakes of the Old Left, mixing up questions of civil rights and foreign affairs. In so doing, we would isolate ourselves from the mainstream of American politics. In mainstream thinking civil rights and foreign affairs constituted separate intellectual and political domains. In such respects, our "Letter" perhaps suffered from what Jules Pfeiffer called "premature morality."

Violence, "ours" as well as "theirs," constituted another problem. In 1964, nonviolence was taught, adhered to as much as possible, embraced on practical if not always spiritual grounds by most people active with COFO. After all, the Student *Nonviolent* Coordinating Committee provided a majority of the shock troops for movement activities.[10] Still, we survived nights in rural and small-town freedom houses, like those in Harmony and Mileston, only because armed black men guarded us from the worst excesses of the Klan and its many allies. Though the films I showed emphasized the virtues of nonviolence, I was under no illusion that nonviolence, though the dominant ideology, was always the prevailing practice, especially among older black Mississippians. After all, they had been defending themselves and their families against night rider terrorism—and would continue to do so long after the volunteers and even civil rights activists had departed. "Picking up the gun" was not some ideological abstraction but, for some, a practical necessity.

In 1965, Klan violence continued, though less visibly than earlier. The catalogue of such incidents was much shorter than the book of mayhem gathered during Mississippi Summer, 1964. But there were still incidents in 1965. For example, a white minister in Jackson was shot after enabling an integrated pre-school to use his church. Posy and a male staff member were arrested and roughed up because they insisted on awaiting the return of the sheriff at Natchez police headquarters.

We were driving from Natchez to Jackson one night with three black guys in the back, going to an MFDP meeting. We'd been warned not to stop for gas at white stations—they're Klan places. On the road only a mile, the guys say we're being tailed. They know the car well, one says. When we slow, the car behind slows as well, doesn't pass. By now we're on the four-lane to Washington, Mississippi. I turn suddenly through a cut in the medial strip; the car behind goes up one cut and also turns. I speed up, find another cut, turn again; I think we've lost him, but no, I see him close behind again. By now, I know the car too. Another turnaround and we gain maybe half a mile. The guys in the back suggest a quick turn after a curve onto a side road; it takes us into a long arc at seventy miles per hour. Back on the highway a quarter hour later, we're clear. I can speak now: "Who was in that car?"

"J. Rouse."

"Naw. His name Robinson. The chief's nephew."

"It's Rouse."

"How you know?"

"I use to work for him."

"What is he?" I ask.

"A Klan."

"What would he do?"

"Kill us."

"Naw, he all alone."

"But he got a radio. Could call others to meet him."

We're doing eighty, thirty miles out of Natchez. I can breathe again but the menace is clear.

Or again, the chairman of the Natchez NAACP, George Metcalfe, who in our absence had filed the petition requesting that the school board develop a desegregation plan, had been bombed in his car, parked in the lot of the Armstrong factory where he worked. He survived, but lost both his legs. Angry black people are out on St. Catherine Street the evening of the bombing; younger people are throwing rocks and shouting threats. We join Ed Pincus and Dave Neuman, who are making a film, *Black Natchez*, and are filming events in the city. We meet Katie, tall and lithe, in a nice-fitting dress with a yellow pattern and high heels. She likes to talk: "We can't find work unless we kneel and say yassuh and be like Uncle Tom," she says. "I use to work at Jefferson-David, the hospital. Now they don't want no part of me." Police cars pass by in the street. Katie's voice is loud enough for them to hear: "But I know one thing. The Negroes are not goin to run no further. Ever see a cat get up to a stone wall an he can't run and he can't climb no further?" Some of the passing cars are filled with white men not in uniform. "It's hard to tell whether they're Klan or cops," I say. Katie responds, "Honey, it's all one. They jus Klansmen up under the star." We laugh and we're still laughing when she says, "White people I can't stand. They made me what I am, which is nothin."

The idea of armed self-defense was not unfamiliar within parts of the Mississippi black community.[11] In more or less rural Mississippi, nearly everyone possessed at least one gun. As Katie put it: "I get to meetins alone. I've got my rifle in the car an my two pistols an I don't mind shootin. . . . I believe in fightin. If anyone fights me, I fight 'em back." Pointing across the street to the triangular gas station, she tells us how a white policeman had pulled in, a black guy in a Chevy right behind. "The Chevy must'v went over a bottle cause it went up in the air and smashed near the police car. Cops jumped out with their guns, and Otis," the black guy, "told them no one had thrown it. The cop said, 'you callin a policeman a liar, boy?' 'Naw,' he say, 'I jus wanna get the story straight. My father own this station.' The cops was pointing their guns right at him. They look up and see this Negro standin there with a machine gun, jus like this," and she cradles her arms lovingly. "They say, 'well, it's time for us to be movin out.' A Negro standin there with a gun—a machine gun—up jus like this—jus like the white man's—an it wasn't no shotgun neither."

One evening we crossed the Mississippi River with the filmmakers Ed and Dave to meet in Arkansas with the Deacons for Defense and Justice. Middle-aged men, low-keyed and friendly, they spoke of their military training, the necessity for maintaining discipline, a secret membership roll, and not giving the cops any excuse to make trouble. They didn't criticize devotees of nonviolence, but neither did they glamorize maintaining their "necessary" armed presence. Their view might have been expressed by a saying of a friend, who had escaped from fascist Argentina; he said: "the wolf eats him who makes himself a sheep." It was there, in Arkansas, that we learned that such an armed self-defense group had been organized back in Natchez and we heard about the armed guards deployed by Charles Evers, the head of the local NAACP chapter.

On our way out of town at the end of summer, we stopped at the freedom house to say goodbye to Posy. When she turned on the kitchen light, we saw a large black gun on her pillow at the end of the couch. While the founding of the Black Panther Party for Self Defense was still a year away, the groundwork for the Panthers had long been laid. Meanwhile, the Watts uprising of August 1965 and its bloody consequences warned us against romanticizing even defensive violence.

Florence and I attempted to write about these paradoxical matters. The movement, we were learning, was full of contradictions—"the road to hell is paved with good intentions." But who needed to hear that from us? It was easier to write about the Voting Rights Act, just passed. But the *New York Times* could do such reporting better. As for nonviolence, SNCC was having its own struggle with the idea: An aspiration, tactic, or way of life? We didn't have much to add—it was certainly not *my* place to write about the armed self-defense I had observed.

So we made our way back North. Florence settled in again at her tenured job in the English Department at Goucher College. I turned to Chicago, a new venue, to advance the peace education program of a regional Quaker office. And to try playing a useful role in the rapidly developing antiwar program of SDS.

The summer had begun with an ephemeral event and, in a sense, did not end until much later in the fall. Sometime in June of 1965 a group of us antiwar campaigners, including the folk-singing trio Peter, Paul, and Mary, along with Norman Morrison, myself, and others, staged a small action, too mild to be designated a "demonstration," *inside* the Pentagon around lunch hour. The trio sang a couple of peace songs, we passed out a leaflet, more singing followed, and eventually we were politely led outside to the parking lot.

I can find no confirmation of our action in public records, though it lives vividly in my memory. Peter Yarrow, whom I asked, drew a blank, adding, "that doesn't mean it didn't happen." But I did briefly describe the event in a June 1965 letter to Sue Gottfried: "We held a speak-out, which as you probably read did go inside the Pentagon, where it was just fascinating (ending with 150 people linking hands and singing 'We Shall Overcome'). Everyone very polite, but profoundly uninterested, I suspect. We're not pinching them yet, though some, like Paul Goodman and Chris, feel their permissiveness to be a sign of weakness." In retrospect that statement seemed to me at once true and false.

Some months later, on a lawn adjacent to the parking lot to which we had been led, on November 2, 1965, Morrison made his own excruciating antiwar statement by immolating himself under Robert McNamara's office window—the second American, after Alice Herz, to do so. It may be that Morrison had become obsessed with the Pentagon. Certainly, he had come to feel that ordinary protest was useless in stopping the ever-larger and crueler American war machine. Whatever the truth about Morrison's motives and mental state,[12] he had correctly identified the liberal American heart whose beating created deeper and more and more ferocious involvement of American troops in Vietnam.

Chapter Six

THE DRAFT

From Protest to Resistance?

The young man has been wandering around the reception room, nervously scanning the pamphlets and flyers on conscientious objection. Now he comes back into the office—can we talk about whether he should apply for C.O.? "You see," he apologizes, "I probably don't qualify."

"We usually let the draft board or the courts decide about that," I say. "Why should a guy rule himself out?" I try not to let the question sound routine. "Why do you think you don't qualify?"

"Well, I'm against this war . . . but I'm not a Quaker or anything—you know, that kind of pacifist."

"You don't have to be a Quaker to qualify. Why are you against the war?"

"Well, that's it. I'm against it on political grounds, and that doesn't seem to make it."

"What do you mean by political grounds?"

"I mean, I'm against American policy in Vietnam."

"Yeah, but why?"

"You know, like we say we're for free elections, only we didn't let them have elections in 1956."

"So?"

"What do you mean, 'so?'"

"I mean, why are free elections important?"

"Well, because people should be able to make up their own minds about their government."

"Why should they?"

"Isn't that right?"

"Sure, I think so, but I want to know why you do. Why should people be free to make up their own minds about their government?"

He sits there working it out for himself. Nineteen, perhaps twenty. A sophomore or junior maybe, "safe" from the draft board for two years anyway, but not "safe" inside himself from what's happening in Vietnam.

"I guess," he says finally, "it has to do with human dignity . . . you know, that men have certain rights, like liberty . . . and life. And you can't take those away from them."

"Is that what you mean by 'political objection'?"

The young man concerned about conscience and conscription has overcome enormous anxiety in order to come to our office. But he's full of doubt. He worries—is it unpatriotic, an act of cowardice to question the draft? But now he's here, feeling, maybe, like a devout Baptist in a porn shop, checking out the·literature while thinking about the next step: in this instance talking with someone, a counselor, about his thoughts and doubts. My job as the counselor is to help a wary individual dig through the pat phrases and attitudes he and his classmates casually throw around. I want him to get to the real, the "conscientious" objections that usually underlie the chatter about the war and "draft-dodging." And I need to avoid substituting my own conscience for his.

Our conversation, like thousands of others going on all over the United States, typifies the problem all of us—young men, their families, counselors, even politicians—had around 1965–66. Like the young man, we were being forced by the war and our roles in it or opposing it to reexamine the categories of morality established by law and society. Everywhere we turned, those categories were quietly exploding: in counseling centers, college lounges, pastoral offices, and dorm rooms. The young men, even those who sought us out, came to different conclusions: many, with barely a scuffle of mind, joined up, as they were expected to. Others, after much struggle, gave in to the pressure to conform. Some followed the path of conscience wherever it might lead: to conscientious objection, to court, to jail, to Canada. A few, an increasing number right then, declared their intentions not to go. Period. Exclamation point. But most Americans, late or soon, had to revisit the values informing American policy abroad. Inspired perhaps by the critical approach to law and custom of the civil rights movement, the young increasingly asked: Why are we in Vietnam?

Like most of the young men coming for counseling, I too was confused. What are the connections, if any, between the civil rights movement, with its emphasis on nonviolent direct action, and the rapidly
growing but still unshaped peace movement? Could liberal politics,
which seemed to me to have failed at the 1964 Democratic National
Convention in Atlantic City, work somehow to end the crisis of Vietnam? Who might become instrumental in changing American policy
in Asia? Working-class men and women, many of whose unions supported the war? Or young people who, for reasons both of self-interest
and morality, had begun to question it? Was our primary antagonist
General Lewis B. Hershey's Selective Service System or capitalist icons
like General Motors, which SDS president Paul Potter had, in the April
1965 demonstration, left unnamed? More personally, could I recon-
cile the priorities of a pacifist organization, American Friends Service
Committee, which paid my salary, and a largely nonpacifist group, Students for a Democratic Society, to which I was increasingly drawn by
virtue of its antiwar program? And, if we were ever able to identify just
what it was we needed to change, what tactics—demonstrations, counseling, producing new pamphlets, sabotage, electoral politics—offered
realistic opportunities for success? For reasons I address in this chapter, I chose to commit my resources, organizational and individual, to
the problem of the draft.

Somewhere in the archive of the Chicago regional office of the American Friends Service Committee, there may be a picture of three men
in a row that captures for me this moment in antiwar activism. I'm at
one end, Thích Nhất Hạnh, the Vietnamese Buddhist monk, is at the
other end, and Martin Luther King Jr. is there between us. The picture
was taken sometime in mid-1966, when Dr. King had come to Chicago
to lead a campaign to desegregate the city's notoriously separate and
unequal housing. I had just introduced him to Nhất Hạnh at the AFSC
office, where King was attending a meeting with AFSC Housing Program staff; they played a critical role in the Chicago campaign. A few
days later, during a march, a white citizen of Chicago would hit King in
the head with a rock.

Many in the peace movement tried to persuade Dr. King to come
out against the war on Vietnam. Ultimately, he did so, on April 4,
1967. Meanwhile, a struggle was going on within the peace movement,
largely framed by two questions: "Does nonviolence have a role in
foreign policy?" and "which side are you on?" Nhất Hạnh, a player in

that struggle for a number of years, represented what some thought about as a "third way" to end the war: not by the victory of the United States and its Saigon puppet and not by a victory of communist forces, but by the ascendancy of Buddhists and others faithful primarily—if not exclusively—to nonviolent means of resolving differences. While Nhất Hạnh was a lovely man and a persuasive leader, I doubted that his cause could succeed. It was opposed not only by the governments of the US and Saigon—at that moment headed by Generals Thieu and Ky—but also by the National Liberation Front and North Vietnam. Besides, most Americans, however much they responded to Mississippi Summer and the Selma-Montgomery march, remained dubious about nonviolence as a tool of foreign policy. They didn't see the relevance of the struggle for civil rights to the anti-communist crusade upon which America's leaders were embarked.

Working for an organization committed to pursuing a nonviolent strategy, I tried not to contradict that position when I spoke or wrote. But I came to feel that the chant increasingly heard at demonstrations—"Ho, Ho, Ho Chi Minh, the NLF is gonna win"[1]—was accurate. It seemed to me contradictory, if not stupid, to carry NLF flags at demonstrations in the US. Who was going to be persuaded by that exploit? But I felt resistance to American war policy gradually taking root and flowering in unexpected ways among young men subject to the draft, but also among many older African Americans, clergy, union members, academics—all of those coming together into a peace movement. The question for me, as peace education secretary and full-time activist, was how to foster resistance among ordinary Americans.

"Foster" is a weaselly word here. What many of us activists really wanted was to prevent Lyndon Johnson from maintaining a swelling army in Vietnam. We wanted to undermine the support in America for the invasion of Vietnam. We wanted young men to deny the military, stay out of the draft if they could, refuse it if they had to, and think about Canada, even prison. Before very long, we began considering how to support GIs who wished out too. Aside from "fostering" individual moral choices, we wanted ordinary Americans who worked in a flower shop or a legal office or an auto plant, and who thought of Vietnam hardly at all, to begin chanting "bring the troops home now." If they wouldn't chant, perhaps they could at least show up at a sociable rally for "peace now." We spoke about it less, but we also wanted the Vietnamese to see that they had friends in America who supported their independence. In 1965 or 1966 these did not seem like far-fetched goals.

Escalation of the war was met with escalation of resistance, in poetry among other cultural forms:

What if I didn't shoot the old lady
running away from our patrol,
or the old man in the back of the head,
or the boy in the marketplace?

Or what if the boy—but he didn't
have a grenade, and the woman in Hue
didn't lie in the rain in a mortar pit
with seven Marines just for food,

Gaffney didn't get hit in the knee,
Ames didn't die in the river, Ski
didn't die in a medevac chopper
between Con Thien and Da Nang

In Vietnamese, Con Thien means
place of angels. What if it really was
instead of the place of rotting sandbags,
incoming heavy artillery, rats and mud.

What if the angels were Ames and Ski,
or the lady, the man, and the boy,
and they lifted Gaffney out of the mud
and healed his shattered knee?

What if none of it happened the way I said?
Would it all be a lie?
Would the wreckage be suddenly beautiful?
Would the dead rise up and walk?
        (W. D. Ehrhart, "Beautiful Wreckage")

Yea as I walk through the valley of death
I shall fear no evil
For the valleys are gone
And only death awaits
And I am the evil.
        (Stan Platke, "And Then There Were None"[2])

While resistance was flowering, so too was rage. Our opposition seemed to have no visible effect on the president's escalation of the war. Escalation, resistance, rage—what else might we do to break into that cycle of ruin?

That apocalypse was not yet upon us in 1965–66. Still, we raged against the smart but senseless war-makers who led our government. We raged as we read the US casualty lists printed daily in the *New York Times*, lists that omitted the thousands of Vietnamese fatalities. There had to be paths toward peace, as yet untrodden. But those of us working in the movement struggled. In what direction should we lead? As a full-time activist, with significant organizational resources, I worried about where to lead.

How should I, as a middle-class activist of the period, define my political and professional roles? Once again, I had given up a cushy academic post to work full time in the movement. Fifty years later that would have condemned me to permanent academic exile. But not in 1965. Universities were expanding. Returning to their embrace seemed and was indeed possible. Still, what were the values that prompted me to leave Smith College and once again throw in my lot with Quakers motivated by their peace testimony? What was the purpose of the minor position I had taken on in SDS? Like many of today's progressives or socialists, I had to confront the question: What did it mean to think of myself as a "radical," rather than, as I had long done, some sort of "liberal"? And what did "radical" imply about the peace activism I had chosen to do full time in Chicago? Who would counsel the counselor?

To begin with, I needed to come to grips with my old identity as a "liberal." Steeped in the writing of TRB columns in the then-liberal *New Republic* of the 1940s and 50s, I was passionately committed to civil liberties. My inoculation against communism had been worn out in the 1950s by observing the firing—irrational, I thought—of my mildly leftist or even communist professors at NYU. I fit easily into the rapidly growing SDS because it remained—at least from the perspective of many of its new recruits if not, perhaps, its initial leadership—a "liberal" organization. An instance: At the second demonstration against the Vietnam War organized by SDS, in November 1965, the main speaker anticipated possible reactions to what he has been saying about US policies in Vietnam, Zimbabwe (Rhodesia, as it was then called), apartheid South Africa, Watts, and Mississippi. "What do you

make of it?" he asked. "Some will make of it that I overdraw the matter. . . . And others will make of it that I sound mighty anti-American.
To these I say: Don't blame *me* for *that*! Blame those who mouthed my
liberal values and broke my American heart."[3]

The speaker, the late Carl Oglesby, had recently been elected
president of SDS. Like me, Oglesby was older than most of the students active in SDS; indeed, he had worked a number of years for a
defense contractor, Bendix. He had children, as I did, and like me he
had begun to focus on his "liberal" values as the war escalated. At the
first national demonstration to end the war in Vietnam, seven months
before, on April 17 of 1965, the then-president of SDS, Paul Potter,
had given the main speech.[4] "We must 'name the system,'" Potter said,
which had created, maintained, and was now escalating the war in
Vietnam. The crowd of some 25,000, far larger than expected, took up
his refrain, chanting: "Name the system, name the system."[5] Now, in
November, Oglesby was doing just that.

Or was he? The term he evoked, not to my ears an ideal slogan
for a demonstration, was "corporate liberalism." The central fact about
"corporate liberalism," Oglesby insisted, was this: "With about five percent of the world's people, we consume about half the world's goods."
In the face of this addiction to a "stolen and maybe surplus luxury,"
"humane" liberals must not only name the system but also "describe it,
analyze it, understand it, and change it."[6]

This agenda has now been pursued by more than five generations of progressive Americans like me. Today, Oglesby's evocation of
"humane liberalism" may seem to us as quaint as the Gilbert and Sul-
livan lines about how "every boy and every girl / That's born into the
world alive, / Is either a little Liberal, / Or else a little Conservative."[7]
But Oglesby does not pose "liberalism" against "conservatism"; conservatism seemed to have been routed with Barry Goldwater in the 1964
election. "Liberals" were themselves carrying out the policies Oglesby
deplored. In fact, much of Oglesby's speech, and also Potter's, constitutes a critique of liberalism. "To understand the war," he said, "it
seems necessary to take a closer look at this American liberalism." For,
he argued:

> The original commitment in Vietnam was made by President Tru-
> man, a mainstream liberal. It was seconded by President Eisenhower,
> a moderate liberal. It was intensified by the late President Kennedy, a
> flaming liberal. Think of the men who now engineer that war—those

who study the maps, give the commands, push the buttons, and tally the dead: Bundy, McNamara, Rusk, Lodge, Goldberg, the President himself. They are not moral monsters. They are all honorable men. They are all liberals. But so, I'm sure, are many of us who are here today in protest.

                                                      (*New Student Left*, 313)

What, then, is this thing called "liberal," I had begun to wonder. At the April demonstration, the singer Phil Ochs had skewered liberalism in his song, "Love me, I'm a liberal." But then one of the heroes of liberalism—of SDS and of myself, the columnist I. F. Stone—had insisted that he was, indeed, a "liberal," and would be long after those espousing "radical" ideas had moved on. More and more I had to ask, especially after Mississippi, Selma, the antiwar teach-ins, and now the increasing resistance to the draft, where does this leave me?

As a scholar of American culture, I could, with Oglesby, trace the idea of liberalism to Thomas Jefferson and Thomas Paine, who, he says, "first made plain our nation's unprovisional commitment to human rights" (313). That legacy, distorted by a system of corporate—still "corporate" not "capitalist"—power, dominates resources worldwide, violently resists progressive change, and uses Cold War anti-communism as a rationale to "hold together our twin needs for richness and righteousness" (319). But if liberalism, or at least its corporate version, has become a dangerous and destructive force, it is not one from which Oglesby, like most of us in his audience, wishes simply to separate himself. On the contrary, his anger derives from the knowledge that Kennedy, McNamara, Johnson, and the rest have "mouthed my liberal values, and broke[n] my American heart." Emotionally and intellectually Oglesby places himself, and most of us who heard him, squarely in the traditions of American liberalism, which he seeks to redirect toward what he calls "a humanist reformation."[8]

In this respect, Oglesby's intellectual position was familiar to me, close to the view dominant in my academic field, American studies, in the mid-1960s: critical, not quite disillusioned, hopeful . . . liberal. The argument is still within the family, so to speak. The rage that would, in a very few years, produce the slogan of the Weathermen, as they then called themselves, "bring the war home" and lead to the Greenwich Village townhouse explosion in which three young members of the SDS were killed building an anti-personnel bomb—that rage was still only beginning to percolate. Moreover, Oglesby's critique of "corporate liberalism" and his effort to separate that retrograde ideology from humane liberalism, stand at the beginning of a process. Subsequently, we've seen the word "liberal" become a Rush Limbaugh curse and an anchor round Hillary Clinton's neck that helped to deepsix her 2016 campaign.

To return to Oglesby's language, prominent in his rhetoric and my own at the time are "corporatism," "radical," "revolution," "communism," "anti-communism," even "humanism," and obviously "liberalism." But never one word, now so familiar, so resonant, so daunting: the word "imperialism." This omission designates the point in American intellectual history at which Oglesby, and with him a generation of activists and intellectuals like myself, stood in the mid-1960s.

Of course, I knew about imperialism from my literary training, and even about the specific opposition to it, "anti-imperialism." Henry David Thoreau, Margaret Fuller, and even Ralph Waldo Emerson, about whom I'd written my dissertation, were hostile to the Mexican War and the transformation through the Treaty of Guadalupe Hidalgo of a third of Mexico into what now constitutes the Southwest of the United States. James Russell Lowell, attacking the Mexican War in a poem I enjoyed but could never manage to teach, wrote:

> Ez fer war, I call it murder,—
> There you hev it plain an' flat;
> I don't want to go no furder
> Than my Testyment fer that.[9]

Congressman Abraham Lincoln, in a comment about the then-president, James K. Polk, and relevant to our own leaders, said: "Trusting to escape scrutiny by fixing the public gaze upon the exceeding brightness of military glory, that attractive rainbow that rises in showers of blood—that serpent's eye, that charms to destroy—he plunged into war."[10] An angry Mark Twain, late in his career, wrote anti-imperialist works like "To the Person Sitting in Darkness" (1901) and "The War Prayer" (1905), texts I liked to teach.

Many other intellectuals and writers like William Dean Howells, Edgar Lee Masters, George Ade, and Ambrose Bierce became active in the Anti-Imperialist League of the late nineteenth and early twentieth centuries. To be sure, a very few post–World War II intellectuals, like William Appleman Williams, deployed the word and certainly the concept of imperialism. Nevertheless, right into the 1960s, "imperialism" was largely a term of the Left—it was the jargon, at least in the US, of Leninist pamphlets and marginal left-wing journals.

The invisibility of the word *imperialism* for much of the twentieth century reflected a liberal cultural consensus: that America had been and remained "exceptional." We were *different* from the imperial powers resident between the Irish Sea and the Caucasus.[11] The continued enthusiasm of people around the world for American ideals, so ironically reflected in Ho Chi Minh's decision to model some of the Vietnamese Declaration of Independence on that of the United States, reinforced this concept of American exceptionalism. Political candidates celebrated that difference through much chest-thumping and nationalist rhetoric. Even the American studies I encountered as a graduate student, since its beginnings in the 1940s, generally reflected the ideology of American exceptionalism. The field fêted American democracy in more restrained but not dramatically different ways from those of twentieth- or twenty-first-century Republican politicians.[12]

But by 1966 American exceptionalism had become a matter for more than academic debate. Not only was the idea of exceptionalism the central ideological tenet of liberal academicians and of my field, American studies, but of US policies at home and abroad. The idea of exceptionalism, in fact, underwrote the Vietnam War, as it does American dogma in the Middle East and Latin America today. It enabled American policy-makers to persuade themselves, as well as a majority of the population, that the bombing of straw shacks, the machine-gunning of water buffalo, the burning of Vietnamese children with napalm somehow served not merely the national interest but also a wider set of democratic and humane values, which "we" were chosen to sustain. To attack the war, it became imperative to question the rationales offered for it. In addition to American exceptionalism, these included notions like the "domino theory"—the argument that if Vietnam "fell" to communism, the rest of Asia would, by rapid steps, go too. Our leaders fed us the claim that the US somehow "owed" it to our South Vietnamese "allies" to sustain their "independence," which looked to me suspiciously like US installed despotism. Then, too, why did Cold War anti-communism tie up the hands of our presidents and the minds of our people? These issues constituted a kind of "curriculum" not only for the increasingly large demonstrations of the time, but also for on-campus teach-ins, new courses on Vietnam, and whatever programs I could develop as peace education secretary in Chicago.

Programs for whom? Who was the audience for our efforts? Initially, I focused on helping organize a "labor for peace" group. Sidney Lens, an active writer, labor organizer, and independent leftist, who was supportive of SDS and other New Left organizations, encouraged this effort. A few years before, I had invited Lens to talk at Hobart and William Smith Colleges, where I had run the lecture-artists series. He had the ability to compress his formal presentation while leaving key questions hanging. His audience would want to ask those questions, he knew. And they did. A clear writer, he had composed one of the better "Beyond Deterrence" pamphlets, titled "Revolution and Cold War," for the AFSC. He believed that at least some of the labor movement could be persuaded to come out against the war, despite the hostility of the AFL-CIO (American Federation of Labor and Congress of Industrial Organizations) of George Meany and Jay Lovestone. Lens introduced me to many progressive union leaders: Jesse Prosten and Charlie Hayes of the Packinghouse Workers (UPWA), the most left-leaning union in Chicago, and Ernie DeMaio of the United Electrical Workers (UE). UPWA actively supported the civil rights movement—it had helped to finance the Selma-Montgomery march, for example, and it would back Dr. King's efforts to change the segregated pattern of Chicago's housing. The union, after considerable debate, passed a motion at its 1966 convention calling for an end to hostilities in Vietnam.

But antiwar activism was slow going in the union world, both politically and personally. Much of the AFL-CIO accepted, indeed supported, the war. The image of patriotic hard hats pushing around soft-minded hippie peaceniks became a popular meme in the mass media. That aside, these progressive unions had much more pressing issues to deal with. The meat-cutting industry was undergoing profound technological changes, and within a very few years the Packinghouse Union would dissolve into the Amalgamated Meat-Cutters and be no more. The United Electrical Workers led a difficult organizational life outside the AFL-CIO, constantly raided by other unions, especially the IUE (International Union of Electrical Workers), which had been set up as a kind of anti-communist alternative to the UE. Many members of these unions opposed American imperial adventures, and significant numbers of active unionists participated in antiwar actions. But unions would themselves probably not provide the cutting edge against the war when the tyrannies of the Taft-Hartley law that threatened their very existence loomed so large and immediate.

I had joined the teachers' union at the University of Massachusetts in 1959, and for years I proudly carried my card in my wallet, along with one from SDS. Much later, I would become a local grievance officer and the vice president for academics in the union of SUNY faculty and professional staff, United University Professions. But I'd had very little contact with active working-class unionists like those in Chicago. When I began working with these guys—and they were mostly guys—I learned a great deal and enjoyed myself too. Older and far more experienced than I, they took a certain pleasure in teaching me the ins and outs of the union arena, as well as something of the history that had brought them to the current ambiguous crossroads. Few of us could then have imagined how over the decades to follow working-class America would come to feel scorned and abandoned by policy-making elites.

In any event, my training was that of a college teacher; I knew students in their teens and twenties, and that cohort seemed like the logical place to put my resources. With the SDS national office having moved from New York to Chicago in 1965, at about the same time that I landed there, and with my election to its National Interim Committee (NIC), I looked for ways to combine my obligations to the AFSC, which was a pacifist organization, and to SDS, which was not. Most important were the material conditions of the war, which had moved the Selective Service System front and center. President Johnson had committed US ground forces to the war early in 1965, and then escalated the American military presence from 23,000 "advisers" in 1964 to 543,000 troops by 1968. As a result draft calls had gone up markedly, from about 100,000 in 1964 to nearly four times that number by 1966.[13] In 1967–68, for example, draft calls increased by 61,900 to a total of 346,900. Meanwhile 1.6 million men received educational deferments in 1965 and some 380,000 had been given occupational deferments. More critically, "of the 298,559 men who entered service in 1967, 11,363 did not return from Vietnam."[14] I was increasingly persuaded that a focus on the draft would be central to the success of the peace movement. Many in SDS were pushing the organization to adopt a program to oppose the draft and encourage resistance to it: their popular slogan was "build not burn." Emboldening resistance to the draft seemed the best way to construct resistance to the war. So it was . . . for a while. But as we will see, the draft proved a slippery foundation on which to build an antiwar movement.

The initial national demonstration against the Vietnam War that SDS had organized in Washington on April 17, 1965, came just a month after the first Marine Corps combat battalions had come ashore on the beach near Da Nang. The November 27 demonstration was even larger. Growing numbers of young men, particularly on campuses, became interested in the organization's political stand against the war or, perhaps as much, their own status as potential draftees. Draftees, it soon became clear, constituted the bulk of combat fatalities. Therefore, it made sense that draft counseling would be one of our main projects in Chicago. We wanted to reach not just the people brought up in traditional peace churches, but any and all young men who doubted the war—on religious, political, or moral grounds. Influencing that larger constituency required rethinking the tools available to us and to potential draftees.

For example, the traditional poster addressed to "men of draft age" and put out by the Central Committee for Conscientious Objectors (CCCO) assumed that young people already knew the meaning of "CO," presumably from their peace churches. But more and more men opposed to the war were not members of the Society of Friends, the Brethren, Mennonites, or other such Christian groups. Many were not Christian at all or even religious in any traditional sense. To inform such men we needed to create posters that did not assume a religious background or prior knowledge about conscientious objection. We changed the posters.[15] We also needed literature that did not restrict conscientious objection to narrow groups of Christians. So I drafted a SDS pamphlet, "Guide to CO."

On the cover of my pamphlet were the lines from Barry McGuire's "Eve of Destruction": "You don't believe in war / So what's that gun you're totin'?" In the text, I tried to avoid any particular pacifist ideology so it could usefully be read by men and women of any persuasion. All the same, Paul Booth, then national secretary of SDS, looked at my working draft and patiently explained where, despite my care, I had fallen prey to existing assumptions, particularly that young men would ultimately have to be categorized as pacifists to qualify for CO status with their draft boards. The final version of the pamphlet does not foreclose the possibility that requirements for becoming a CO might evolve, along with attitudes toward the Vietnam War—as indeed happened. Ultimately, the Supreme Court ruled that men could become conscientious objectors if their beliefs played the same role in their lives that traditional religious training and doctrine played in the lives of others clearly eligible for CO status. My own view was that we ought to support anyone willing to take a stand for peace and against the war, whether or not he "qualified" as a CO from the perspective of the draft board. The pamphlet was widely circulated to SDS chapters, on campuses, and in developing draft counseling operations like ours.[16] It proved very useful.

Related materials began pouring out of the Chicago AFSC office, other Quaker and religious centers, and the SDS Chicago headquarters. I produced a leaflet describing the "AFSC Information Program on Conscientious Objection and the Draft," and other handouts on "Counselling C.O.'s," "Alternatives to Military Service," "Student Deferments for Conscientious Objectors and Others," "Background Information on Conscientious Objection and the Draft." SDS issued an article by Jack Smith from the *National Guardian* on "Facts for Draft-Age Youths Who Object to War." The Central Committee for Conscientious Objectors distributed a particularly useful "Fact Sheet on Vietnam and the Draft," and the Board of Christian Social Concerns circulated "General Suggestions to Registrants." The War Resisters League had a widely circulated flyer. Someone—perhaps the Boston Draft Resistance Group—sent round a leaflet on "Political Counseling." "Counseling," it said, "acts to keep men out of the military. Political counseling gives consciousness as to the whys and wherefores of draft resistance: it explains the modes of resistance in a system where the individual feels powerless, a pawn in other men's games."[17]

Draft counseling centers, on college campuses and beyond, spread rapidly across the country. The de facto leader of our counseling effort in Chicago, Joe Tuchinsky, was even appointed to a formal position by the dean at Roosevelt University. An ever-larger number of students and their families needed help with the draft. While seeking such advice could feel challenging to a draft registrant—he might hear "coward," "traitor" echoing somewhere in his head—counseling was carefully legal. We did not urge young men to resist the draft. That wasn't the role of most counselors. Instead, we tried to lay out the meaning of the often baffling categories maintained by Selective Service: I-A, IV-F, II-S, I-O, and the like, some eighteen in all. Our goal was to help registrants understand their options.

Of course, the very act of talking about and demystifying Selective Service categories and procedures meant that young men were beginning to assert some control over their lives. They would themselves decide instead of assuming that their elders—parents, teachers, draft board members, congressmen, the president—would, and should, tell them what to do. Nor would we. To take control of their own lives was a political act, akin to the goals of a freedom school education. To be sure, there were never very many applicants for CO status (perhaps one in six hundred registrants), much less young men who were categorized as I-O or I-AO—the CO groupings. Even if all those interested in CO obtained that status, or refused induction, the US military would have had plenty of draftees and "volunteers" that the draft helped produce. In 1967, for example, only 7,234 of the 298,559 men who were drafted failed to report for duty that year.[18]

But that was not our point. We wished to introduce into the process of military recruitment questions about its purpose—war—and alternative assumptions about national goals. We wished to delegitimize the nationalist and anti-communist ideology that underwrote the draft, the military, the war itself. To talk CO was to talk interference: to intrude flamboyant music between the speeches of Lyndon Johnson and the ears of the kids he intended to send to the rice paddies of Vietnam.

Some in SDS, for a number of reasons, remained suspicious of promoting a "liberal" position like conscientious objection in the first place. The other word missing from Oglesby's speech and much early SDS rhetoric was *capitalism*. Wasn't that the system, as Potter had said, to be named and also fought? Promoting conscientious objection diverted individuals and organizations from anti-capitalist efforts. And even if one was not ready to enlist in socialism's final conflict with capitalism, and saw ending the war as a sufficiently engrossing task, radical draft resistance, not just conscientious objection, was already stirring, and not just among pacifist groups. I had observed radical draft resistance in 1965 among black Mississippians. By 1966 it had spread to elite University of Chicago students. Gradually, a range of individual actions were translated into such organizational forms as the Resistance and the Boston Draft Resistance Group, as well as support organizations such as Support in Action in New York and, nationally, Resist.

Meanwhile, an increasing number of young men visited our counseling facilities; others wrote to their draft boards that they intended to refuse induction. Burning draft cards in public became a feature of demonstrations. We lined up attorneys to take cases that would soon emerge. Materials about the Selective Service began finding their way to college campuses, to high schools, and even to tables outside a few draft boards. We drove to Ann Arbor to leaflet about the draft at a high school dance and at an auto race track, where we were not warmly welcomed. But our actions were covered by Stanhope Gould, a CBS national news producer. Our small resistance world expanded rapidly.

There were those who saw—who still see—draft counseling as subversive, if not downright traitorous: young people should go when called, no questions asked. Subversive, yes! Or so we hoped. Our literature and counseling services helped legitimate questioning the draft, and thus the war. Even the American government. Maybe capitalism. The effect of counseling, as our critics maintained, may have been to undermine conventional ideas about the "land of the free and the home of the brave." Guilty we were, and happily so. But beneath the legal niceties, the cool language of our pamphlets and flyers, frustration and anger accumulated: What did one have to do to resist, to reverse the escalation of war and the murder of innocent Vietnamese?

On the other side, supporters of the war, and some fighting in it, were asking: How can we shut down these cowardly commie sympathizers? I remain surprised that it took so long for the murderous violence of the war to come home to America: from the emergence of draft resistance in 1965; to the police riot at the Democratic National Convention in Chicago in 1968; to the murders of King and Kennedy, the 1969 "days of rage" of the Weathermen, and the police killings of Black Panthers Fred Hampton and Mark Clark; to the 1970 bombing of the math building at the University of Wisconsin and the massacre of student protestors at Kent State and Jackson State Universities. The channels of protest remained open . . . but they led nowhere. Frustration mounted. Rage simmered. The same war continued.

ଔ   ଔ   ଔ

In 1966, I thought the path for ending the war ran through the tangle of the draft. The unfair and arbitrary system presented a bureaucratic nightmare that belonged in a Marx Brothers storyboard more than in a Marxist diatribe. Events in late 1966 and early 1967 seemed to confirm my focus on the draft. These included two conferences in Chicago and revelations about the Selective Service's "channeling" memorandum.

The first of the conferences, at the University of Chicago, was organized primarily by Sol Tax, a professor of anthropology there. Political and intellectual heavyweights like Margaret Mead, Milton Friedman, Harris Wofford of the Peace Corps, Senator Maurine Neuberger, Congressmen Donald Rumsfeld and Robert Kastenmeier, cartoonist Bill

Mauldin, and Ted Kennedy (briefly at the end) attended.[19] The conference also included staff from the President's Commission on the Draft, from congressional committees, and of course from the Pentagon and the Selective Service itself, all of whom were expected to carry back to Washington ideas produced by the "experts." Initially, the meeting seemed to have been put together to promote "national service," the idea that all young people would be required to serve their country—some in the military, some in venues like the Peace Corps or Vista or in a job corps. A number of the invited participants had written papers extolling some form of universal service. Margaret Mead believed universal service held the promise not only of equalizing obligations to the nation but also providing education and training that too many young Americans did not, she felt, adequately obtain in schools.

If promoting national service had been a major intention of the conference organizers, that goal was rapidly disrupted,[20] along with the seating and speaking hierarchy. The windowless, fluorescent-lighted conference room was arranged into three square tiers of green felt–covered tables. At the innermost tier—complete with place cards, microphones, and signal lights to have the mikes turned on—were forty invited important participants. At the other two tiers sat some eighty-five representatives of veterans groups and peace, religious, and labor organizations, as well as twenty-five or thirty students and a few dissenting University of Chicago professors. We in the outer tiers had paid sixty bucks for meals and for some 1,500 pages worth of papers, materials, and documents. But we were neither prepared nor willing to sit passively through summaries of the papers and discussions just among the "experts." We responded impatiently to papers that did not adequately address the relationships between the draft and the Vietnam War; ditto for papers not scrutinizing existing assumptions about the "national interest" and "manpower requirements." We expected reactions to the fundamental question stated by the keynote speaker, Professor Geoffrey Hazard: "Do we need a large army, and if so, why?"

Rather quickly, in good sixties style, participants demanded and obtained basic changes in format and agenda. The disorderly discussions that followed did not focus on statistics and econometric issues associated with the allocation of manpower, as some of the organizers had apparently hoped. Rather, they engaged many of the issues facing decision-makers and young men dealing with the crazy-quilt system then in place.

The conference did not end with a set of resolutions. As the organizers pointed out, reasonably, participants represented no one but themselves. Still, certain ideas were widely shared: first, that the draft, as it was presently constituted, should be ended. The entire structure of wildly different draft boards out of touch with young people, the unfairness of student and other deferments, the narrowness of the conscientious objection criteria—these and more anomalies made the Selective Service System an ineffective bureaucracy—or so we thought. Harris Wofford, then associate director of the Peace Corps, summed up the prevailing view:

> A system which encourages a cynical avoidance of service, relies primarily on compulsion, discriminates in favor of students enrolled in formal education, uses grades as the criterion of who will go to kill or be killed, turns college or graduate school into a refuge, corrupts American higher education, turns upside down the sensible order of calling younger men first, throws a shadow of uncertainty over most men until they are twenty-six or older, treats men in the same category differently according to the vagaries of local boards, permits the calling home for induction of Peace Corps Volunteers still serving overseas, drafts former Peace Corps Volunteers while others who have not served at all are deferred or passed over, provides no alternatives for men with a conscientious preference for non-military service, requires conscientious objectors to prove some kind of direct line to God, leaves women out, and leaves unmet so many national needs for service—requires fundamental reform.[21]

Voluntarism was the focus of an intense discussion: if there was to be any form of service, including military, it should be freely chosen by the young people performing it. The Pentagon had, up to that point, resisted the notion of a volunteer army as far too expensive and unwieldly. But at the conference, arguments from right, left, and center supported the idea. Milton Friedman claimed that the present system seemed less costly only because it imposed an indirect tax on those serving by paying them minimal wages. People on the left argued that a voluntary force would inhibit the president's tendency to use draftees in unnecessary military adventures. Hindsight underscores how what seemed to be perfectly reasonable reforms in effect supported quite different goals from those at which they aimed. A volunteer army, for example, has in no way subdued military adventurism.

Indeed, the focus of antiwar activists on the draft itself led in directions that contradicted our primary goals of halting American imperialism.

Meanwhile, nearby, a very different kind of conference had been assembled around the increasingly popular slogan "we won't go." While the formal University of Chicago conference focused on "reform" of the system, this one was concentrated on "resistance" to it. The "We Won't Go" conference, which drew about five hundred people, had been organized primarily by students at the University of Chicago, many of them potential draft resisters. It featured speakers like David Mitchell and Jeff Segal, who would soon be jailed for nonco-operation with the Selective Service. John Sumrall, a CORE organizer from Quitman, Mississippi, cited the refusal of the Democratic Party to seat MFDP delegates at the 1964 convention as evidence that "I'm not a citizen. If they didn't recognize me as a citizen then, then I'm not a citizen now, and I'm gonna' remain that way." Next, Staughton Lynd, a historian, active pacifist, and important mover of Mississippi Summer, placed the resistance of 1966 in a historical context. Others active in the meeting included James Bevel, one of King's associates in the Southern Christian Leadership Conference; Arlo Tatum, the executive secretary of the Central Committee for Conscientious Objectors; Dick Flacks, one of the founders of SDS, and subsequently a professor at the University of Chicago; and a variety of draft resisters—men who had turned in their draft cards, publicized letters to their draft boards saying that they would not go, or otherwise had set themselves on a collision course with the government.

The conference included three workshops: on legal problems, resettling in Canada, and the roles of women. All three workshops displayed the early stage of the "We Won't Go" movement. The women's workshop rapidly moved into a discussion of organizing a housewives' boycott for lower prices. The legal workshop focused on questions of how to resist the draft and yet not face a five-year jail term. Draft resistance was considered an individual concern, pitting a private citizen against the social and political muscle of government agencies. And the heavily attended Canada workshop went round and round on technical and personal questions—often asked repeatedly—that people had about emigration.

The core question, seldom addressed, was—to use the locution of the later feminist movement—how to make the personal into the political. In one sense, as feminists were to insist, the personal is always already political: society and politics, not just private psychological forces, shape one's life. In the women's movement, the issue became understanding one's sense of anomie, depression, and frustration—what Betty Friedan called the "problem that has no name"—as derived not from some inner maladjustment but from the potency of society's gender arrangements. Here, the problem involved translating personal acts of conscience into a social movement that challenged government policies, to make individual acts of principle into a strong political movement.

In their different ways, both the draft reform and the "We Won't Go" conference greatly increased the visibility of the problem of the Selective Service System. Rage against the draft had already been rising, especially on campuses, because the Selective Service demanded that an undergraduate maintain good grades to retain his student deferment. If a faculty member gave a young man an F or D, or even a C, he might be subjected to the draft and sent to Vietnam. In Nam, draftees constituted the vast majority of infantrymen and, by 1969, half the combat deaths.[22] Kyle Longley comments that many grunts "were thrown into combat; an astounding 997 men were killed on their first day in Vietnam."[23] Students, like those at the University of Chicago who organized the "We Won't Go" conference, had already been demanding that their institutions *not* send grades to the Selective Service office. These demands generated significant campus protest and conflict with administrators and some faculty.

The publication in *New Left Notes*, the SDS newspaper, of the Selective Service memo on "channeling" by Peter Henig[24] dramatically escalated fury with the draft.[25] The "channeling" memo had been included in packets of material prepared by the Selective Service and provided to local draft boards throughout the nation. It explained how the mechanism of *selective* service was designed to encourage young men to pursue forms of study and of work desirable from the point of view of those who wished to control the allocation of manpower for the nation:

> The young man registers at age 18 and pressure begins to force his choice. He does not have the inhibitions that a philosophy of universal service in uniform would engender. The door is open for him as a student to qualify if capable in a skill badly needed by his nation. He has many choices and is prodded to make a decision.
>
> The psychological effect of this circumstantial climate depends upon the individual, his sense of good sportsmanship, his love of

country and its way of life. He can obtain a sense of well-being and
satisfaction that he is doing as a civilian what will help his country
most. . . .

In the less patriotic and more selfish individual it engenders a
sense of fear, uncertainty, and dissatisfaction which motivates him,
nevertheless, in the same direction. . . . Throughout his career as a
student, the pressure—the threat of loss of deferment—continues.
It continues with equal intensity after graduation. . . . The loss of
deferred status is the consequence for the individual who acquired
the skill and either does not use it or uses it in a non-essential activity.

Is this a parody? Who can imagine a government bureaucracy
arrogating to itself such control over the lives of young Americans?
What kind of individual would not feel rotten about his student or
even occupational deferment? The memo blithely concluded that
"the psychology of granting wide choice under pressure to take
action is the American or indirect way of achieving what is done by
direction in foreign countries where choice is not permitted." Students gasped in disbelief or with outrage whenever I read that particular sentence. Where were American ideals of fairness? Of *difference*
from totalitarian societies? "Hell no," young people responded, "we
won't go."

Students' furious reactions to the Selective Service System and the
rapid increase in draft resistance[26] encouraged me to stay with this
work. Humor helped too. Tuli Kupferberg and Robert Bashlow's hilarious pamphlet *1001 Ways to Beat the Draft*, and some of the more arcane
methods of draft dodging they proposed,[27] provoked smiles and guf-
faws. But just as we recognized the vulnerability of the draft as a mechanism for pursuing the Vietnam War, so the national administrations,
both of Johnson and Nixon, came to recognize the Selective Service as
a liability. Slowly, they introduced changes both in conscription and in
other military policies that reduced the leverage that antidraft activity
provided for the peace movement.

By 1969, the Nixon administration had set up a lottery system,
based on one's birthdate, that established the sequence in which men
might be called for induction. The lottery provided somewhat more
predictability than the uneven hand of local draft boards. However,
those in the lower registers of the lottery, whose numbers would almost
certainly never come up, got a free pass. Not surprisingly, many of
these lucky ones turned away from antidraft agitation since they were

no longer personally threatened. Thus, the very individualistic character of the draft came back to haunt us. Moreover, by changing military policies—for example, toward "Vietnamization" and bombing rather than ground war—Nixon was able to reduce US casualties from a high of 16,899 in 1968 to 6,173 in 1970 and 2,414 in 1971.[28] Again, the administration managed to reduce the personal stake in the antiwar movement of many men and their families.

Where did this leave our movement? In fostering resistance to the draft, we did not necessarily develop sustained opposition to the war, nor to the underlying American policies from which it grew. Liberals and conservatives alike continued to believe in American exceptionalism, in the right of the United States to play the role of arbiter of peace and war in the world; they still do.[29]

A couple of months after the 1966 summer encampment of the Chicago region AFSC on Lake Geneva in Wisconsin, the executive director, Kale Williams, called me into his office. He had a problem with me that had led to his decision to end my employment. I was, as peace education secretary, the leader of the camp. And yet I was living there in sin with Florence. He was apologetic, yet firm: my behavior was outside acceptable norms for a good Midwest Friends organization. What, he asked, did my mother think of it? (My mother?!) I could stay on into the spring, by which time I would presumably be able to find another job. Meanwhile, I could continue work for a while, though I figured he was not altogether happy with my emphasis on draft counseling and activism. Perhaps he thought that the conscientious objector status I was seeking to foster, if it was not exactly inherited, was not designed to provide nonbelievers with a route to escape service. And clearly peace *education* secretaries weren't generally thought about as organizers of "resistance."

I was outraged. British Friends had recently published a booklet called *Toward a Quaker View of Sex*, counseling against judgmental conclusions like those to which I was being subjected.[30] My behavior hardly transgressed the reasonable ideas discussed in the *Quaker View*, which urged Friends to be open to changing situations, even while upholding appropriate traditions. Who were Florence and I harming by living together without benefit of clergy or of Mayor Richard J. Daley? My mother? Was Kale hiding dissatisfaction with my work behind disapproval of my shacking up? Could he be that unhappy with our relationship? Absurd. I would not wait until the spring to leave. I might not have a salary, we concluded, but I'd be gone from the AFSC by January.

Florence could return to her tenured position at Goucher, we would move back East, and I'd find some appropriate job.

Meanwhile, we planned ways to stretch our funds in Chicago. We took to going to very late-night cheap movies with Todd Gitlin and Nancy Hollander, who had been working in an SDS-sponsored project in Uptown. We began resurrecting graduate school cuisine: stuffed cabbage and spaghetti and meatballs, though veal had gotten too expensive for veal and peppers. And we seized every opportunity to speak or write. These opportunities fortunately multiplied in 1967. Now that I was soon to be unemployed—and, as the employee of a not-for-profit social service organization, not eligible for unemployment benefits—I could begin writing about these issues. Florence, Dick Flacks, and I quickly composed our first piece soon after the December conferences for the movement magazine *Liberation*.[31] We wrote a major article for the *New York Review of Books*[32] that reached an audience far beyond that of *New Left Notes*, *Liberation*, or *La democracie nouvelle*, for which I had also produced essays. Over the next few years, we continued to write about the draft and its opponents, including a long chapter in the book *The Conspiracy of the Young*,[33] as well as about other activities of the growing peace movement. In time, I would return to full-time work in the antiwar movement, but for now I was pleased to be writing and speaking about it.

My unemployment early in 1967 and my experience with a movement organization led someone to propose me as a candidate for executive director of the newly forming National Conference for New Politics (NCNP). NCNP was an ambitious effort to create an umbrella organization that would somehow unify civil rights (and by now black power) with antiwar and other New Left activity, and to put the resources of a union of diverse movement activists behind progressive candidates for local and national office in the coming 1968 election. It would have its founding meeting later in 1967. After some calls and a letter or two, I flew to Boston with Florence to be interviewed for the job. I met with Marty Peretz, who would later buy the *New Republic* and take it in a more conservative and Zionist direction, as well as a gentleman who owned an auto-distribution company and supported movement activity, and one or two other white men. The interviewing group did *not* include Julian Bond, then a Georgia state legislator and former SNCC leader, who was theoretically co-chairman of the NCNP steering committee.[34] The more we talked, the clearer it was to me that the meeting being planned for Chicago over the Labor Day weekend was a disaster in the making. Identity politics was increasingly important, yet a group of white guys, like the ones with whom I was talking, were making all the basic decisions. Harsh disagreements over controversial issues like black power, the future of Israel/Palestine, the role of women in such an organization, and the very idea of a "radical" form of electoral politics had not been discussed at sufficient length among an appropriately broad group. Certainly the organization's leaders, much less the constituencies they wished to organize, hadn't come to agreement about these issues.

It's important to know what one wants to come out of a big meeting *before* going into it. That was not the case here. People seemed to think that acrimonious differences among comrades would magically be resolved in response to the urgency of the issues and the solidarity that movement activity promoted. A naive vision, I thought. The Chicago meeting *was* going to be a big one, both in terms of the movement leadership attending and the numbers of activists being assembled. The huge plenary assembly would overwhelm the possibilities offered by small-group processes. Conflicting goals would thus be harder to address. Did I want to take on the chief leadership role in such an organization? To place myself in the eye of a tornado? I might be masochistic but not mad. "No thanks," I said, and began planning to move back East. Which we did.

But the question here isn't personal. Rather, it's the impact of the Chicago convention. As Simon Hall has pointed out, there is very little research or writing about the NCNP, as if movement scholars were allergic to it. One reason, which Renata Adler's nasty *New Yorker* article about the convention makes clear, is that many of those participating in the organization, and especially in the conference, put their worst face forward. Why mock them further? Adler has already done it. The meeting exacerbated a split between some Jews and some African Americans active in the movement. The black caucus at the conference proposed a thirteen-point set of resolutions that, among other things, called for black participants to have the same number of votes as the majority whites, and they attacked Israeli policies. NCNP adopted these resolutions after long and sometimes embarrassing displays of self-abasement by some white participants. That apparently led Marty Peretz, one of the main sources of financial support for NCNP, to write a long, long diatribe in *Commentary*.[35] He argued:

Those of us in the radical community, then, for whom Israel's rights are on the same moral plane as the rights of the Vietnamese, have drawn a kind of moral cut-off line on this issue; other radicals cannot deny or reasonably plead against it in the name of unity. For certain anti-Israel positions cast a shadow over the intellectual probity and political responsibility of men and movements which had commanded serious attention and strong loyalties as a result of their early and forthright stand against the war in Vietnam.

Over the years, Peretz would increasingly commit himself and the resources provided by his spouse, Ann Farnsworth, to Zionist causes. This occurred most notably when he bought and began directing the liberal journal the *New Republic*. Peretz was hardly alone in feeling that the NCNP conference had worked against the unification of progressive activities, even though a very small minority agreed with him that "Israel's rights are on the same moral plane as the rights of the Vietnamese." Most antiwar activists were more likely to see Israel's treatment of Palestinians as resembling America's attack on the Vietnamese.

True, many on the left felt a certain devotion to Israel. At the beginning of the Six-Day War of 1967, when Israeli authorities were—rather successfully—putting out the story that they had been attacked and were about to be massacred by massive Arab armies descending on them from Syria to Egypt, Florence and I asked one another where we might volunteer. That idea evaporated within a day or two. But it was born of a sentiment akin to that which propelled Peretz into Zionism. That sentiment would drive other liberal journals away from collaboration with African American activists and from those who, even fifty years ago, regarded Israeli policies as a form of settler colonialism. NCNP brought to the surface what would continue to be a significant fracture on the Left.

A similar division emerged between activist women and the leadership of the conference, but with more positive consequences. A group of women met during the conference to develop a set of resolutions on feminist issues having to do with property laws, control over their own bodies, abortion, and equal representation on conference committees. When they tried to bring their resolutions to the floor, the chair ignored them. "Cool down, little girl. We have more important things to talk about than women's problems," he said to one of the outspoken women who had come to the platform. Shulamith Firestone was the "little girl" being patronized. Reasonably enraged, she, Jo

Freeman, and a number of other women hurtled from the NCNP conference to start up the first feminist organization in Chicago, Westside. Before long, a number of the original consciousness-raising groups sprang from that source.[36] Belittling the concerns of feminists was not, alas, unusual in movement circles of 1967.

NCNP did not succeed in unifying civil rights and antiwar activists. Nor did it manage to develop a significant electoral presence for the upcoming 1968 campaigns. Criticizing NCNP now, I feel like a nasty crow pecking over a long-decayed corpse. At that moment the task of unifying black militants, antiwar activists, feminists, and the New Left cadre would have defied the Buddha himself. The problem wasn't that racism, patriarchy, American imperial ambitions, and the dominance of corporate capitalism were separate matters, as many liberal commentators maintained. Rather, the trajectories of these oppositional movements carried them into quite different if sometimes overlapping terrain. Could a campaign of draft resistance help transform the racist and economic oppression of poor African American communities? Could it help women win control over their bodies? Would a demand for black power sustain draft deferments for students increasingly anxious about becoming victims of the war machine? Movement rhetoric of the time, like "conservative" bombast of the 2010s, tended toward extremes. No one wanted to be outdone, at least in talk and even sometimes in action. Moreover, we encountered a concerted campaign by the FBI and local "red squads" to infiltrate meetings, disrupt proceedings, and—as later would be revealed—to steal organizational files, including address lists.

It's always easy to say in retrospect "that was not the time," even if, in fact, it wasn't. But you never knew until you tried. That's what we were shortly to learn in the Morgan Community School project, which for many of the same reasons would be less than a shining success story.

Chapter Seven

VISIONS OF FREEDOM SCHOOL IN DC

(For Bob Silvers)

Florence Howe and I moved back East from Chicago in the spring of 1967. She took up her tenured position at Goucher College and I moved into a new educational venture: as *associate* director of the Morgan Community School. Fortunately, one of the families involved with the school project offered us their top-floor bedroom while we looked for an apartment. Alice Jackson, who had been a student at the 1964 freedom school that Florence had organized at the Blair Street AME church in Jackson, had come North with us at the end of summer 1965 to continue her high school education at a good school and ultimately to attend college. Now she joined Florence in searching for a place for all of us to live.

The two followed a variety of leads, but without success. We were puzzled. It never occurred to us that people, seeing Alice, who is black, with Florence would assume that she and I were a "mixed" couple. We expressed our bewilderment to one of the friends with whom we were staying. Looking at them, she said, "they are probably seeing you as a 'mixed couple.' You'd best not go together." That proved to be sage advice. Florence alone soon found a lovely flat on Biltmore Street, a block into Adams-Morgan from the Calvert Street Bridge and a quick walk to the Morgan Community School. It had one bedroom and an indoor sleeping porch, which was Alice's when she was with us. When the windows were open and the breeze blew in the right direction, we could hear the sea lions barking at the Washington Zoo. At the end of the tumultuous 1967–68 year, when we left Washington for Baltimore, closer to Florence's job at Goucher, we showed the apartment to a man who would become its new tenant. He was a police reporter for the *Washington Post* named Carl Bernstein.

Adams-Morgan, later to become DC's hip neighborhood, was in 1967 racially diverse—sort of. White, upper-middle-class professionals lived west of 18th Street and across Rock Creek, while blacks, mainly poor, lived east of 18th Street. Further east, the neighborhood was haunted by drugs and violence. Two elementary schools served Adams-Morgan: the John Quincy Adams School, which had been the segregated white school and remained basically middle-class; and the Thomas P. Morgan School, the neighborhood's segregated black and 80-plus percent poor school, named after a nineteenth-century white man who had once served as the DC police commissioner. When I first received the statistics on students at Morgan, I noted that four percent were listed as "other than African American," although all the students I saw were black. When I inquired at the DC public schools headquarters about this seeming anomaly, I was told—foolish of me to ask—that the 4 percent were "obviously African."

A number of graduates of Antioch College had settled into the comfortable blocks between 18th Street and Columbia Road—whites with a commitment to school integration as good social and educational policy. Where better to pursue that goal than in their very own neighborhood? These Antioch alums and active black members of the biracial Adams-Morgan Community Council had a model in mind: make the Morgan School, say, 13–15 percent white, increase the resources beyond those provided by the district, and develop a new and imaginative curriculum. If they could achieve such goals, performance by *all* the students—black, white, rich, poor—would improve, and a persuasive case could be made for school integration right in the nation's capital. They turned to the Antioch-Putney Graduate School of Education to work out a plan of action.

That plan, set in place long before I came to the project, involved transferring control over the school to the "community." Community in this case meant the Adams-Morgan Community Council, with Antioch College as its agent and, de facto, the controlling authority. Like other reformers in those years, the Antioch group saw decentralization, aka community control, as *the* means for transforming dysfunctional, segregated urban schools, which were failing to educate a huge portion of their mainly poor black and Latinx students. An enormous battle would soon be fought over the question of community control in

Ocean Hill-Brownsville in Brooklyn. That was in the future and would involve much more powerful forces than those in Adams-Morgan.

Our plan seemed modest: one elementary school, whose teaching force and principal would be strengthened in a number of ways by Antioch-Putney interns studying for their master's degrees; by Antioch undergraduates working during their co-op periods; by community "interns" functioning as teaching assistants; and by Antioch hires like the project director and associate director, me. We would run a three-week summer institute with teachers, interns, and community members to develop a fresh educational program. We would also petition educational publishers to provide materials to pursue the goals of integration, about which everyone, of course, agreed. The superintendent of the DC school system, Carl Hansen, regarded the project as a small demonstration that, if it proved useful and didn't cost one dollar more than a regular school, might be imitated elsewhere. The Antioch vice president in charge of the negotiations supported that position. Today, such an arrangement would be called a "charter school." That is, the school remained within the DC system and was funded by taxpayer money, but control of the curriculum, teachers, and the budget, along with the organization of the space, were placed in "private" hands. The District of Columbia continued to issue the checks for teachers' salaries and to pay for the supplies and books, such as they were. But those of us working for Antioch decided how books, supplies, and teachers would be used.

What would guide our decisions? First of all, the dreadful reality of the district's schools. A team of observers from Teacher's College/Columbia had been gathering material for a study of those schools; here is one striking comment:

> The child spent most of his day paying the closest possible attention to his teacher, following her directions, responding to her questions, and obeying her rules. The children were not encouraged to talk to one another, either formally or informally—indeed, the principal technical criticism the observers had of the language program was that it did not seem to deal with speech. And the sad fact is that in spite of all this, the children don't really learn to read, as the test surveys have repeatedly shown.[1]

Many of us who had joined the project in the spring or early summer had been reading extensively about British "infant schools" and other child-centered experiments pursued by educators like James Moffett and Sylvia Ashton-Warner. Though I did not know it at the time, comments attributed to Albert Einstein about his own education in Aarau, Switzerland, would have summarized our outlook: "It made me clearly realize how much superior an education towards free action and personal responsibility is to one relying on outward authority."[2] How, then, to create opportunities for "free action" and "personal responsibility"? How to avoid the authoritarian structures that remained the norm in Washington, DC, schools?

The configuration of the Morgan School building suggested an organizational strategy: four classrooms were grouped at the ends of long corridors on each floor. Each set of four classrooms, we decided, would constitute a largely ungraded unit within which we would encourage more or less free movement of students. Rather than having self-enclosed classes, each room in the unit would be focused on different learning opportunities: for example, arithmetic and science in a math lab, reading or story listening in a "quiet" room, drawing and music, miscellaneous activities. Children could undertake tasks and participate in lessons as they were motivated to do so. They would *not* sit stiffly and silently in rows of desks with their hands clasped, tracking the teacher with their eyes. Of course, such a conventional classroom, standard for DC, was the classroom that the children's parents had experienced. And expected for their children.

A proposal we filed with the National Science Foundation summarized the experimental character of our instructional plan:

> Instead of the self-contained classroom, we are planning for team teaching in a complex of four rooms, each of which will hold one or more "activity centers." Instead of grades, the seven hundred and fifty children will be organized into seven overlapping age groups—five to seven year olds, six to eight year olds, seven to nine years olds, etc. Each group of about 120 children will work with a differentiated team of approximately nine adults: one coordinating teacher, associate teachers, interns in the Antioch-Putney M.A.T. program, "community interns," undergraduate students on work-period assignments, undergraduate practice teachers, and National Teacher Corps interns. Such an arrangement will permit us, with no increase in personnel costs, to have present about one adult per 12 children.[3]

Our intentions were clear: a break with the authoritarian and unsuccessful organization of teaching in the DC schools, but one, we were regularly reminded, that would not fundamentally change the allocation of funds.[4]

The first bumps in the road appeared early in the summer: the project director, whose name has happily been lost to memory, never materialized, nor did a secretary for the project. I became the project director, even though I had not been in an elementary school since graduating from P.S. 64 in the Bronx in 1943. Almost immediately, the school's principal and almost all of the teachers decamped; they decided that their futures could not be trusted to this unshaped experiment so they moved elsewhere.

In this new situation, I became the de facto principal, telephone operator, and recruiter of a new staff—including a principal—as well as project director. During my free time, I served as fundraiser and contact point with outfits such as the Educational Development Center, from which we begged for new curriculum materials and plans. I signed endless forms, negotiated with DC school bureaucrats about fixing toilets and painting rooms, and I hired a young Antioch co-op student as maid-of-all-work, though I didn't know how I would pay her. In fact, Florence constituted such staff as I had—for which we were later charged with nepotism. (That would almost become a source of mirth, given my fate at the Chicago AFSC.) Meanwhile, I struggled—without success—to develop a research design, as well as a plan for the pre-service institute for all the school personnel before classes began. I became allergic to the ring of my phone.

The difficulties we faced illuminate the aspirations of the freedom schools in the 1960s and other educational "reforms" today.[5] First, the "differentiated" staffing plan, nice in theory, turned into a huge problem. The Morgan School originally had twenty-eight regular teachers and three specialists. Under the plan adopted at an early stage of negotiations, that number would be reduced by eleven. The salary money thus "freed up" would be used for eleven Antioch interns in the master's program and fourteen community interns. These, presumably, would more than make up for the smaller number of full-time, experienced teachers.

Not so. The community interns had little if any formal teaching preparation. They were certainly devoted to the children. But like many people in the community, they probably would have preferred that the kids sit down and shut up. One of the interns—who loved to cook and therefore knew a lot about measuring, balancing, and boiling—became adept at using the science experiments we'd obtained from the Educational Development Center. The Antioch master's degree candidates, like Teach for America recruits today, displayed enthusiasm and dedication. But they knew little about curriculum development and less about classroom management, critical in a school of poverty like Morgan. Moreover, their training, I belatedly discovered, focused on secondary, not elementary, education. These Antioch interns, almost all white in a largely black school, were brave and often quite political. One, a draft resister, was snatched from the front of his classroom by FBI agents as a prologue to a visit to the school by Vice President Hubert Horatio Humphrey. Committed and eager as they were, most of the interns were not ready for the rigors of an inner-city school, especially without two vital features of Mississippi Summer: the stability of a well-crafted curriculum and the active support of the local black community.

The Mississippi freedom school curriculum, which had been created over many months by very experienced and committed professionals, had two principal virtues: First, it addressed the political conflicts of the world that students actually inhabited, a world in which segregation, the Mississippi power structure, the activities of the movement, and the Holocaust, as well as mathematics and writing by black authors, all played significant roles. Second, it provided inexperienced teachers with intellectual and social support. Curriculum—the materials we wanted our students to know, or at least to study—was essential to our success in Mississippi. Unfortunately, at Morgan in 1967, we began in haste, without a familiar and well-integrated curricular structure, much less one rooted in the world in which the students lived.

I continue to believe in the soundness of our organizational plan. Grounding teaching in students' desires to learn, which they have in abundance, still seems right to me. Liberating students to do what they can do and valuing what they bring into the educational enterprise are powerful instructional virtues. For example, one of our interns at Morgan developed a curricular unit around the Poor People's Campaign in Washington. He set up a "poor people's corner" where he placed many questions and related materials on cards. Here are some of his materials: "What is the 'War on Poverty'? Is it helping people? See page six in 'Poverty' by Sargent Shriver. How does the welfare system help to break up families? See fact card number seven. Pretend you are on welfare. You have five children. Welfare gives you fifty dollars a week; your rent is twenty-five dollars. How would you spend the rest? Would you have enough to live decently?"[6] Good teachers, supported and encouraged, produce such curricular materials; these help bring what students know and feel into the learning process.[7]

At the Morgan Community School, the odds leaned against such an experimental plan. We—and I in particular—had very little experience of elementary education, and absolutely none of this particular school. We did not know the students, their parents, the teachers who had been working there, or the new teachers we hired. We were white intruders in a predominantly black school. In that respect, we resembled many of today's educational "reformers" and state-imposed superintendents descending on unfamiliar schools with their battery of tests, Teach for America recruits, and their desire to stir things about. We needed the initially promised year of planning. Instead, we were forced to squeeze our preparation into a conflicted three-week institute. Focused on abstractions about how children learn, we largely ignored the particular circumstances of this particular community at that particular moment in time.

For example: most of the school's basal readers showed happy, smiling white kids in 1950s suburban settings. They had been handed down from white schools where they were no longer used. Florence consigned a bunch of them to the furnace to heat the water for the bathrooms, and their replacements were very slow in arriving. In retrospect, I see that we might have asked students what *they* thought of these cheerful white narratives. Their responses might have provided an interesting lesson in critical pedagogy, even if the kids looked at nothing but the pictures. But in the rush of the opening moments that lesson didn't occur to any of us.

Second, we spent very little time with the Morgan parents, who were entrusting their children to us. Mississippi's 1964 freedom schools, in contrast, were rooted in the black community. The black community caringly embraced the mostly white volunteers: they housed us, fed us, and protected us. They saw freedom schools, meeting in their church basements or community halls, as a valuable resource. Freedom school students canvassed for the Mississippi Freedom Democratic Party; they circulated and sometimes wrote newsletters; and they helped prepare adults for the arduous task of registering to vote. The freedom school students experienced possibilities for action that were radically different from those their parents had struggled through.

In Washington, organizing of the black community had slipped into low gear since the "community school" arrangement had been put in place. While the Adams-Morgan Community Council and especially its chair, Bishop Marie H. Reed, had taken control of the community's school, its committee on curriculum was moribund; another committee seemed stuck searching for a principal. No one was consistently out there talking with members of the community about what *they* might expect to see happen in the Morgan Community School and how our plans might relate to their hopes and expectations. That explanation might have become my role had I remained solely the *associate* director. I did send around a long memo before the opening of the school trying to explain "team teaching," "activity centers," "ungraded" groupings, and our other innovations. Most parents, I'm sure, found it puzzling—at best.[8]

Further, while Morgan was now a "community" school, it did not develop the programs a poor and marginalized community needed. Such schools, David L. Kirp has written, "open early, so parents can drop off their kids on their way to work, and stay open late and during summers. They offer students the cornucopia of activities—art, music, science, sports, tutoring—that middle-class families routinely provide. They operate as neighborhood hubs, providing families with access to a health care clinic in the school or nearby; connecting parents to job-training opportunities; delivering clothing, food, furniture and bikes; and enabling teenage mothers to graduate by offering day care for their infants."[9] At the Morgan Community School, community "control" did not translate into community services. Thus, the relationship of parents to the school remained unchanged, as did their expectations that the school would continue to do what schools had always done: help both to educate and discipline their children.

We did not alter the relationship between parents and the school, except in the limited form of employing community interns. That was a good thing to do. But it did not change the dynamic by which parents sent their children *to* the school, as distinct from involving parents *in* the school. It is not clear that we could have done so even had we conceived "community school" in such participatory terms. Most of the parents, and especially the black parents, were poor, busy trying to make a living, and often alienated from schools that had not served them well. Should we be asking them to help us do our jobs? The answer is probably yes, but that would have required not only thinking differently about how the school might work for the community, and especially the parents, but also implementing such plans. We lacked the resources.

Third, a three-week institute, like today's brief Teach for America course of study, was inadequate for planning a major departure from local, familiar educational practices. Three weeks would have provided, under the best of circumstances, only a small gesture toward organizing the school and designing a curriculum almost from scratch. But the circumstances were not the best, despite the hard work of the institute staff. I had asked Carolyn and Arthur Reese to be key players at the institute. The Reeses, African American teachers in Detroit, had run a successful if slightly stiff freedom school network in Hattiesburg, Mississippi, in 1964, and they continued to be active in the state through the American Federation of Teachers in succeeding years. We had encountered them again in the summer of 1965 when they had demonstrated to us their method of drawing people to confront their own racial attitudes. How did *we* dress, they asked, when coming to eat at a restaurant in the black community, as we were doing? Sloppily, we had to admit, deeply embarrassed, but newly enlightened.

In the Mississippi freedom schools, many students were involved in canvassing or in other movement activities; the very act of coming to a freedom school displayed a courageous choice. Not surprisingly, the volunteers respected the kids, and the resulting dynamic countered whatever residual doubts about educating poor black students volunteers might have carried with them from their racially isolated upbringings. In Washington in the summer of 1967 we had no movement activities helping reshape the outlook of our teaching staff—traditional teachers as well as interns. We had to focus on the profound doubts our teachers brought to the project, especially about whether *these* children could benefit from our innovative methods. A significant portion of the readings, films, and discussion was devoted to this problem.

We asked: Could we overcome the self-contempt so many of the students—*and* their teachers—had long been taught. As one illustration, we had shown a film in which a little black girl stroked the long, straight hair of her white teacher. Why, Carolyn Reese asked, "hadn't the teacher reciprocated? Why didn't she make the child feel that she was beautiful too?" Wasn't black beautiful? After a certain amount of hemming and hawing, one of the black teachers said: "But how could she reciprocate? She couldn't say the child's hair was beautiful—it isn't. It's all kinky and nappy, bad hair." When the term began, that teacher was among the first to claim that experiments like ours, while they might be all right for suburban kids, wouldn't work with "these children," who needed discipline, control.[10]

The Reeses effectively raised such issues at the institute. They brought years of school experience and profound commitment to equal education. In addition, they made sure that their appearance inspired respect and also hewed to a conservative ideal in their dress: Arthur always wore a jacket and tie and Carolyn a well-tailored dress. Still, they were perceived by many in the community—especially in the white community—as fostering a black power project that differed from, if it did not altogether conflict with, community norms. Why, they might even be encouraging two of our young teachers who wore Afros! That "black power" charge probably derived from the widespread arguments in the national press: What did Stokely Carmichael mean when he used the phrase during the Mississippi March Against Fear the previous summer? The Reeses expressed their understanding of the situation, accurately I think, in Arthur's evaluation of the institute: "None of the participants seemed able to participate in direct confrontation with the factor of race as a major determining factor in American socio-economic political and educational dynamics."[11] He pointed to the underlying and largely unexpressed conflict between the educational goals the white, powerful but small minority of parents held and the aims of the vast majority of black parents in the district. The whites saw some inherent conflict between teaching that black is beautiful and the educational aspirations they had for their own children, like learning a foreign language. They saw Florence and me as white fellow travelers of black power undercutting their ideas about how the school should serve their (rather few) children. Inevitably, racial tensions emerged as central to the institute—a good thing in itself, though such discussions overwhelmed the development of curriculum.

All the same, I remain persuaded that our strategy was sensible. Speaking of the approach of the Union, New Jersey, school system, David L. Kirp comments: "Building relationships between students and teachers also takes time. 'The curriculum can wait,' Lisa Witcher, the head of secondary education for Union, told the high school's faculty . . . . 'Chemistry and English will come—during the first week your job is to let your students know you care about them.'"[12] Excellent advice, particularly for those teaching younger students. Attitudes about race, especially beliefs about beauty and intelligence, are central to persuading children of color that "you care about them." Students will never trust teachers who regard them as repulsive or stupid.

The white parents active in the Adams-Morgan Community Council kept tabs on our institute. They realized that they would have to invest not just their collegiate ties and perhaps some money in the plan, but their children as well. Understandably anxious, they registered their discomfort. During the third week of the institute, arguments exploded one evening in the storefront headquarters of the community council. When we attempted to explain what we were about, one of the white mothers said: "If you organize a curriculum to teach Negro children to be proud of the fact that they are black, where does that leave my children?" The meeting came apart. Some of the black staff left in tears. Then an old drunken man came through the front door and launched into a lecture on the importance of education. Things never calmed down after that.

Yes, the whites in the community were unhappy. And after the term started, the black community began expressing their doubts about what we were doing. People in Adams-Morgan saw this bunch of young and mostly white folks coming into their school and . . . well, disrupting it, rather than helping discipline and educate their kids. The school had become a "community school," but it did not seem theirs. "We" seemed like intruders rather than supporters of community customs. One fourth-grade kid, when he was asked who his teacher was, said, "I ain' got a teacher; I got a white boy."

The Morgan Community School struggled with Antioch's differentiated staffing plan, our too-brief training institute, and an in-process curriculum. Without a settled teaching force, we were vulnerable to criticism from many quarters. Whites in the community discovered that their kids were paying their lunch money for protection. Black parents heard stories about children racing wildly through the halls. Besides, why was our best science teacher a "community intern"? "Why is *that* woman teaching *my* child?" I remember an overwhelmed teacher asking me one afternoon to read to a restive group of eight- and nine-year-olds. The kids were more interested in who I was than in what I was trying to tell them. We had fostered that curiosity but often without knowing how best to respond to it. At long last, a new principal, Kenneth Haskins, was actually appointed. Then Antioch began to pull back, and soon enough I was out of a job.

In fact, my job closed twice before it closed. One late Friday afternoon in September, the head of Antioch's operation in Washington came into my office to tell me that my job was no more. I'd soon be reassigned, he said. A frantic weekend followed, featuring much support from teachers and interns at the school, none of whom had been asked by Antioch about my effectiveness there. Nor, as it turned out, had the decision-makers in the community council been asked. By Monday, the decision had been reversed. But if I was going to survive, not so Florence. She had developed a plan, partially funded by Teachers and Writers Collaborative, to work with two groups of teachers and their students on language arts. This was a particularly sensitive matter. One of the ways that adults, including teachers, undermined black students' sense of their own value was to treat their language, like their hair, as deficient: an "incorrect," low-level dialect. Students heard the incessant "correction" as an expression of their deficiencies. A creative language arts program had to speak both to students' needs and teachers' training. As we put it at the time, "a reading-writing-speaking program" has at least two goals in mind: the first addressed "the pleasure that children may gain from exploring—in language—their own feelings and ideas and comparing them to those of other people." The second concerned learning about language, self-expression, and reading, which the Washington, DC, system was notoriously deficient in accomplishing. We planned to instruct teachers not to rely on the negative and unsuccessful reading methodology imposed by the DC system, and correction, correction, correction. Instead, the teachers would use a variety of tools, including "role-playing and dramatics, writing one's own books, illustrating them with paintings or photographs one has taken, reading each other's books," or those in the vastly expanded library we were creating. The plan was sensible, helpful to the teachers (many of whom had never taught or even studied reading), significantly funded, and consonant with our fresh design for the school.

But, Florence was an outsider, who had not adequately consulted with the "community." Worse, this female outsider rejected the idea that a wife should work as a volunteer rather than as paid staff, especially in a project in which her husband—as I was perceived—was a leader. In addition, the notion that black children should read and write about their own lives, rather than those of white kids whose suburban experiences and mores were deeply alien, threatened white parents, especially those whose relationship to the school was that of the volunteer wife who felt that a curriculum emphasizing black pride meant her children would be left out. The inevitable friction of the community school project led to my firing and then reinstatement. But

Florence was completely pushed out. We were, Antioch announced, guilty of nepotism, and she would have to go. Enraged, she felt like a goat sacrificed to patriarchal power. She was being martyred to outdated masculine ideas about "nepotism" that had long been used to exclude women from professional work.

My own reprieve proved temporary: within a month, I had been permanently "reassigned," though not to anything in particular. Perhaps I could write grant proposals, the Antioch vice president proposed—a mode of composition I was good at. But the college rapidly withdrew from its promises about adult afternoon and evening programs, additional staff, and the other requirements for making Morgan a true "community school." Within the year, Antioch's involvement was over and I was out of my job. Alas, the college's interest in becoming a player in urban education remained.

After its withdrawal from the Morgan Community School, someone at the Antioch-Putney Graduate School of Education devised a plan to intervene in the Baltimore public schools. They selected a high school and developed a program to place a dozen or so Antioch master's degree interns at the school. The interns, I was told, would work with parents in the black community to demand a new and improved curriculum that would challenge the existing, wholly black teaching faculty and force it to change. The Antioch authorities proposed that I direct this catastrophe in the making.

Clearly, importing a bunch of young, inexperienced, and mainly white master's degree candidates into a volatile school situation could come to no good end. It would alienate not only the teachers, but also the school's administrators and, very likely, the parents as well. I declined the offer, even though I felt small pangs of guilt because Antioch would be paying my salary for the second year of my contract. But I didn't suffer for long. Antioch's insistence on starting up such a foolish program (and others later on) derived from its financial need to expand its graduate offerings in order to stay ahead of its costs. Ultimately, this shell game would lead to the college's bankruptcy.

A year later, when I began teaching at the University of Maryland, Baltimore County (UMBC), Florence and I went looking for a house in Baltimore. One place, recently put on sale, had an attractive office in the basement. On the desk there I noticed Antioch-Putney stationery. I inquired of the seller of the house; it turned out the stationery belonged to the poor fellow who had taken the job I had rejected. The project, the seller explained, had collapsed, and he was now headed out of town.

Like any ill wind, the end of my position at the Morgan Community School blew open new possibilities. Now something of an expert on school decentralization and community control, I began to write about those conflicts.[13] The previous year, I had gone to Cambridge to discuss with Noam Chomsky the possibility of organizing a call to resist the war and the draft. The call might be modeled on the appeal of French intellectuals for soldiers to refuse orders to pursue the war in Algeria. Others had also begun to plan such a statement. Those efforts came to fruition in the "Call to Resist Illegitimate Authority" of October 1967, released just as my job at Morgan was evaporating. I could return to draft resistance and antiwar organizing. Florence and I also began writing more extensively about the draft and draft resistance, especially for the *New York Review of Books*.[14]

But the Morgan Community School has continued to haunt me, especially its implications for today's school "reforms." Schools rarely are, but they should be and can be, community resources. By closing so many schools of poverty in Chicago, New Orleans, Baltimore, and elsewhere, today's reformers have "blundered" badly. Instead of concentrating resources for community development through schools, they have further weakened already dispossessed communities by closing down these potential centers. They have argued that, according to high-stakes tests of doubtful validity, students in the schools are not making adequate "progress." But even if that were true—and the results of such exams were accurate, which is highly dubious—the solution would be to invest *more* and more imaginatively in schools as resources for people of every age in a community. Disinvesting from schools undermines the intellectual and cultural resources of a community; it also eliminates jobs.

Ironically, one of the holdovers from the early days of the Morgan Community School project is an expansive civic center on the site. When the ancient and dilapidated Morgan School was finally torn down, it was replaced in 1977 by the Bishop Marie H. Reed Community Learning Center, with a child care facility, public health clinic, adult education classes, and a swimming pool, in addition to the elementary school. A new building, now being constructed on the site, will sensibly maintain the community focus.

I am not arguing that schooling alone will break the "poverty cycle." It will not. But schooling, as freedom schools showed us, can be instruments of empowerment. The Baltimore Algebra Project, described in Jay Gillen's *Educating for Insurgency*,[15] teaches students not only algebra but also prepares them "for organized acts that will render . . . [the] system unworkable, and compel change" (132). What the students and their mentors want to change are, among other matters, the systematic starvation of public education, particularly of schools that serve poor and working-class children. Courts order the state to provide adequate funding, mandated by the state constitution, to the Baltimore schools, for example. But when that funding is not forthcoming, Baltimore Algebra Project activists demonstrate: they march on Annapolis, engage in a hunger strike, and carry out "die-ins" at meetings of school authorities. They stage actions to extend student bus tickets to 8 p.m. so that all can participate in the math tutoring central to the project's work. They organize against police violence, no small matter in Baltimore and elsewhere; they put forward alternative narratives about the causes of young people's anger from those offered by the powers that be. Older students teach algebra successfully to younger students; they also develop sessions on public speaking, civil disobedience, organizing tactics, and the other skills necessary for pursuing their goals in the public arena. While teaching mathematics, they demand quality education as a "constitutional right," no less important than the ballot.

One might argue that the approach of "reformers" to schools today constitutes not a "blunder," to evoke the word I used above, but a calculated effort to turn public education into a private profit center. Three examples: First, whatever else charter schools do, they all funnel public taxes into private control, and that has generally meant private profit.[16] Second, for-profit colleges[17] like Corinthian Colleges, ITT Technical Institute, and DeVry University have used needy students as conduits for sucking up government funds in the form of payments for tuition and other costs without delivering meaningful educational results. The schools and their owners profit, the government pays, the students lose out. A third, lesser-known device for turning education into private profit involves transferring control over tests from teachers and schools to giant corporations, which create, promote, sell, deliver, and grade high-stakes exams—an ever-larger market given the testing demands imposed by federal and state mandates. This hugely profitable venture includes the more hidden but insidious collection and sale of computerized data, a la Facebook, about shopping, surfing, and even the doodling preferences of children and their parents to vendors wishing to peddle their products. This subsidiary bazaar has become an even bigger market than that for exams.[18]

Drawing on our experiences in Washington and elsewhere during the school wars of the late sixties, Florence Howe and I examined the meaning of supposed "failing" schools in "How the School System Is Rigged for Failure."[19] Describing the schools as "failing" assumes that they have not succeeded in the mission of educating students. On the contrary, we argued, systems like the tracking practiced by the Washington, DC, schools, in fact *succeeded* in implementing an altogether different but primary goal: sorting students by class and race. We wrote, "schools institutionalize and maintain privilege in America." Tracking "harms some children, depriving those we call 'deprived,' making them less competent, less able to reach, let alone to use, the instruments of power in US society. In the light of tracking, schools become for such children, not the means of democratization and liberation, but of oppression" (18).

We need to approach today's claims about school "failure" in a similarly systematic manner.[20] What do those who control school systems and chant "failure, failure"—often governors and mayors—actually *succeed* in doing? On the one hand, they launch a startling number of students, especially young people of color, into the school to prison pipeline and, for the "lucky" ones, into the armed forces. On the other hand, they open endless entrepreneurial opportunities. The goal of "reforming" schools through charters, vouchers, and other devices like state-controlled districts creates a huge flow of public revenue into private hands. Privatization of schools may not always be the primary goal, though it is an ideological imperative for some self-appointed "reformers." But the attack on schools and teachers as "failing" has traction *because* there is money to be made. The bottom line in America remains the bottom line.

Antioch-Putney's misshapen Baltimore project in the year following the Morgan Community School fiasco offers a case in point. Antioch needed such projects to overcome the deficits posted in previous years and to pay its administrators. Today, we see the same dynamic at work in miserably unsuccessful online for-profit charters like the Electronic Classroom of Tomorrow (ECOT) in Ohio or in religiously inflected schools like the Gülen-run[21] networks of charters. These charters, whether for profit or not, siphon taxpayer funds out of public education and into the pockets of owners, managers, and contractors.[22] If state laws forbid profiteering from educational services, managers nevertheless use devices like renting space they already possess to their own schools and carrying out other real estate deals to obtain hefty financial returns. The boards that authorize charters need to ask not only how they might better serve students, but who will make money from the enterprise, how much, and for what, if any, educational purposes. Because the funding for charters comes from local sources—that is, from public school resources—public schools themselves face cuts in many programs, especially those like history, music, and art that are not subject to high-stress exams. Extra-large classes and the disappearance of counselors, nurses, and librarians also result from taxpayer funds being drained off into private profit.

Resegregation of schools is another consequence of "reforms" touted by super-rich entrepreneurs to pass responsibility for the education of black and brown children into private hands. Rann Miller has argued that "state governments must be held accountable for the education of Black and Brown children. School privatization has allowed state governments to avoid their obligation to educate children of color, especially poor children."[23] No wonder the NAACP has called for a halt to the expansion of charter schools, along with closer examination of what charters do and do not accomplish. An end to for-profit charters, especially those using online methods, is long overdue.

At the Morgan Community School we were not able to provide minority children with a transformative education. We could have done better. As we saw in the Mississippi freedom schools in the summer of 1964, education can support and empower students and communities in the ongoing struggle for a democratic, peaceful society. It seems to me a lesson for the future now being contested.

Chapter Eight

RESISTING

The night before October 2, 1967, at my mother's Washington Heights apartment where I had grown up, I kept thinking, "This will be big. This will make a difference." Then I worried: Was I indulging an adolescent fantasy, like rooting for the old Brooklyn Dodgers to come from behind in the bottom of the ninth, as I had often done in this very room? The event wasn't a ballgame but the formal release the next day of our "Call to Resist Illegitimate Authority." Signed by hundreds of famous and not-so-famous academics, writers, and intellectuals, the call committed us to breaking the draft law by urging potential inductees to say no to military service. In response to this big display of civil disobedience, the war-makers would react. But would the intervention of this "Call to Resist" begin to reverse the momentum of America's war on Vietnam? Could anything do that?

I had spent much of the last four years ever-more enraged by what my country was doing in that faraway Asian nation and desperately seeking something—a statement, an action like the freedom rides, a commitment of my life and "sacred honor"—to bring about change. I wish I had a way to get this page physically hot to make my readers feel the fury with which I thought about the president, his advisers, the generals, and, yes, even the marine privates who were making Vietnam a place of torment and misery.

Now, at the distance of half a century, even an effective documentary like the Ken Burns and Lynn Novick film history *The Vietnam War* cannot make that fury sufficiently vivid. Poetry perhaps:

> The same war
> continues.
> We have breathed the grits of it in, all our lives,
> our lungs are pocked with it,

the mucous membrane of our dreams
coated with it, the imagination
filmed over with the gray filth of it. . . .
                    (Denise Levertov, "Life at War," *Poetry Magazine,* June 1966)

But even Levertov's intensity fails before the tide of "hard rain" that
was engulfing us. I'd been working for pacifist organizations. But now
I felt that, given the opportunity, I'd lay nonviolence aside to somehow
decapitate America's warmongering leadership. I was hardly alone.

Half a year earlier, I had flown from Chicago to Boston to meet
with someone Paul Booth of Students for a Democratic Society (SDS)
insisted I had to talk to, Noam Chomsky, a linguist at MIT. All I knew
about linguistics were the distinctive rhymes I'd charted in Wyatt's
poetry for Professor Helge Kökeritz's class a decade earlier. Chomsky
and I sat down over coffee at Bickford's on Mass Avenue. What did he
think of a statement by hundreds of professors and well-known intellectuals urging men not to serve in the military and on the battlefields
of Vietnam? In fact, he had been thinking along such lines. French
intellectuals like Jean-Paul Sartre and Simone de Beauvoir—the only
names of the people he mentioned about whom I knew something—
had done this kind of action at the time of the Algerian War. The
1960 "Manifesto of the 121" had presented the war led by the Algerian National Liberation Front as a legitimate anti-colonial struggle;
it called for an end to torture and the recognition of conscientious
objectors to military service. The manifesto, Chomsky thought, had
helped bring about a change in outlook in France, encouraging formation of a front against the continuation of the war. What might be
done to create an equivalent in the United States? How could we transform the predominant sentiment among Americans who, even if they
did not wholly support the war, were not prepared to take a public
stand against it?

As it turned out, people at the Institute for Policy Studies in Washington, notably Marc Raskin and Arthur Waskow, and others in New
York—sparked by Robert Zevin, a professor of economics at Columbia—were considering similar ideas. During the half year while I had
been toiling in the basement of the Morgan Community School, discussions had led to drafting a document, the "Call to Resist Illegitimate Authority."[1]

Now, in October, we were about to go public with our call. Fortuitously, I had been set free from Morgan and from any other Antioch

assignment. Tomorrow, at the New York Hilton, we would hold a press conference broadcasting our call to the world. At my mother's, lying awake in my old bed, I felt hopeful: perhaps we, too, might divert the war-makers from their lethal course and save something of the values we liked to attribute to America.

October 2, 1967: some thirty of us draft-resistance supporters have gathered in the Beekman Room of the Hilton, a small, colorless function room, designed for such doings. Our group includes some of the most prominent American intellectuals: Chomsky, William Sloane Coffin, Paul Goodman, Dwight Macdonald, Ashley Montagu, Benjamin Spock. But almost no one from the press—and not a single TV camera. We had assumed that the spectacle of Dr. Spock and the famous Yale clergyman Bill Coffin urging and, in a sense, committing civil disobedience would have brought out the cameras. But it did not. The press seemed as uninterested in our form of protest as the administration— at least for the moment. The *New York Times* a few days before had run a story partly about the call, and that was all that was needed from the point of view of the "newspaper of record."[2] Our speakers delivered their brief speeches, drew the analogies between our action and that of the French intellectuals who had urged French soldiers not to serve in Algeria, and deplored the immoral, unconstitutional, and filthy war on Vietnam. Chomsky spoke for all of us:

> After the lesson of Dachau and Auschwitz, no person of conscience can believe that authority must always be obeyed . . . those who refuse to serve in Vietnam are at the forefront of the struggle to salvage what remains of American honor. Their refusal is an act of courage and high principle.

Mitch Goodman announced the draft card turn-in planned for Friday, October 20, at the Department of Justice in Washington, DC. We handed out our call, bearing the signatures of a few hundred professors and intellectuals, with hundreds more to come. We then decamped for Columbia University, where Robert Zevin had arranged for us to hold the first formal meeting of what was by then called Resist at the Faculty House.

The key organizer of Resist, Zevin had brought together the three initiatives to produce a call for American intellectuals, professors, and writers to aid and abet draft resistance. To start a small organization, he had rented an office and hired its one staff member, Herschel

Kaminsky. He also set up a monthly pledge system to provide Resist with a regular income. My son David, who was then nine, sent a dollar each month; others contributed more. A bit later, Zevin would become a crucial player in forming the United States Servicemen's Fund, which, despite its anodyne title, was dedicated to fomenting GI antiwar activity. Behind the spiffy brown tweed jacket and tie, befitting the financial advisor he would become, was a man dedicated to finding concrete ways of contesting America's war policy.

Later, our unsuccessful press conference would play a significant role when the government decided to indict Spock, Coffin, Mitch Goodman, Marc Raskin, and Michael Ferber—the "Boston Five," as they were later known—for violating the Selective Service Law. Meanwhile, at Columbia we felt hopeful. We talked about what a new, small organization of clergymen, professors, and poets could actually do to interfere with America's immense war-making capacity. What could Denise Levertov and Allen Ginsberg achieve against Robert McNamara and Walt Whitman Rostow? How could SDS, the Resistance, the Fellowship of Reconciliation, and a Philadelphia draft-counseling group challenge the authority of General Hershey and his hundreds of local draft boards?

Some urged the expansion of draft counseling, which I supported as a means of undermining the draft and thereby the war. Others favored militant actions to make draft resistance more visible; still others wanted activities that involved ordinary Americans, not just those willing to break the law. While we didn't agree on any clear strategy, our initiative and the other actions planned as part of Stop the Draft Week energized our thinking. I found myself elected as "national director" of this new, and soon to be noticeable, organization.

Plans for a draft card turn-in at the Justice Department provided an initial set of actions for the newly constituted Resist. Mitch Goodman had little idea of what needed to be done to bring it off there in DC. Since I lived in Washington and had organizing experience, I volunteered to help as my first Resist action; so did Louis Kampf. Mitch displayed much fervor, but wasn't an organizer, much less a bureaucrat. He had written one of the best novels about the Second World War, *The End of It*, and had early on become a significant figure among New York writers opposing the war. Headstrong and enthusiastic, he leavened the tendency of intellectuals to lose themselves in the predictable language of protest. Mitch always seemed to be at the edge of some direct action, like striding down the aisle and calling out

Hubert Humphrey at the National Book Awards ceremony for "burning women and children in Vietnam," an exploit which endeared him to me.

As a result of the arrangements made at Columbia, Mitch and the poet Denise Levertov, to whom he was married, came to stay with Florence and me at 1940 Biltmore Street for the days before the draft card turn-in and the Pentagon demonstration scheduled for October 21. For many months thereafter, I became the person the District police contacted whenever some antiwar street demonstration came onto their radar. I wasn't very helpful. While I knew people organizing some of the protests, I didn't have any authority in the organizations involved. Still, I became a "consultant" of sorts for groups needing to obtain permits, agree on march routes, and establish liaisons with the cops—when they wanted to.

We planned the draft card turn-in in two stages. At the beginning of Stop the Draft Week, October 16, draft resisters would burn their cards or hand them in to Resist members and other supporters in different parts of the country; these supporters would bring the cards to DC to be deposited at the Justice Department. That part of the plan worked reasonably well: on the morning of October 20, the people involved assembled at the First United Congregational church, and draft cards were brought together and stuffed into Dr. Spock's brief case. The group marched to the Department of Justice, where on the steps additional cards were ceremoniously added. Florence and I were giving a talk at a long-scheduled meeting of the Baltimore Teachers' Union so I never found out exactly what happened after. Arthur Waskow said that he was part of a small delegation that had expected to give the cards to US Attorney General Ramsey Clark but were shunted to some assistant, who had to be persuaded by Waskow pounding the briefcase on a table to accept the cards as evidence of a "crime." My own absence might have been one reason why I was never indicted with Spock, Coffin, and the others—though perhaps that's only an expression of what Mike Ferber termed "subpoena envy."

Denise Levertov drew energy from the young men—those burning or turning in their draft cards—who constituted "the Resistance," as they now were calling themselves. The war enraged her, as her poetry powerfully demonstrated: "delicate Man," she writes,

> Still turns without surprise, with mere regret
> to the scheduled breaking open of breasts whose milk

runs out over the entrails of still-alive babies . . .

these acts are done
to our own flesh; burned human flesh
is smelling in Viet Nam as I write.

("Life at War" *Poetry Magazine,* June 1966)

For Levertov, these heroic guys of the Resistance constituted the vanguard of opposition to those monsters carrying out the brutal "acts" she catalogued. Supporting their efforts registered seriousness; she was impatient with those who held back. We'd known each other slightly for many years—I'd written an enthusiastic review of one of her early books in the *New Leader* back in 1961, and I was moved and impressed by her recent antiwar poems, like "Life at War," which she recited to powerful effect at readings of Poets Against the War. But as the poem itself suggests, her rage, which I largely shared, left little room for strategic thinking about building various forms of opposition to the war. One was with the Resistance or hopeless, from Denise's perspective. She could not accept that draft resistance was not the only path to ending the war. Insisting on its absolute priority, as she did, led to conflicts within the peace movement. All the same, the card turn-in clearly infuriated the president, and the wide circulation of the "Call to Resist Illegitimate Authority" challenged many of the "liberal" intellectuals in Johnson's camp.[3]

Mitch and Denise were with us the next day when we took off for the Pentagon demonstration. The Yippies had promised to levitate the building magically, and while we somehow doubted their powers, we were game to watch them try. The march on the Pentagon was in any event a ragtag affair. After crossing the Memorial Bridge over the Potomac, we lost track of the leaders—perhaps they had been loaded into police vans and from there into Norman Mailer's famous book, *The Armies of the Night.*[4] Spotting an opening through a fence to one of the building's entrances, we and hundreds of others charged up a grassy slope, through some bushes and scraggly trees, and headed toward the Pentagon mall. A line of soldiers in battle gear confronted our weaponless battalion. Using rifle butts in our chests as clubs, they pushed back, but other demonstrators circled past that line. They were met by troops in gas masks and bayonets, who promptly attacked. Experienced people provided instructions: "tear gas rises, keep your heads down, don't rub your eyes, wet your handkerchief and cover your face with it. Throw the canisters back if you can." We dodged in another direction, arriving at the mall where foreign dignitaries might ordinarily be greeted. Now it was occupied by a long line of military policemen blocking access to the building. Our response? We sat down, along with a thousand others, for the next fourteen hours.

Florence and I wrote about these adventures at the Pentagon. Initially, we had been called on by demonstration leaders to contradict the administration's assertion that troops had never used violence or gas (American troops?!), only demonstrators (who were probably commies from the North!). Or, as Robert Bly was to put it in *The Teeth Mother Naked at Last,*

First the President lies about the date the Appalachian Mountains rose.
Then he lies about the population of Chicago, then he lies about the weight of the adult eagle, then about the acreage of the Everglades . . .
He lies about the composition of the amniotic fluid, and he insists that Luther was never a German, and that only the Protestants sold indulgences . . .[5]

Mitch Goodman, bullhorn in hand, asked how many were willing to stay. "Hell no, we won't go!" came the response, the movement's then-favorite chant. We began talking to the troops, fellows as young as most of the demonstrators: "Join us." "We love you," someone called. "You know this war is wrong. Join us." We talked about the failures of the war, the resistance of the people of Vietnam to the Chinese, the Japanese, the French, and now us. When we mentioned the folly of what had become US policy, the sergeant in the rear responded with "you don't hear nuthin, you don't say nuthin." Rumors flashed up and down our line: a soldier had dropped his rifle, but had been hustled away. Perhaps, someone said, it was 1917 and the troops would begin to throw down their weapons and cross the line to revolution. Or was it 1905 in Odessa? Would these Cossacks we sat in front of come down on us, firing as they attacked? In fact, there was no high drama. Periodically, a patrolling sergeant would kick a soldier's boots from behind so that they were pushed under a protestor seated in front of him; the protestor would then be seized, dragged through the line of soldiers, clubbed, and taken to some holding pen or jail.

Meanwhile, as evening fell it grew colder. Even those who had come dressed for jail with extra underwear shivered. People grumbled. "Think how uncomfortable it is in Vietnam," a voice countered.

A collection was taken up for food and coffee. When our supplies arrived, they were hoisted up the wall by ropes that had demarcated areas off-limits to us but which some enterprising demonstrator had repurposed. Other demonstrators used the ropes to scale the embankment. So we sat, and we talked, and we sang, and we shivered.

The soldiers stood, mostly at parade rest, occasionally bringing a rifle butt down on a marcher, who was then dragged through the line. A sergeant walked along the line of troops, emptying his canteen on the seated demonstrators. "Row, row, row your boat, / gently down the stream," they responded.[6] Our numbers gradually melted away as it approached 4 a.m., then 5 a.m. The Pentagon's strategy was becoming clear: attrition, not mass confrontation. Nothing to produce a headline, attract a camera, or even a *Washington Post* reporter. We sat and talked at the troops and each other. We sang. We shivered. Around 6 a.m., we stood up and thanked the soldier in front of whom we had been sitting and with whom we had exchanged an occasional smile: "We appreciate your restraint." "Hope you have a nice walk home," he responded. He was the only government person to speak to us during those hours of the sit-in.

We got back to the apartment, weary and bedraggled. Mitch and Denise greeted us. Denise hoped that we, or some of our cohort sitting in, had received Florence's Irish woolen blankets that she had happily thought to send us to fend off the night's cold. No. We hadn't seen them. Could they have ended up in the trash we saw being swept up by the Pentagon's garbage-removal truck? Within minutes, it was clear: no media reports of our Pentagon sit-in; no recovery of Florence's beautiful blankets from amidst the sandwich wrappers, soda bottles, abandoned backpacks, and miscellaneous trash. So it was.

A couple of months afterward, in late December, Florence and I, with my two kids, David and Daniel, on winter break from school, moved temporarily into Phyllis Ewen's apartment on Putnam Avenue in Cambridge. The kids were with us on school holidays and had already accompanied us to political gatherings, like the SDS convention in Clear Lake, Iowa. David often sat in at meetings. Discerning the rhetoric of such moments perhaps taught him the skepticism and inner calm that mark his work today as a Washington journalist. Dan even then preferred music; political arguments bored him. We schlepped bags of files along with winter clothes, for Florence and I were already deep into writing a book about the youth movement, *The Conspiracy of the Young.*[7] The cover photo of clean-cut late teens and twenty-some-things provided a hilarious contrast with pictures of spaced-out young people adrift along the Haight. My salary agreement with Antioch enabled me to have my first sabbatical for writing, in this case about freedom school, draft resistance, "channeling," schooling in America, "the White Problem for Black Youth," and the like. We mined the articles we had been writing for the *New York Review of Books.* Florence, meanwhile, between class preparations, was busy drafting a 120-page chapter on free universities.

Louis Kampf had rented an office for Resist on the second floor of 763 Massachusetts Avenue, directly opposite the Central Square post office. We had come to Cambridge to help turn Resist into a functioning organization. Not a moment too soon. Just as the fateful year 1968 began, the "Boston Five" were indicted on charges of "conspiring to counsel young men to violate the draft laws." Overnight, Resist became a hub for movement actions and as many direct "support" activities as the lawyers would allow us to conduct. Immediately, Chomsky wrote a letter to supporters asserting that if the five were guilty, we all were guilty: "We stand beside the men who have been indicted for support of draft resistance. If they are sentenced, we, too, must be sentenced. If they are imprisoned, we will take their places and will continue to use what means we can to bring this war to an end."[8]

In fact, Chomsky was named as an "unindicted co-conspirator." Louis spent most of the night calling contacts across the country. The money rolled in to Resist, and I found myself as the director of an unexpectedly significant national antiwar organization. Fortunately, Louis had organized a large number of faculty, from MIT, Tufts, Harvard, UMass/Boston, and elsewhere, whom we designated "area people." They established and maintained an informational and fundraising network with draft-resistance support groups across the country. At the same time, Helen McCormick, a former librarian and active Quaker, came into the office as a volunteer and became Resist's first full-time Cambridge staff person. Tall, thin, and soft-spoken in that way of New England Quaker women, Helen took the Quaker peace testimony as a personal imperative. She organized us.

Our monthly newsletter focused on resistance activities across the country. We provided literature on draft resistance and counseling to local resistance support groups; we helped mount an "academic day of conscience" around tax time; and we backed and publicized a Berkeley initiative for a "Vietnam commencement." We also set in motion a new legal defense fund. We began to plan summer organizing institutes, antiwar poetry readings, a speakers' bureau, and other initiatives designed to make antiwar activity more visible and more a part of the consciousness of average Americans.[9] Challenging the government's rationale for escalating the war remained our goal.

By the time the trial of the Five began on May 20, 1968, however, events had overwhelmed our hopeful program: first and foremost, the Vietnamese had launched the Tet offensive. They suffered huge casualties, but their attacks unmasked as lies the assertions about "progress" in Vietnam made by the American military and the president. By the middle of February, over five hundred Americans and untold numbers of Vietnamese were being killed every week. Then on March 12, the New Hampshire presidential primary made it clear that the American people had had enough of Lyndon Johnson. A few days later, on March 16, Bobby Kennedy announced his decision to run for president. Soon Johnson gave up the electoral ghost.

Then on April 4, 1968, Martin Luther King Jr. was murdered in Memphis. The response to King's death was overwhelming: major rebellions occurred in virtually every large American city. When King was shot, we were staying at my mother's in New York, seeing her through an illness; it was many days before we could return to a Washington still smoldering in the aftermath of the assassination. America seemed to be coming apart faster than Vietnam. On campus, later in April, the student occupation of buildings at Columbia University and the subsequent police bust suggested the depth of campus rage and resistance to racism and the war. In Paris, student and worker activism approached the very edge of revolution. The question for many people opposing the war and the draft was, what next? How could we bring an end to American destruction of Vietnam? To the racism that corroded American democracy? In our crowded Mass Avenue office, what could we do in response to the daily horrors confronting us? Our call said "resist!" But every day we had to ask ourselves, resist what exactly? And how should we begin?

For starters, we had to resist the lawyers. We—that is, those of us active in Resist—wanted to use the trial of the Boston Five to dramatize opposition to the war. That was, after all, our *raison d'être*. But the lawyers' job was to get their clients off, and some coordinated set of actions involving them, or even us, would suggest that the government's conspiracy charge had substance to it. Marc Raskin's advisors were reluctant to make the trial a political event, especially because he had not been involved in "overt acts," like draft card turn-ins. His role was only—it didn't seem so "only" to me—helping compose and circulate the "Call to Resist Illegitimate Authority." In fact, he, Noam Chomsky, Donald Kalish, Arthur Waskow, and Robert Zevin were the signatories of the initial letter of August 3, 1967, asking people to sign the call. In any event, Raskin was found innocent of the government's conspiracy charges while the others were "guilty as charged." We congratulated Raskin's lawyers on the innocent verdict, however curious; one factor may have been that government attorneys confused the thin Raskin with his colleague at the Institute for Policy Studies, the full-bodied Arthur Waskow. At one point the government attorney referred to a "Mr. Waskin."

None of the "Call to Resist" defendants was ever incarcerated, but as we all knew, draft resisters were serving terms of two to five years. It seemed unlikely that the government would actually jail America's favorite baby doctor, but one never knew. US policy led to acts at least as insane, and much more awful, in Southeast Asia. So we limited our public actions and barely involved the defendants in them. Many equally well-known signers of the "Call to Resist" in Boston had not been indicted, though the government termed them "co-conspirators." The trial attracted a good deal of financial support, which encouraged my sense that we were effectively fomenting opposition to the war. But the judge in the case severely limited testimony about the war. It proved impossible in court to advance our argument that the precedents of the Nuremberg trials obligated the defendants and their supporters to disobey the "illegitimate authority" carrying out the attacks on Vietnam.

We also had to resist the resisters. A number said angrily, and with a certain logic, that a *support* organization, Resist, should not be raising money based on their actions, much less deciding what activities to back with these funds. We should, they said, simply channel money to the Resistance. But, we pointed out, there were many forms of resistance, some of which involved people less able to gather support than the largely middle-class white men in the Resistance. The argument heated up. Ultimately, we invited a number of leaders of the Resistance to a Resist steering committee meeting held at my mother's apartment in Washington Heights. They sat on the piano bench, three or four of them, irritably reading the applications and supporting materials from a variety of organizing projects—some in black and working-class communities, some in areas of the country hostile to resistance of any sort, and others from projects just getting off the ground. Chomsky suggested that some Resistance guys in the Boston area come to the Resist office and read proposals we had earlier supported; a number did. In the end, the Resistance activists agreed grumpily that having Resist provide such projects with seed money and, occasionally, a second grant for a mailing or flyers or a newsletter made good political sense.

We also had to deal with the movement's engrained sexism. At the first meeting at Columbia, Sondra Silverman, the only woman present, was promptly elected to the steering committee. Hip to the issues, she jokingly apologized for not also being black. We knew that Grace Paley, who was involved with a vigorous group, Support in Action in New York, was also willing to serve on the Resist steering committee. Susan Sontag joined for a while, as did Florence Howe. Otherwise the committee, however distinguished, remained male and white and the staff largely female, as Hilda Hein pointed out. Resist was not a center for contesting gender and racial issues within the movement. On the other hand, it did support controversial organizing projects of groups like the Black Panthers and a number of lesbian collectives and other feminist organizations. Resist's rendezvous with identity politics would come later.

After the indictments, we concentrated on broadening the resistance of American professors, students, intellectuals, and writers against the Johnson administration. Johnson had his brain trust, people like Robert McNamara, McGeorge Bundy, and Walt Whitman Rostow. They provided the intellectual rationales, such as the "domino theory" and the notion of "free-market" economic "take-off," for American policy in Southeast Asia. Our obligation, as we saw it, was to question such folly, to undermine the credibility of these "whiz kids" of carnage. We would hold them accountable for the murderous consequences of their abstract policy decisions. The long history of Vietnamese conflict with China, we argued, undercut their portrait of the war as a battle against Chinese and Soviet expansionism. We questioned the fundamental metaphor of Southeast Asian countries as mechanical dominos ready to "fall" should Americans withdraw their arms. We showed how American advice about the Vietnamese economy and military had again and again misconstrued their society, especially the demand, in a country of peasants, that those who worked the land should own it.

Most of all, we tried to organize thousands of the nation's intelligentsia to call out the administration's policies and the draft laws as unjust, unwise, and immoral, and to insist that they would no longer comply with them. We hoped civil disobedience would gather strength from Americans of every persuasion, many of whom were slowly beginning to doubt the war policy. The policy-makers would have to listen. Or so we thought. At first.

We were amazed by the support of so many colleagues and friends. At an open meeting in New York's Town Hall, organized mainly by Grace Paley and Sandra Levinson, we planned to invite members of the audience to come to the stage to sign the "Call to Resist" and thus to commit civil disobedience. Uncertain that people would come forward, we arranged for well-known figures like Allen Ginsberg, Robert Lowell, and some members of the Resist board to step up first. When the time came, hundreds of people rushed to the stage to sign, nearly trampling our pacesetters. All the same, the Boston Five trial did not mark a big step forward from protest to resistance. It did expose our rage against the war and against American racism; it probably persuaded some people that "our" intellectuals made more ethical sense, maybe even practical sense, than those who had given themselves to Johnson and later to Nixon. Still, though eternally optimistic, I kept asking myself: How could we get in the way of the American war machine? How could we get the American people to slow it down, bring it to a halt?

College faculty devoted to the peace movement filled our office. The "area" people, a host of volunteers, and eventually paid (not much) staff carried on an energetic program aimed at bringing the draft and thus the war into question. If only the administration could see how dedicated and spirited we were, I thought. Of course, they did: the FBI had established an office overlooking ours in the post office across Mass Avenue. Later we discovered that they had been sorting through our garbage. Good luck with that! But what difference would it have really made had McNamara and company understood our politics, our values, even our commitment?

Many years later, during my first visit to Vietnam, I'd climbed down into the Cu Chi tunnels, now a major tourist attraction. Imagine discovering three underground levels with sleeping quarters, cooking facilities, schools, clinics—and all largely impervious to American bombing. I remember commenting: "They should have invited McNamara to see these tunnels. He would then have understood how impossible a task he had imposed on American GIs. Maybe he'd have packed up and gone home." But of course, that was a dream. America's "leaders," or at any rate our commanders, had so thoroughly persuaded themselves of their virtue and wisdom, of American moral "exceptionalism," that nothing short of military catastrophe—as was happening—could have changed their minds.

After the conclusion of the trial, a new way to use it to pursue an antiwar platform presented itself: working with Noam Chomsky to write a reflection on the case for the *New York Review of Books*. Writing with Chomsky was for me unlike any such opportunity before or since. Florence and I drafted a modest article emphasizing the by now well-developed points of draft resistance as a means for undermining the war policy. That was what the trial was about, after all, and while the judge might keep the war out of his courtroom, we were under no such constraints in the pages of the magazine. We sent a draft to Chomsky. The next morning, we received back a new article, perhaps four or five times longer. In it, Chomsky had extended enormously the discussion we had had about the applicability of the Nuremberg principles to the Boston Five case, and more generally to draft resistance as a moral and political imperative for those opposing the war. We were blown away. First, by the encyclopedic detail he arrayed to make his argument. But also by the speed and grace with which he had written—clearly, we were working with a person different from thee and me. We might not command legions of marines, but the peace movement could deploy superior intellectual resources. Alas, that was not enough.

Resist, draft resistance, a legal appeal from the Boston Five conviction, the intellectual efforts to counter the abysmal ideas of LBJ and his advisors—all these continued. But so did another set of antiwar activities in which I joined: direct nonviolent (mostly) actions in the streets and on American campuses. Our goals did not differ from those of Resist, but other priorities shaped what we activists did. Frustrated and angry, we believed it essential to carry out visible antiwar agitation. Only in that way would the widening opposition register among Americans everywhere. Also, we understood that such direct actions put pressure on politicians, local or national. We had learned from experience on campuses that administrative responses to local pressures were often ill-considered and sometimes over the top—they alienated possible allies and drove others toward us. We hoped overreactions and stupid mistakes by the administration would lead to alienating that "doubtful majority" and to moving more people into partisan opposition. Indeed, that would happen with Nixon's "plumbers" and the

Watergate break-in that led directly to his removal from office. Many direct actions, unlike most gloomy trials, were fun—until they weren't, and the police took to attacking, manuals for making bombs circulated, and the National Guard started using live ammunition. Even so: a friend, I will call her Eliza, and I were part of an upbeat Baltimore contingent that liked to participate in demonstrations—locally, in New York, in DC, wherever the action happened to be.

In Baltimore, where I was then living, I came prepared for action: heavy leather boots, my white crash helmet, a gas mask of early World War II vintage. I left the chain links home. Running up Charles Street, I spotted on a corner a seemingly abandoned Baltimore Police Department motorcycle—no cop in view. Should I push it down, maybe pry open the gas cap, set it afire? I hung between fear—registered as adult caution—and manly desire, gave in to the former, regretted it for days after. Especially after I was busted for trying to protect a fellow demonstrator (and Vietnam vet) from a pissed-off Baltimore cop. But then again, the Baltimore Police Department and its bikes were not my enemy, though I never could abide the phrase "our brothers in blue."

In DC I joined a loose-jointed demo organized by activist friends. For some reason we were outside the Justice Department when the tear gas canisters began raining down. Intrepid souls picked some up and heaved them toward a person they claimed was John Mitchell, who was looking down on us from an enclosed balcony. We at least had the pleasure of seeing people inside the building wiping away tears as we fled onto the National Mall. The next day the papers ran stories about Mitchell's wife, Martha, observing the demonstration and mocking what she described as a liberal communist revolution underway. We hitched a ride to the outskirts of DC, and everyone in the car was coughing before we'd gotten halfway to the Maryland border. Tear gas particles stick. A few days later when we picked up our coats from the dry cleaners, the owner asked "wherever have you been? Everyone in the store had to rush outside when we began to brush down your coats." Tear gas sticks. What was it like, then, under clouds of the stuff in war zones of Vietnam?

Another Washington action in 1969: Eliza and I were part of a major demonstration, the "counter-inaugural," directed against Nixon and Spiro Agnew. The Baltimore contingent played a large role. As the demonstration marched down Independence Avenue, we made our way to the front, I got up on a parapet, and like some cartoon of a Bolshevik agitator, flung my arm again and again toward the part of the Smithsonian Institution where the Agnew party was being held. The whole march turned in that direction. We knew what our governor was really like. Soon enough he would be forced to resign for political and financial corruption. SDS members had formed the Weather Underground and were by then courting fights with cops, such as right outside the Agnew reception. Since we weren't up for arrest that day, we wandered away after a bit, then stopped and looked at one another: in our heads, we realized, we were already in bed, needing only to race back to her Maryland house, where we could throw off our clothes.

I had never before appreciated how much of a turn-on street action could be. A cheerful reinforcement of desire. A way to turn my talk into action. Not everyone's definition of fun, not always, and not everywhere. A few years ago when I joined a picket and leafletting rally directed at Bank of America in New Mexico, I felt the exhilaration again, with people waving back at us: "Go for it." We seemed to be making change, however slowly.

We *were* making change, in ourselves, in those around us, in an America at war. Why did we march, risk a nightstick across the back, a lung full of gas, an indefinite tomorrow? Or, as at Kent State and Jackson State, the bullets of the same callous power that had been unleashed on Vietnam? Whatever the pleasures we derived from our actions, we weren't playing at fun and games. It seemed to us that we carried forward *the* most meaningful of American traditions: the tradition of dissent, and the right and duty of revolution, if that became necessary. We tried to make it clear that an America at war could no longer be governed peaceably, that business as usual became impossible while the same war continued. If those making decisions about war would not heed the appeals to "give peace a chance," perhaps they would respond to the noise of turmoil sounding louder across the campuses and in the streets of America.

In the summer of 1968, Florence and I moved from Washington to an apartment near Johns Hopkins in Baltimore. There we became increasingly involved in the Baltimore Defense Committee (BDC), the local movement organization that carried out actions against the war and others directed against racism in the city and county. One of the first feminist journals, *Women: A Journal of Liberation*, was connected to the BDC. And there, we came into the orbit of the Catholic radicals who constituted the "Catonsville Nine."[10]

The Catonsville Nine action is probably the best known of a series of physical attacks on draft board files. Earlier, the "Baltimore Four," one of whom was Father Philip Berrigan, poured a combination of human and animal blood over draft files in Baltimore. And in Milwaukee, a group that came to be known as the "Milwaukee Fourteen" used homemade napalm to set on fire some twenty thousand draft records, including about six thousand 1-A files, on a small grassy area opposite the draft board. In each case, the clergymen and lay women who participated stood singing and praying while the files burned or were otherwise compromised. These actions embodied militant nonviolent protest. They perhaps marked a transition from protest to resistance. In the places attacked, resisters stopped the draft from being carried out. As I wrote at the time, they kept "oppressive institutions from functioning, preventing illegitimate authority from controlling and maiming lives."[11]

Inevitably, these militant nonviolent actions produced controversy within the peace movement. One of the slogans of the Catonsville Nine—"some property has no right to exist"—took aim at a central assumption of capitalism, the sanctity of property. The actions were themselves seen by some as implicitly violent. But for many of us involved with the BDC, the burning of draft files seemed, miraculously, both nonviolent and revolutionary.

At the events built around the week of the Catonsville Nine trial we saw new developments in the movement, which carried us where we had been unable to go earlier in the year at the Boston trial. The Catonsville Nine encouraged demonstrations in the streets of Baltimore and held forums at St. Ignatius church. Their lawyers, led by William Kunstler, well known for supporting movement activism, agreed with that strategy. Each evening's forum had a somewhat different emphasis: the first, with Harvey Cox in the lead, focused on American imperialism. Noam Chomsky traced the character of American imperialism through its manifestations in the Philippines, Thailand, and elsewhere; Dorothy Day explained the inspiration for radical Catholic direct actions; and Blasé Bonpane, one of the clergymen who had been expelled (with two of the Catonsville Nine) from Guatemala, spoke from personal experience about guerilla resistance there. Tuesday night, twenty-five men there in Baltimore burned their draft cards during a forum devoted to "revolution and risk."

These forums resembled intense teach-ins. They paralleled the testimony being given in court by each of the Nine explaining their actions. The judge allowed the Nine considerable opportunity to explore with him the relationship between the judicial system and the war, as well as US imperialist activities in places like Guatemala, where a number of Catholic radicals had served. To be sure, when it came to instructing the jury, the judge said they were only able to consider the acts the defendants had committed, not their reasons for carrying out such acts.

At each evening forum and at a Saturday rally in Baltimore's federal plaza we took up a collection. That was my role, perhaps because I was a professor with hair going grey. I struggled to explain in different and, I hoped, compelling ways our need for money to continue the work of the Nine. No doubt they would soon be headed for prison, and we needed to carry on. On the last day, at a rally in the plaza, I argued that we had in significant ways become a community of believers and activists. I hoped that everyone there would put some money into the hats we used to gather contributions. But, I added, if there were members of our community who faced serious wants and needed funds, they might consider taking a few bucks *out* of a hat. That proved a mind-blowing idea.

During the week, we needed to talk about any course corrections with those of the Nine who were not already in jail for earlier actions. They came, along with the leadership of the BDC, to our apartment for a quiet but intense discussion: eighteen to twenty people, mostly sitting on the floor, talking about where things might be heading. Afterwards, Dean Pappas, tall, blonde, and curly headed, modeled like a classical Greek statue, encountered one of our neighbors in the hallway as he headed to the elevator. "Young man," the old woman said in her nasal voice, "you smell bad." Responded Dean, "you ain't no bed of roses yourself, you old fart." We received an eviction notice the next morning.

What was the impact of the actions in the streets, in the courtroom, and at St. Ignatius? Had the Catonsville Nine succeeded in moving from "protest" to "resistance?" Or did their actions simply hasten the demise of a fading institution, the draft? Nixon would win the presidential election (though not the votes of Maryland) in about a month. Meanwhile, divisions in the nation were widening, particularly between young people and those Nixon celebrated as "the silent majority."

Few of us fully understood the political jujitsu that marked Nixon's first term. Nixon's "secret plan" to end the war involved three key elements: first, Vietnamization. On the whole, Americans did not fret over Vietnamization of the war—let the wogs kill the wogs, so long as our own boys were being brought home, however slowly, or left to pursue their private lives. Second, the draft lottery and movements toward a volunteer force succeeded in undercutting the effectiveness of draft resistance as an antiwar strategy. American casualties declined, yes, as did draft calls. Our own efforts to end the draft, as in the National Council to Repeal the Draft, were effectively turned against a more fundamental goal: ending not only the war but also the ideology of American exceptionalism and the righteousness that underwrote it. And third, while we spoke of moving from protest to resistance, Nixon, like LBJ before him, portrayed "resistance" as unlawful. The young movement—driven wild by frustration and a commitment to ethical values that America claimed but seldom practiced—gave the politicians abundant evidence to sustain that argument. We were breaking the law.

Through such actions, Nixon managed to some degree in dividing the antiwar movement, but not, for many a year, in ending the war itself. Casualties—American and especially Vietnamese, Cambodian, and Laotian—continued for another seven years. And in Southeast Asia they continue to this day, thanks to unexploded ordinance, the effects of Agent Orange, and the widespread disruption of civilian life produced by the war. While American GIs usually faced the war for twelve or thirteen months, Vietnamese civilians faced it day after fiery day for years. Terrorizing civilians, I came to understand, had become a primary object of the ongoing war.[12] As Mrs. Phung Thi Tiem told Martha Hess in an interview:

> That evening buildings were destroyed, everything. Many people were injured and entire families were wiped out—from the youngest to the oldest. In one family, five generations were killed together, the baby inside its pregnant mother, the son, the mother, the grandmother and the great grandmother. In one family there were nine children, and their parents died. We spent that week digging out the shelters, looking for missing people. The smell of the dead was terrible. We collected the bodies in one place, and the wounded were taken to the hospital. To be fair, the Vietnamese didn't send troops

to invade America. Never, never forget. We remember the war. We remember our losses. All the little children—nine years old, thirteen, they had committed no war crimes for the Americans to come and kill them. When they died in the bombings, their eyes popped out from the compression. Their bodies were mangled. Small children and old people. They lived here, and worked their whole lives here. They never sent troops to America. They never took one plant, one leaf from America. Why did the Americans come to destroy everything, to kill the people, to kill small children, to kill even pregnant women—why? Don't the American people even know why?

Americans had begun asking the same questions. Indeed, getting Americans to ask such questions was the major concern of the peace movement. The war-makers had the bully pulpit of the presidency, the assurances of success pronounced daily by the generals, and the patriotic suppositions about their country's morality. Most Americans accepted those views, at least at first. They believed the messages of anti-communism inculcated by virtually every cultural institution in the United States. They knew the sacrifices young Americans were making on the fields of valor—or shame—in Vietnam.

We in the peace movement had . . . the truth.

That truth about the American mission in Vietnam had been framed early on in the struggle against the war by ex–Green Beret Donald Duncan: "The whole thing was a lie."[13] Now, half a century later, we have the knowledge brought by overwhelming, authoritative sources. Millions of Americans have by now seen the powerful film about the Vietnam War made by Ken Burns and Lynn Novick. I question much about the film, especially its failure to portray accurately the antiwar movement.[14] But Burns and Novick are clear about one thing: young GIs, dedicated to their country, were betrayed by the mendacity and incompetence of their leaders, civilian and military. While the film focuses on the American scene, it makes a parallel case, accurately or not, about the Vietnamese soldiers and their leaders.[15] Johnson, Nixon, McNamara, William Westmoreland, and down the chains of command, lied and lied again to the men and women they sent into battle, to the American people, to the Congress, and often to one another.

The same conclusion emerged in serious exhibitions like that at the New-York Historical Society (2018), as well as in new scholarly articles and books based on recently available materials from US and

Vietnamese archives. We in the peace movement argued, as far back as the 1950s, that an American military presence in Vietnam violated international and domestic law. Our military, we argued, sustained a corrupt and immoral puppet government in Saigon. America's blind anti-communism, we said, would never lead to peace but to an endless war whose victims were predominantly civilians. Sad to say, we were right, and those who served successive administrations were, by virtue of ignorance, mistakes, or intent, fatally wrong.

Chapter Nine

A NEW UNIVERSITY?

In the spring of 1969, after a year and a half of steady activity with Resist, I decided to return to academe. During that time, I had written parts of *The Conspiracy of the Young*, coauthored a number of articles for the *New York Review of Books* and other periodicals, and added my body to many protests. I was weary. Our disruption of the 1968 Modern Language Association convention in New York—to which I will turn shortly—offered a kind of bathetic climax to the increasingly murderous events of 1968. I felt I needed the steadiness and, yes, the salary of a regular job.

I had very mixed feelings about moving full time into movement work, which was one of the options for me at this time. To support my children financially, I needed a regular income. But, the idea of raising the funds for my own salary gave me the creeps. Nor, as a depression baby, could I live with the prospect of being broke five or ten years down the road. I worried: When the war crisis passed and people returned to their normal lives, would they support someone who didn't have a "normal" life? I enormously admired Dave Dellinger as a person and a movement leader. But I couldn't accept the economic uncertainty that marked a life like his. Perhaps it was my petty bourgeois upbringing. Or maybe changes in the movement turned me away. The sectarianism dividing the movement seemed loony to me, especially as bombs rained down on Vietnam, Laos, and Cambodia. I couldn't accept factionalism, given what the American military was doing in Southeast Asia. But even if one didn't join one or another group, one had at least to pay the various lines some heed in order to maintain credibility in a divided movement and to sustain the momentum of antiwar activity.

The university was familiar terrain—both enjoyable and politically ambiguous. True, we academics helped reproduce the structure and culture of American capitalist society. But maybe we could change that. Maybe we could provoke students and colleagues into questioning racism and patriarchy and the exceptionalism that underwrote America's culture of war. Education, as I had learned in the 1964 freedom schools, could help liberate and empower people. I knew my way around this academic world, and the credentials I brought to a position in the English Department of the University of Maryland, Baltimore County (UMBC)—a Yale degree, a considerable record of publication—had resonance there.

A new institution in the Maryland system, UMBC had, after considerable argument, been located in Baltimore County rather than in the city. That location, and Baltimore's limited public transportation system, prevented many urban students from enrolling. Mostly the students were white and often working class. Many had a conservative view of what teaching was about, though less so than the apprehensive administrators. Administrative anxiety would lead to trouble for me over the two let's call them "interesting" years, 1969–71, I taught at UMBC.

Florence and I bought a large, old house on Greenspring Avenue, near the Pimlico racetrack, with a giant oak in the front yard and perhaps a half acre in the back. It cost about $28,000. Florence's Goucher salary was maybe half that, mine more or less the same. Settling into a home seemed like reentering the abode of the everyday. But even had I wished to do so, I couldn't: not then, not later, not ever. I had stepped out of the realm in which I had been shaped and had entered another one that, as part of the movement, I was helping to form. The office of The Feminist Press, soon to be conceived, occupied one of the bedrooms on the second floor of our house. The regional organizer for the New University Conference (NUC) and his activist spouse would come to live on the third floor. I was secretly asked by a movement friend (later said to be a police agent) to bury weapons covertly in the land behind the house (I didn't). I never left my post with Resist and continued writing *Conspiracy*, as well as articles for the *New York Review of Books* and other journals. One contribution Florence and I thought we could make to movement activity was to write for an influential audience about the draft, the war, and resistance to them.

UMBC at the time consisted of raw poured concrete and red brick buildings with rigid oblong windows, linked by concrete paths often bordered in brick. Like many of these new campuses, it seemed a site waiting to happen, to sprout grass and trees and students at frisbee. As has come to be. A room I was twice assigned had all forty or so seats bolted into the concrete floor, as if to say "so much for your seating these kids in a circle." One term I managed to change rooms with a colleague who liked order and a fixed syllabus. The other term I spent wondering what the registrar who allocated space had against me, or perhaps against new, flexible ideas about teaching and learning.

Some movement activities followed me into UMBC like Marx and Engels's specter haunting Europe. Women's studies tested our resolve. When we came before the faculty meeting to ask for recognition of a program, one of the older gentlemen said, with what might have been a disarming honesty, "I've never heard of such a field. What does it do?" Nancy Henley, a psychologist who was leading our effort, responded cheerfully:

"That could well be the case. But that will certainly change. They've now been set up at Cornell, San Diego State, and other places. There will be dozens in a year or two. So we'll all know about them soon.

"As to what they do, they study women, our work, our minds, and the art of women . . . and men, of course. I'll be happy to sit down and share with anyone recent scholarship that's already changing many fields, like my own."

Students at the back of the room applauded her; we were proud but restrained.

When I was asked to teach a new advanced English Department elective, I invented Revolutionary Literature—perfect for the moment, I thought. Or maybe not: there were more revolutionary failures, like André Malraux's *Man's Fate* and Ignazio Silone's *Bread and Wine*, among the books I taught than successes. We looked at a number of films, most unforgettably *Memories of Underdevelopment* and *The Battle of Algiers*. I saw the latter so often that I could visualize what was on the screen by hearing the music. My favorite works were Lu Xun stories, particularly "A Madman's Diary" with its striking final line, "Save the children," and Fyodor Gladkov's remarkably feminist novel of 1925, *Cement*.

The course hinged on Raymond Williams's somewhat formulaic distinction between bourgeois culture, which he described as individualistic, and working-class culture, which he defined as collectivist. Williams's otherwise useful contrast got me fired. The students understood individualism well enough—it was what they aspired to practice in some half-baked way: be distinctive, be yourself and no one else, wear some T-shirt or hairdo that marks you as you. But collectivity— that was an elusive concept for them, something they associated, reasonably given American ideology, with communism, the Soviet Union, a world of unions and kibbutzim that they neither knew nor wished to find out about. Their schooling, with its individual tests and grades, and uniformly separate results, established Williams's bourgeois culture as the unquestioned norm. Collective achievement had been left behind with kindergarten.

To push against this "common sense," I proposed an option for their final exam: they could write their own individual answers to the questions in the usual way, or they could work as a collective to compose a single set of answers for which I would award them a collective grade. The conventionally smarter students wrote their own exams. The others discovered many of the difficulties of collective work. I had numerous phone calls:

"Jack isn't coming to meetings. What can we do?"

"Your problem," I'd say.

"Jill wrote a lousy section for the exam. Can't we cut it and substitute something else?"

"Your decision," I'd say.

"We don't agree on why workers in that story rejected the union. What do we do?"

"Work it out, or maybe write about why it's difficult to come to conclusions," I'd tell them.

The students learned far more trying to work collectively, I thought, than simply by reading about it in my assignments.

The dean didn't see it that way, or so he claimed. He fired me. Before he did so, Nixon had invaded Cambodia and students protested by trying to block Baltimore highways. I had met with them to talk strategy, and I picketed with them. The dean's rationale for getting rid of me seemed a bit implausible. I went to see him. Inside my very large fake-leather briefcase I carried a tape recorder. The dean explained himself: "Until you arrived," he said, "we never had students demonstrating and carrying on." Good, I thought, I've caught him in a lie—that's not his public story. When I got back to my office, I rewound the tape and began to play it. I heard footsteps. Nothing else. Evidently, I had turned the tape machine on only when I left the dean's office and so had recorded the sound of my shoes on the steps leading down from his building to mine. Fortunately, I was never called upon to carry out technological tasks for the movement, though I became useful at home with running toilets, frozen water pipes, and plants needing to be repotted.

At UMBC we started a chapter of the New University Conference (NUC). That project, along with writing, became my primary movement work. It consumed as much time as my teaching. The NUC was one among a number of late-sixties efforts to create an "adult" alternative to the collapsing SDS. I lived through a "Back to the Drawing Board" conference, ridiculously disrupted its very first night by three loud guys from the Haight who called themselves "diggers." Periodically, a "Movement for a Democratic Society" would emerge, aiming to activate people who no longer saw themselves as "students," or never did. The NUC was part of a wider effort among radical faculty and graduate students to transform universities and the intellectual work done within them. In virtually every academic field in the United States and in Europe, especially in the humanities and social sciences, radical activists started new organizations or transformed existing peace research groups. The new societies included the Union of Radical Political Economists (URPE), the Sociology Liberation Movement, the Radical Philosophy Association, and the like. Such groups generally met at the conventions of the larger existing professional societies, held independent sessions, often published newsletters, and provided academic "homes" for those struggling to unify their academic work and their political values.

In the fall of 1968 the NUC had become the umbrella for those of us interested in somehow radicalizing, or at least stirring up, the staid Modern Language Association. At its convention in New York's Hilton and Americana hotels[1] (an enormous fifty-story place that is now a Sheraton), we handed out buttons saying "Mother Language Association"; we put up posters on the Americana's slick walls with slogans like "The Tygers of Wrath Are Wiser Than the Horses of Instruction"; we pressured the MLA to allow us to present Noam Chomsky in an unscheduled teach-in on the Vietnam War at a huge forum in the Trianon Ballroom. We also joined with the organization's liberals to move the 1969 annual convention out of Chicago because of the police riot at the Democratic National Convention. Ultimately, we elected Louis Kampf, who had been arrested for protecting one of our posters from the hotel cops, as the MLA's second vice president. He would thus succeed after two years to the presidency—much to the horror of the sad MLA brass, which had before the vote announced the presumed election of its chosen candidate. We organized ourselves as a Tactics Committee, which met many times a day in Dick Ohmann's room at the City Squire Hotel, the "overflow" hotel across Seventh Avenue from the Americana. Among our more consequential actions was backing an initiative to set up an MLA Commission on the Status of Women. It became an important center for feminist activism in higher education.

The Americana lobby—spacious, with high ceilings, wide couches, and fancy crystal chandeliers—provided a handsome opening venue for the NUC. Most off-Broadway casts would have envied us. Organized just a few months before at a meeting at the University of Chicago, the NUC had played a visible role in protests at the American Sociological Association meeting in Boston that fall. I staffed a Sociology Liberation Movement table there for some hours—I think while the insurgents were having it out with the sociology establishment, which was loudly threatening them with arrest.[2] In New York, we played out a three-cornered drama with the MLA hierarchy, hotel officials, and our band of well-dressed (dresses, ties, and jackets) revolutionaries.

One dramatic moment occurred in the hotel lobby when we demonstrated against the Americana, which had had our comrades arrested defending our posters. The MLA leadership—John Hurt Fisher, Henry Nash Smith, Maynard Mack—pleaded with us to move elsewhere. In the middle of the lobby we sat in a loose circle on the floor discussing whether or not to move. Meanwhile, the New York Police Department's "tac squad" silently and menacingly entered the hotel and formed up into a large black-clad wreathe around the walls. Bruce Franklin, who had served as a navigator and intelligence officer in the Strategic Air Command, and who would later be fired from Stanford for allegedly "urging and inciting disruptions of University activities," remained standing. He conducted the meeting according to parliamentary rules—requiring raised hands (even by the frantic MLA brass), no speaking out of turn, letting all sides be heard before a vote. We finally did vote to move to a back part of the hotel to negotiate with the MLA and the management about dropping charges and apologizing for attacking our posters and busting our folks.

A few days later, a *New York Times* editorial condemned us for "adolescent public display" and "public invective." We wrote to and ultimately met with people from the editorial page. What a good moment! Being dissed by the *Times* called attention to the NUC, like a hostile drama review—just make sure you spell our names right. It helped place us on the map. Thank you, Abe Rosenthal, A. H. Raskin, and

company, who finally agreed to print our letter (which I drafted) calling out their inaccurate reporting and irrational hostility. Thus, aided
by the *Times*, the MLA, the NYPD, and the Loews Corporation (which
owned the Americana), the NUC grew rapidly. Fred Pincus and Marty
Ehrlich estimated that by 1970–71, some sixty chapters had emerged,
with about two thousand members.[3]

The rapid growth of the NUC demonstrated the desire of younger
faculty, graduate students, and others who worked "in, around, and in
spite of universities"—to use Michelle Russell's formulation, which got
incorporated into NUC's founding statement—to find or create an
organization that could carry forward our politics. By the end of 1968,
SDS—in which many of us had worked—was well on its way to implod-
ing. The "good guys" in SDS, whom I liked and admired, had come
to speak in a violent language of revolutionary struggle; their actions
seemed to me unhinged from American reality, despite their adop-
tion of a Bob Dylan phrase to name themselves, "Weatherman." The
"sectarians," especially Progressive Labor Party members who paraded
themselves as "communist cadre," variously attacked the Chinese government, revisionists from some red planet, or the Vietnamese, whose
struggle had for the better part of a decade provided a moral and
political center for the movement.

The Mobilization Committee to End the War, in its various con-
figurations, got people onto busses for giant rallies in New York,
Washington, San Francisco, and elsewhere. But it didn't offer an
ongoing program, or even a slogan, more substantial than "give
peace a chance." Those joining the NUC were committed to ending
the war. But many of us also wanted to transform our teaching, our
universities, our professions—preferably all three. Almost everyone
initially involved with the organization had been active in civil rights
work and remained committed to the movement's antiracist goals.
The NUC seemed to provide a structure for working toward these
objectives.

And it did for a while. But the NUC was caught up in a number
of fatal tensions that led to a deterioration even more rapid than its
rise. As Pincus and Ehrlich have also pointed out, by 1972 membership
had declined to around three hundred, the organization was broke,
and its last convention voted to pack it in. Why, after such a brilliant
rise? First of all, it remained unclear whether NUC members should
think of themselves as a revolutionary vanguard or as a group of professors and grad students dedicated to radical change in our university

workplaces—and ultimately, in the wider society. Were we "radical teachers" or people active in a radical movement who happened to be teachers? The organization didn't come to firm conclusions. If we were radical activists, we would join other activists, whatever their work, in demonstrations such as that at the 1968 Democratic National Convention in Chicago. Nothing wrong with that—though I didn't support that action—but it led in a different direction from radicalizing our university work. It ignored our teaching and research as factors in defining our politics. The actions we organized at the American Sociological Association meeting or at the Modern Language Association convention saw our professions as starting points, and change in them as a critical goal.

From the opening whistle, this conflict divided the NUC. At its founding convention in Chicago, I'm told, Staughton Lynd urged the assembled academics to leave their comfy university precincts and undertake more direct revolutionary activity among working-class people, like those in the Mahoning Valley, where he was now active. At the final plenary, Louis Kampf responded by urging participants to focus on transforming their work and their institutions so as to build a socialist future. I'm not sure where I would have come down in this debate at that particular moment. Florence and I were in Skiathos, my first time overseas, eating wonderful grilled Greek octopus and trying to finish writing *The Conspiracy of the Young*.

The idea of being part of a "revolutionary" vanguard struck me as absurd—there I was enjoying a mortgage, two children, and even a writing career. Nevertheless, I retained my tenuous link to the Weathermen, even after they went underground. Once every three or four months, I would get a call: that meant I should go to a particular public phone box in Flushing, Queens, at a particular time. From there, I would get another call about another time at which my contact would join me walking the streets around Grand Central station. It was a workable although pretty meaningless plan for sustaining an "underground." I'm told that I even spoke at an NUC meeting about the need to retain such ties. Some of these underground folks were good friends. The ongoing war, which had now moved from Johnson's bloody hands to Nixon's, made all of us furious. At the same time, many of us—myself included—were drawn to a kind of romance with the idea of personal transformation through activist politics. Our goal, as Mao urged, was to cross from our daily activities as teachers and intellectuals over to the revolutionary side. Yes, we would!

Conflict over who we were, or might become, also affected NUC's recruiting activities. Were we trying to bring in established faculty to construct a broadly radical organization? Or should we aim to include activists whose relationships to universities were, at best, tangential? In Baltimore, for example, we had enlisted Alice Rossi, a long-time feminist leader, a founder of NOW, and a major figure among university sociologists. Was her participation a good thing for a developing organization, as I thought, or a hindrance to sustaining a "truly" radical program?

At another time and in another place, a well-built organization might have pursued both broader political goals—ending the war, for example—as well as changes in work, workplaces, and economic authority. The United Electrical Workers (UE) provided one such model. But in the late sixties, and throughout the movement, differences in emphasis became differences in values, credibility, principles. "Which side are you on?" came to differentiate not a "union man" from "a thug for J. H. Blair," but an acolyte for one sect from a devotee of another.

The NUC proved no exception to such enervating conflict. At the National Committee meeting (a small convention, SDS-style) in Baltimore, we decided to exclude delegates who were affiliated with the Progressive Labor Party. Progressive Labor was an offshoot of a series of splits from the Communist Party and maintained a sectarian culture hostile to parliamentary democracy. The group was notorious for infiltrating organizations (notably SDS) and recruiting members for its own purposes—purposes that had already been decided upon by its own leadership and which might or might not accord with the host organization's commitments. In this particular case, as I recall, Progressive Labor had decided that the NUC should devote itself to pushing academics to leave the confines of the university and join the industrial workforce in order to promote therein a brand of communism. National Committee members who had been around the movement for a while urged kicking them out since they were shamelessly disruptive of any discussion that did not promote their goals.

I was a bit skeptical. Should we tell a bunch of academics, some of whom I knew, that they couldn't play in our yard? We threw a party at our house the night before this purge was to happen. At one point, I stood watching a small group of people talking in the kitchen. Among them was Hilary Putnam, a well-known professor of philosophy at Harvard and active in Progressive Labor. He was dressed like a working-class stiff, smoking, his pack of cigarettes wrapped in the end of the sleeve of his t-shirt. Soon enough, he dropped the butt on the kitchen floor and ground it into the linoleum. I asked myself: "Did I want to work with an organization which prized such a thoughtless jerk? Let's be rid of him—and them." The next day I was part of the group barring access to the Progressive Labor members.

The NUC also struggled with conflicts between national and local priorities. To have an impact on national policies, like the war, the organization needed to have a national profile—like the one we secured through the MLA actions in New York. We decided to sponsor a "Week Against Campus Militarism," designed to combat the ROTC, military research on campus, and the like. I actually wrote the proposal and supported the idea. But people in some chapters saw it as an effort of the national office to impose a program on local organizers. They had other priorities, like defending members who had been fired or starting a women's studies or a black studies program. Why put time and energy into someone else's idea of the organization's purposes? Our differences in priorities were never fully resolved. They came down to a fundamental question: What was the NUC about?

That question could not be answered in any simple way, partly because the very nature of universities was at issue in countries around the world. In the United States, one major focus of dispute concerned "open admissions"—that is, what criteria would determine who got into college and how that affected the curriculum. The NUC tried to develop a program, OUTS (Open Up the Schools), that spoke to this basic concern about who had, or should have, access to higher education.

In China the Cultural Revolution was taking place just as the NUC rose and fell. The Chinese experience interested me from the time I was in grammar school. Fascinated with what the Western press referred to as the "agrarian reformers"—that is, the communists—in China, I sometimes found brief paragraphs about them in the *New York Times* or in the *Herald-Tribune,* and I would bring them to class for show-and-tell. That nebulous interest led me to reading, including one of Agnes Smedley's books, *Battle Hymn of China.*[4] My revolutionary literature course at the University of Maryland, Baltimore County included Lu Xun, which meant that I had to explain to students in what ways he *was* revolutionary.

The course also included a useful theoretical piece, Mao Zedong's *Talks at the Yenan Forum on Art and Literature.* It's not exactly a thrill a minute to read, but Mao provided me with a weapon against critics who promoted artists I disliked, like Jackson Pollock, Mark Rothko, and Willem de Kooning, and theorists with whom I disagreed, like Clement Greenberg. When we came to start the magazine that would be called *Radical Teacher*, I proposed, only partly in jest, that we name it "The Pear," after Mao's comment on learning about social revolution: "If you would know the taste of a pear, you must change it by eating it."

A few years later, in 1974, I became part of the second delegation of Americans to go to China after Nixon's opening. I remained very enthusiastic about what I saw in China, even as the Cultural Revolution was winding down. At a school we visited, someone in our delegation asked what they did with a teacher who did not work out; did they simply fire him? The deputy director rejected the idea. "That would only mean he would do damage at another job. No, we try to work with such a teacher to change what he does." Sounded good to us. At a hospital in Guangzhou, someone asked what medical problems were of particular importance to them. "Back pain," was the answer, given the hard labor that peasants and workers undertook. Such answers—along with works of persuasive art like the Rent Collection Courtyard sculpture, the absence of advertising that exploited women's bodies, the ending of foreign concessions in cities like Shanghai, and the use of formerly "white" parks for local t'ai chi practice—these and other parts of our trip registered positively with us. They spoke well for the Chinese liberation struggle.

Nor was everything ideology and solemnity. Toward the end of our trip, at a banquet in a Peking duck restaurant, I tasted the best dish I have ever eaten: duck webs and tree fungi in an anise sauce. But the climax of the event came when the waiters paraded to our table with a large silver salver, placed it before our host, and ceremoniously lifted off the cover. Our host, on whose left I was sitting because I was making a presentation of Agnes Smedley papers, then grandly lifted with his chopsticks and placed on my plate the duck's head, complete with beak and eyes. What do I do now? I could not ask others on the delegation: they were half-seas over from the 50 percent alcohol banquet drink, *maotai*. I tentatively addressed my chopsticks to an eye and was rewarded with an approving nod by our host. And so I went on, uncertain where to continue and when to stop.

Later, I would learn about the violence and stupidity of the Cultural Revolution, its brutalization of people from every class, and its fundamental goal of consolidating Mao Zedong's political power. But

I remained persuaded of the importance of its effort to alter the class base of those who studied—and taught—in universities. Universities play a powerful role in opening paths for upward mobility to students. The question of who can get into and graduate from college was deeply conflicted in the late sixties—not only in China but also in the United States, France, Britain, and elsewhere. It remains so, as we know. How to change access to college, curriculum, admissions standards, the allocation of funds, and whom you hire to bring about such change—or avoid it—were subjects of passionate dispute in the NUC, and *over* the NUC. What were we about?

For Florence and for me, that question and everything it implied about direction, program, and membership came to a head at the 1970 NUC Convention at the University of Michigan. Among our tasks as members of the National Committee through the 1969–70 academic year was gathering and editing articles for a newsletter on "radical teaching." This *Radical Teacher* newsletter seemed like a natural project for a "new university" organization. But in Ann Arbor disagreements were rampant about the organization's purposes and the usefulness of projects like our newsletter. Were our efforts, focused on university teaching, manifestations of elitism, as some members argued? Or were they central to the organization's purpose? These differences came to a head with the election of members for the National Committee.

Of the seven men on the National Committee, all but one stood for reelection. Of the seven women, only one—given the reigning anti-leadership ideology among feminist women—decided to run again. This in itself disturbed some of us: another instance of male control, however predictable. The six incumbent men were reelected. The one incumbent woman, Florence, was not. The women, we later heard, hadn't voted for her. In a rage, we left. We drove from Ann Arbor across into Canada and planned to stop for the night at a motel in Ontario. Louis left after us and, amazingly, we met at some diner.

"You left without saying goodbye," he said.

"We wanted to get out of there," Florence responded.

"How did you know to find us?" I asked.

"Someone told me where you were headed. What was the hurry?"

"We were very upset with the election, too upset to stay around. All the sexism in the organization came out."

"I understand. But there's more involved than an election. The organization is less chauvinistic than most."

"Well, it doesn't feel that way to me," I put in. "Why do you say that?"

"You know, most of the demands of the women's caucus were approved. All the committees are balanced. We've come a long way."

"But there's no real equality," Florence said. "You saw that in the election, right? The men are still in charge. I've had enough."

"They're the heavies," I added.

"That's partly true," Louis said. "But that's not the main problem."

"So what is?"

"All the revolutionary BS. Being in some vanguard. A lot of people who don't work in education mouthing off."

"That's all very well. But the organization is sexist, and we haven't really done anything about it. I don't think you get that.

And so it went, there, in Cambridge, and later in Wellfleet on Cape Cod. Louis trying to calm us down, while we simmered, berating one and all for not seeing what seemed so obvious to us: organizational sexism. No doubt, that was one factor, although the NUC had in fact taken unusually feminist steps in organizational practice. But it was also true that Florence, for whatever reasons, was not popular. Moreover, as a "married" couple we constituted a kind of small caucus that ran its own show. A "liberal" one at that, some people said, dedicated not to revolutionary actions, whatever those might have been, but "only" to radicalizing the classroom. The newsletter, some said, showed our true "liberal" colors. Well, suppose it did? In the next few months and years that newsletter morphed into the magazine *Radical Teacher*,[5] which recently published issue number 113, and has remained a vital publication all these years. The NUC died.

Obviously not because Florence and I left it. The NUC died because those who stayed in it did not, perhaps could not, devise an organizational program responsive to the changing conditions of American higher education. The vast expansion of the sixties, which opened possibilities for many sorts of educational experiments, rapidly gave way to the shrinkage of the seventies. Jobs, which had been plentiful, seemed to evaporate—as was notoriously apparent at the MLA 1969 convention in Denver, where candidates found hardly any departments interviewing, much less hiring. The predictions of serious shortages of PhDs in the humanities and social sciences proved utterly false; on the contrary, pundits began talking of a "glut" of qualified job-seekers. State-level cutbacks came to be the order of the day, encouraged by the Nixon administration, which correctly saw campuses as breeding grounds for resistance to its policies. Anxiety about jobs is always the enemy of radical activism. So it was in and around universities in the 1970s.

I should probably have been more cautious at UMBC, especially since we had a mortgage to go with an active, citywide NUC chapter. But I happily pursued my revolutionary literature course up to and past the dean's decision to axe me. Then I was confronted with a decision common to such occasions: Do I try organizing with my colleagues and students to take actions to reverse my firing, or do I seek legal recourse against a doubtfully lawful decision? I was familiar enough with being fired: it had already happened to me a number of times. But it is never easy to contemplate the guillotine looming in the pathway before you. Self-doubt, like Blake's "invisible worm, / That flies in the night," creeps under one's intellectual armor. Perhaps, after all, you did stray from a righteous way. Are your hands spotless? Is your stature upright? They need to be, since recruiting others to carry your lance and shield might forever damage their lives.

In any case I had to ask: What have I done to justify having others take risks for me? Few people—myself *not* among them—are ecstatic at martyrdom. I did not and could not model my activities on those of my Catholic radical friends, who contemplated prison with the same equanimity they brought to praying over draft files they had set afire. That fire was not in my future. But what, by 1970, had I accomplished that might justify a campaign to save Paul Lauter's ass?

Looking back now, fifty years later, I know that my accomplishments have been substantial. They depended upon my walking along the edge without much of a handhold—as I would do many years after UMBC along a mountain trail above the Baliem Valley in New Guinea. I neither tumbled into the river rushing five hundred feet below nor gave in to the impulse to sit down where I was and not move a foot further. I took a proffered stick and, with a little help from my friends, continued along the edge to the next Dani village. There, the sweetly smiling headman, dressed only in his penis gourd, gently took my hand and guided me to the hut where, after observing his village and its garden, we would be spending the night.

Being fired is part of the trek from what *is* to what, academically, might be. Like being dumped, it's painful when it happens. But it can be remarkably liberating, as it has been for me on a number of occasions. Yes, I was grateful for the walking stick, the tendered hand, the hope ahead. All helped me sustain my too easily eroded sense of my own value. I was even grateful for my enemies. Those taking actions against me, I discovered, were not monsters of disorder but frail men able to see only to the next bureaucratic corner, where they could turn away from the difficulties I had strewn along their paths. The American Friends Service Committee executive, the Antioch College vice president, the University of Maryland, Baltimore County dean—I watch them busily clutching the past as it slips away. "Fuck 'em," I say to my friends. "Let the dead bury the dead." Let's think about what might be done *if*—if we would teach differently, from different books, asking different questions of many different students.

That is what I tried to do.

Meanwhile, we went back to the Cape in the summer of 1970. While there, we got a long-distance call from the Baltimore police: a black couple had been seen taking stuff out of our house. Did we know anything about this? The couple, we assumed, were probably Jack and Michelle Russell. Jack was becoming the New University Conference organizer for the Baltimore region. He was about as blonde as a man could be, and Michelle, a black woman, was almost light-skinned enough to pass for white. They would live in our third-floor apartment. Actually, they were moving their things *into* the house, as we had arranged before we had walked out of the NUC convention a month or two before. But such was the racial hysteria among our Baltimore white neighbors in 1970, exceeding even the misguided revolutionary zeal of our former NUC comrades. We told the cops what they could easily accept: don't worry, the "black couple" were taking care of our house for us.

Many years later, it occurred to me that the complainants, who remained unnamed and unknown to us, might have been the FBI. They had our house under surveillance, we discovered, when we got our FBI files: one of their accounts described an argument between Florence and her mother. The reporter suggested that squabble might provide a useful means for exacerbating conflict in our family—a desirable outcome from the point of view of the feds. Perhaps the report about the black couple was likewise an effort to sow discord or find a rationale to inspect our place.

Chapter Ten

A WORKING-CLASS MOVEMENT OF GIs

In June of 1971, I was once more out of a job. My courses at UMBC, including revolutionary literature, received positive student reviews. Mostly with Florence Howe, I continued to publish extensively, including *The Conspiracy of the Young* in 1970 and articles in the *New York Review of Books*. I'd become something of an authority on community control of schools. Good enough credentials for tenure, I thought, especially at a new and not very well-developed college. But the dean didn't want someone who conspired with students to oppose the war, or some man who agitated for women's studies. So I was gone at the end of my two-year contract.

But once again, opportunity emerged from adversity. Florence, who had been elected MLA second vice president and chaired its active Commission on the Status of Women, had become a hot professional commodity. She opted for a new tenured job at the SUNY College at Old Westbury on Long Island in New York, and so I decided to follow whence I'd come—back to the city. I began to look around for employment. One of my movement friends proposed that I should take the reins of the United States Servicemen's Fund (USSF), an organization that supported coffeehouses near military bases, underground GI anti-war newspapers, and other forms of edgy entertainment for guys in the service.

A dubious marriage I thought. I had been 4-F (unfit for military service) and viewed military service through the anxious lens provided by Norman Mailer's *The Naked and the Dead* and James Jones's *From Here to Eternity*. Neither my father, either of my grandfathers, nor anyone else in my immediate family had, so far as I knew, served in any army—not the tsar's, the emperor's, or the president's. It was almost a tradition. Moreover, I shared something of the mainstream peace movement's gut-level but dumb antagonism to soldiers—why hadn't they beaten the draft? Then again, I had some experience raising money for antiwar projects, which the position required. And I was deeply committed to ending the war. So I became "national director" of the USSF.

I soon found an office on Greenwich Avenue in the West Village—inexpensive, up two flights of stairs—and near both the Seventh Avenue and the IND Eighth Avenue subway lines. It overlooked the schoolyard behind the building where Grace Paley, an extraordinarily supportive person and a dear friend, had her apartment. Down the street, a branch of my favorite bakery, Sutter's, offered a delicious oasis where I could have a coffee and a Danish pastry in the morning while quietly reading the mail. If I couldn't live in the Village, I thought, at least I could work there.

Like many people in the peace movement, I knew very little about antiwar activity among Vietnam vets, much less active-duty GIs. I had read Donald Duncan's 1966 exposé in *Ramparts* of South Vietnamese corruption and US military incompetence and deceit. Nothing in its title, "The Whole Thing Was a Lie," or its contents surprised me: "We weren't preserving freedom in South Vietnam. There was no freedom to preserve. To voice opposition to the government meant jail or death."[1] That fit. I had begun to notice more Vietnam veterans joining antiwar marches, beginning as early as February 1966—certainly a welcome development. I remember once in Baltimore running the streets with a Vietnam vet acquaintance; he was sufficiently enraged about the war to get into a shoving match with a local cop. We got busted together.

I'd also been hearing about GIs refusing deployment to Vietnam. The case of David Samas, James (J. J.) Johnson, and Dennis Mora, the "Fort Hood Three," had been heavily promoted by one of the left-wing organizations. But in 1966–67, I was much more directly involved encouraging draft resistance. I had also heard about the doctor, Captain Howard Levy, who had refused an order to train Green Berets in basic dermatology. He argued that the slight knowledge he could impart in a brief course would be used not to provide real medical care but to recruit Vietnamese villagers to the American side. That would involve him directly in the war, which he deplored and saw as illegal. When I was hired by the USSF, we would meet and become friends.

In Howard Levy, the army met its match. Slight of stature and wiry strong, he was one of the most determined men I have ever encountered, especially when he believed he was right. Once set on a course, he pursued it—as he had done, first, by kicking the Green Berets out of his clinic; second, by refusing a direct order, which he knew would lead to court-martial at Fort Jackson, South Carolina; then, by entering Leavenworth Prison for a twenty-six-month term. Howard's resolve could have a comic side: I see him seated in the glassed-in veranda of a Village restaurant engaged in a long dispute with the maître d' about smoking his large cigar. Cigars, Howard maintained, "were healthier to smoke than cigarettes since you didn't inhale." Probably true; however, the maître d' wasn't concerned with Howard's health, but with fielding complaints by customers about the smell of his stogy. In addition to his resolve and courage, Howard was very smart politically. He cut through American excuses for our criminal role in Vietnam. Later, he would be active with HealthPAC analyzing the rationalizations of the medical establishment that help maintain the crazy quilt—but profitable—American health-care system.

After his stint in prison, Howard carried forward a forty-plus-year career as head of dermatology at Lincoln Hospital in the South Bronx. He could imagine alternatives to the US health-care system, just as he had imagined what GIs needed to survive the military. Howard played a key role in the USSF, both as an icon of military resistance[2] and as a source of original ideas about what the organization should undertake. For example, he proposed a kind of antiwar, pro-GI, Bob Hope–type spectacle that would come to be called the "FTA show."[3] Implemented by Jane Fonda, Donald Sutherland, and Len Chandler, among others, it became one of the USSF's main attractions, as well as a lightning rod for controversy.

Once I had rented an office, I furnished it with some ratty pieces from my favorite used equipment store on 23rd Street. I then looked around at our staff and resources and began getting myself up to speed about the GI movement itself. I started systematically reading many of the GI underground newspapers that the USSF helped support, and enjoying their creative names: *Paper Grenade, Short Times, Travisty, Four Year Bummer, Up Against the Bulkhead, Fed Up!, Broken Arrow*. The network of antiwar newspapers, most put out by and for GIs, ultimately encompassed over eight hundred separate titles.[4] The more I read, the more horrified I became. It wasn't that the papers spoke out against the war, mocked the brass, and derided martial pretensions.

Obviously, I shared such views. They told an extended tale of injustice, not only to the Vietnamese, but also to the grunts in the field.

They described draftees blown away on their first day in country. They reported on widespread drug use, endemic corruption throughout South Vietnam, and atrocities carefully hidden—three, four, many My Lais.[5] American ground troops, they revealed, were a decreasingly reliable force in Southeast Asia.[6] This was good news; yet the war continued, leaving in its wake a generation of badly damaged young Americans and literally millions of Vietnamese casualties.

These GI newspapers, and the mainstream press stories to which they led, gave me a handle on the hideous reality GIs faced in Vietnam, as well as the forms of rebellion their disillusion and anger were taking. Some went AWOL,[7] though that was never easy inside Vietnam. Some turned against the military and those who tried to force them to carry out senseless combat missions. Some spaced out on weed and even heroin. Others just said no to patrols. Incidents of "fragging"—in its "classic" form rolling a fragmentation grenade under the tent of a gung ho officer or noncom (noncommissioned officer)—became sufficiently widespread to lead to a congressional investigation in 1973.[8] Fragging and other modes of direct rebellion did not have to be extensive to have effects. Young officers, who were often from different class backgrounds, realized that leading their men into the treacherous jungle or up some obscure hill for murky reasons could be deadly for their troops *and* for themselves. GI papers and coffeehouses spread the "bad news" of declining military capability more rapidly than the TV newscasts most Americans watched. Through them, I came into touch with the grim lives of American guys on the ground in Vietnam.

The GI antiwar movement differed from the peace activism I knew. The work of GIs was war. Civilians who participated in peace actions could, when the demonstration was over, the petition signed, the congressman visited, return to their ordinary jobs as teacher, auto dealer, housewife, clerk. The Selective Service System even provided draft resisters, often middle class, with alternatives: student deferment, conscientious objector status, Canada, or jail when all else failed. GIs, especially the grunts on the ground, engaged in war as their primary, and too often their entire, life activity. As in their working-class civilian lives, they were restricted, constrained by those with authority, and in a constant struggle for a degree of autonomy.[9] Male bonding as civilians—around sports teams, hunting, drinking, girls, cars, and the like—provided forms of sustenance and support, if not solidarity. The military had learned to transform that desire for camaraderie into the battlefield unity so essential to successful combat. Even men hostile to the war sustained that unit solidarity in battle.

One thing that struck me about most GIs and USSF staff was their youth. I was about to hit forty, long past that magical cutoff date beyond which you were supposed not to trust anyone. They were members of another generation and, culturally, of another world. The cultural distance between us registered strongly when I began visiting coffeehouses. The coffeehouses, decked out in psychedelic and rockstar posters, resembled their progenitors in San Francisco's North Beach or the Haight.[10] In ambience and design, they were largely modeled after the first of them, the UFO, started in January 1968 near Ft. Jackson, South Carolina, by Fred Gardner and Donna Mickleson. Coffeehouses, Gardner strongly believed, should be vibrant, comfortable places where GI's were "free to hang out, to read, to play chess or cards, to rap, to dance, to flirt, to discuss what was going on in their lives or the world at large. GIs added their artwork to the walls and hundreds of records to our collection. The UFO was the only integrated place in town, not just white and black, but GIs and students too."[11] In general, coffeehouses were started not by the USSF, back in Northeast cities, but by movement activists—some GIs, some not—who were committed to their fundamentally antiwar purpose and to the kind of hip setup Gardner articulated. The USSF helped support them as much as possible, but each one had its own leadership and unique dynamic.

I thought Gardner's conception of the coffeehouses was right on. They were in tune with the culture of the young guys at the bases, offering a much-desired alternative to the usual bars, whorehouses, cheap jewelry and clothing stores, and pawn and porn shops that constituted "downtown." During the day, they were relatively calm—not Sutters, to be sure, but not overwhelming either. But at night . . . well, at night the music and talk heated up beyond what my older sensibility, and ears, could tolerate. But OK, I didn't need to be part of the scene to appreciate their virtues and the staff's hard work in maintaining them.

In a number of respects, the coffeehouses reminded me of freedom houses in 1964 Mississippi, as well as the Council of Federated Organizations' freedom schools. They legitimated ways of thinking and behaving that contradicted efforts at control insisted upon by the army and the local and national power structures. Those with authority in Mississippi, in Saigon, or in Washington sought to enforce discipline and conformity. By contrast, coffeehouses, like freedom schools,

invited self-expression and making common cause with one's comrades; they helped GIs learn what the powerful preferred to hide, that
racism and violence provided the roots for their control. Again, like
freedom schools, coffeehouses opened possibilities for connecting
learning to actions for change, like organizing a pray-in at a military
base or getting out an underground newspaper. GIs got a taste of their
own political power and the limits of repression. This kind of movement education led to other actions, such as participating in demonstrations. Perhaps most importantly, soldiers learned a different kind
of solidarity from the battlefield unity insisted upon from basic training onward and maintained by the military's structure of authority.
That new kind of solidarity gave meaning to the phrase "GI antiwar
movement."[12]

The coffeehouses were not only places to hang and for holding
cultural events like singers or even the FTA show. They became important off-base spaces for meetings and for political organizing by antiwar GIs. I found on the bookshelves (bookshelves!) radical literature
and on the tables flyers, pamphlets, and GI papers in abundance. The
places I visited made me hopeful. I wished that I could get away from
my bureaucratic responsibilities in the New York office and spend
more time in the field.

For the office was not always a happy place. The USSF, I found,
was overstaffed, with two groups, one in Cambridge and one with me
in New York. Most staff, veterans of the GI antiwar movement and in
some cases of the military too, were courageous and dedicated, as were
the people operating the coffeehouses. However, like their peers in
SDS and other movement organizations of the time, many had joined
one or another left sectarian group. They did not always get along with
each other politically—and often not with me, their putative boss and,
moreover, someone over thirty. Sectarianism emerged as the fly in the
movement's ointment. The problem was not with staff members prose-
lytizing for the antiwar cause—hardly necessary with GIs, either before
and certainly not after they served in Nam. Nor did most staff initially
push some particular partisan line. And on the whole, the work of
raising money and sending it to projects got done. All the same, in
my view, sectarianism became a disease fatal to the enterprise. In one
exemplary case, a coffeehouse turned itself into a "movement center,"
substituting the study of Marx and Lenin for the music and mocha java
that had made the place a favorite GI hangout.

Of course, movement activists needed a political analysis of the causes and consequences of the war. And since a majority of GIs came from working-class backgrounds, activists argued, they required what their schools never provided: an understanding of how class determined who received deferments to go to Stanford and who got assigned to "search and get killed" missions in the jungle. Militants affiliated with various left political parties, each with its own, somewhat different analysis, would help develop such understanding. They might also try to recruit active GIs to their perspective and ultimately to their organizations. Understandable goals. But these soldiers were American working-class guys, for whom the intricacies of Marxism, Leninism, and Mao Zedong–thought were alien, and often alienating, ways of thinking. "FTA" resonated far more with GIs than "primary and secondary contradictions." The culture fostered by readings from the "Critique of the Gotha Programme," "What Is to Be Done," "On Practice," or even the latest communiques from Albanian communist leader Enver Hoxha differed profoundly from that of turn on, tune in, and CYA (cover your ass, a rough military equivalent of "drop out"). Such readings, at the right time, have their value. Unfortunately, USSF staff devoted as much attention to what theory might appropriately be taught to young soldiers as they did to figuring out how a coffeehouse adjacent to a despised military base or airfield during a brutal war could best "FTA."

So there were tensions about organizational priorities and individual responsibilities. Many of these tensions came to focus on the FTA show, which those active on the USSF board saw both as an effective event for projecting GI resistance and, importantly, as a source of needed funds. But some projects unwisely saw the show as an intrusion on their organizing—in fact, especially overseas, as a threat to their safety. A movie had been made of a performance of the FTA show in South Carolina. But Jane Fonda, our star, hated the film. Bob Zevin and I flew to California to talk with her about that problem and future plans for the FTA show. We rented a car, drove up to someone's house off Mulholland Drive, met Sutherland, and waited for Fonda. Eventually she appeared, saying "it's just too hot today. I need to cool off." With that, she stripped, dove into the pool, swam a few laps, and reemerged to the dumbfounded eyes of us Eastern cynics.

We never did resolve the question of using the film. Since I could not understand her objection, I took her to lunch when she was in

New York for the performance of the show at Avery Fisher Hall. Jane was a vegetarian, so in my innocence I figured the place to go was the one vegetarian restaurant I knew of in New York, Brownies, on East 16th Street. Appearing with such a celebrity in a restaurant like Brownie's? Terminally naive. All heads turned. A serious conversation proved impossible; I learned only that Jane thought showing the film would "wreck" her career. I never found out why. Nor have I ever seen the film—few have—or, for that matter, the subsequent one made by Francine Parker of the FTA show performing at various sites in Asia.

Jane Fonda is a determined person, accustomed to success, and effective in organizing people toward goals she insistently defines. Appropriating the form long popularized by pro-war performers like Bob Hope for an antiwar spectacle was a smart move. She was courageous in defying not only the US military but also many of the coffeehouse staff in presenting the FTA show in Asian war zones. I marveled that she did not hesitate to put herself in danger—as she did in going to North Vietnam during the bombing—to dramatize her opposition to the war and her solidarity with the Vietnamese people. Nor was her engagement a one-off political stunt. She sustained her antiwar activity not only with the FTA show but also in collaboration with Tom Hayden and the Indochina Peace Campaign, building public support for the timid congressional attempts to rein in Nixon and Kissinger. In many respects Fonda carried out the injunction Paul Potter stated at that very first SDS antiwar march in 1965: that people had to be "willing to change their lives" to defeat the power of imperial America.

As for USSF, conflict with Jane Fonda turned out to be the least of my problems. The organization itself became an arena for struggle. Seeking a venue for the FTA show in New York, we argued at great length with Sutherland. He had initially insisted on Madison Square Garden, and he wanted to charge the "same price that Cassius Clay," as he called him, had charged for a title bout. When we talked Sutherland out of the Garden, he proposed that losing location, the Felt Forum, the sad behind of Madison Square Garden. Then, grumbling, he accepted Avery Fisher Hall, which seemed to me virtually impossible to fill, even with Aretha Franklin as a co-starring attraction. The two women organizing a fundraising event after the show argued bitterly over the food: dainty canapes or a six-foot hero from Manganaro's. In getting out a newsletter, staff members went to war over the content and the phrasing. Florence and I argued over my small salary; she detested effectively supporting my work in an organization she mistrusted. The IRS, perhaps instigated by the Nixon administration, came down on USSF for "violating" the terms of our tax exemption, though we'd always said we would support coffeehouses, newspapers, and entertainment for GIs. Returning from a trip to projects on the West Coast, I found that the office coffee machine had not been cleaned in some weeks and had sprouted a multicolored jungle of mold. The movement continued, but the organizational prognosis dimmed.

All the same, the GI antiwar movement had a defining impact on bringing the war to an end. No mass rebellion forced a close to Nixon's war. No battle cruiser turned its guns against the American embassy in Saigon. But by limiting and undermining the strategies available to the US government—short of nuclear weapons or the like—the millions of individual acts of resistance weighed heavily against continuing the American assault. As John Kerry did not quite put it, who wished to be the last man to die for a lost cause?[13] Or, for that matter, to kill for it? Even before Nixon took office, American ground troops had become an increasingly unreliable force in Southeast Asia.

By 1967 or so, as recent scholarship has demonstrated, the Pentagon elite and LBJ's advisors knew full well that American "victory" in Vietnam had become a hopeless fantasy.[14] Nixon and Kissinger knew too. That awareness did not keep them from heavy assaults on Vietnam—not to speak of Laos and Cambodia—to force concessions at the bargaining table, bolster their reelection chances, avoid being blamed for "losing" Vietnam, or just fuck over their "enemies." They looked for some measure of success to the ongoing air war.

The air war provided certain advantages: it removed those dropping bombs, napalm, and defoliants from the daily grind of jungle warfare, and from the drugs and racial tensions that had begun to overwhelm ground troops. But the shift to air war did not end GI resistance—nor, despite its ferocity,[15] did it accomplish the goals set out for it by the American military.[16] Air war moved the venue of resistance to aircraft carriers and airfields. To keep carriers from deploying to Southeast Asia, antiwar sailors deployed chains and large tools to screw up critical gears and drive shafts. They circulated petitions, like those in the Stop Our Ship (SOS) movement, demanding that their ship stay in port, away from military action near Vietnam. Coffeehouses, especially those up and down the West Coast, and GI newspapers broadcast the latest details of resistance, and they helped widen the network of GI struggle as it spread to the air force and navy. At USSF, we aided the

newspapers rolling out their stories and assisted the coffeehouses to
stay open for navy and air force activity. And we passed stories about
American military activity, which were being withheld from the public,
on to reporters.

The GI antiwar movement operated like other movement organizations or, for that matter, other complex social groups. Among
students, word about actions spread rapidly from campus to campus—
that was part of the genius of SDS. Administrators imitated the process
and had, in addition, institutions like deans' camp. When the idea of
using retrenchment provisions to cut programs and faculty came along
in the early seventies, administrative networks quickly carried it forward—until a judge ruled that a school could not use the excuse of
"financial exigency" to eliminate departments while the college held
on to its lucrative golf course.

Among GIs, nothing the military started up remained secret for
very long. When the Pentagon decided to use B-52 bomber wings,
flying from Guam, to attack Vietnam, the word rapidly came to staff
in coffeehouses, from there to the USSF, and from us on to the news
media, whose stories were sure to generate further opposition in the
United States and preparedness in Vietnam. I'm sure there were those
in the administration who viewed the process as a form of espionage.
But it was simply GI democracy at work.

Still, the war continued, widening not only into Cambodia and
Laos[17] but also, as we experienced it, penetrating the ghettoes and
campuses of America. Chicago cops had attacked demonstrators at the
1968 Democratic National Convention in what is now generally seen
as a "police riot." In 1969, the FBI and Chicago police murdered Black
Panther leaders Fred Hampton and Mark Clark in their beds. National
Guardsmen and state troopers killed and wounded protesting students
at Kent State and Jackson State Universities in 1970. In response, the
movement departed from the protocols of nonviolence: Karleton Armstrong and others bombed the Army Mathematics Research Center at
the University of Wisconsin in 1970 and, in the process, killed a graduate student. The Weather Underground set off a bomb in a toilet in
the national capitol in 1971, part of an effort to "bring the war home."
Oakland and Berkeley were the scenes of major clashes between movement activists and the police and military.

To some, such events—and many more that anyone who lived
through those years could name—seemed symptomatic of a worldwide transformation of society and politics. Indeed, there were major

changes, especially in gender definitions and relationships and in what we thought was important to read and teach, and thus know about. But the revolution that some thought, or hoped, was upon us and that would sweep the Agnews and Nixons into the "dustbin of history" was not. To be sure, while Agnew and Nixon would indeed be swept away, the capitalist power they promoted gained force.

The movement, about which I have been writing, never really succeeded in moving from protest to resistance. It certainly did not produce a radical transformation of American politics and society. On the contrary, what emerged by the end of the 1970s was what has come to be called "neoliberalism," a program of privatization of public resources like transit, water, and schooling; elimination of government regulations over corporate activity; free trade agreements like NAFTA, which would have the effect of exporting American jobs; and "austerity" in the form of cutbacks in government spending on social programs. All together, these policies increased the role, power, and magnitude of private wealth in the economy and society; and they undercut the socialist revolution envisioned in one form or another by many movement activists. Ultimately neoliberalism was promoted by the Nixons of the time, and then embraced even by the mainstream of the Democratic Party. The movements to end the war, to transform racist and sexist institutions, to advance on a "long march through the institutions of society" continued. But so did war, imperialism, racism, and patriarchy.

In fact, the movement largely fragmented, with different constituencies going in different directions. The slogans of the time register that division: "smash the nuclear family," "black power," "give peace a chance," "Ho Ho Ho Chi Minh, the NLF is gonna win," "make love, not war." The student movement, despite the bloody ongoing war, fell into sectarian competition, with various blocs organizing around their own slogans and ideological stances: "less talk, more action," "worker-student alliance," and the Revolutionary Youth Movement, which itself broke into at least two or three factions. By the 1969 SDS national convention, the organization had come apart. The problem the movement really faced was that which challenges any insurgency: win or disintegrate. When push has come to shove, if you do not triumph, internal divisions, the fatigue of unrequited toil, and the miscarriage of hope will undermine conviction. The banners will sag, the posters crumble. Blame will consume sustenance. Friends will vanish and foes will shove you down. So it was.

In Paris in May 1968, the forces of change seemed about to oust the Charles de Gaulle government and replace it with a socialist alternative. But as we know, that political revolution did not happen, though significant social changes took place in France and elsewhere in Europe. In the US we never came close to the political "final conflict" that would, as the socialist anthem "The Internationale" had it, transform the "international working class" into "the human race." Still, the movement did not go away—demonstrations got bigger, angrier, more militant, as at the Washington Mayday actions in 1971.[18] But the favorite antiwar lyric of that time seemed to me excessively modest: "All we are saying is give peace a chance." I could never sing it.

Disagreements in American society about how and why the US had gotten into Vietnam underlay conflicts within the movement. In mainstream organizations, liberals grown unhappy with the war maintained, in the words of the Ken Burns and Lynn Novick film on the subject, that "it was begun in good faith, by decent people." Miscalculations, mistaken ideas, military rigidity, and corrupt southern allies had left us sinking into the "big muddy." Some who supported the war conceded that it was not communism but nationalism, the general desire to rid the country of foreign invaders, that so forcefully motivated the Vietnamese. This analysis sometimes led to the claim that South Vietnam's leaders shared nationalist goals with Ho Chi Minh and his comrades; and further, that Americans had properly intervened in what was a civil war between southerners and— with a touch of Cold War rhetoric—communist-led North Vietnamese forces. Others on the left argued that "land to the tillers"—a basic goal of the National Liberation Front (NLF) in the south—provided the astonishing motivation that enabled poor peasants to stand up to and defeat in combat not only their landlord-dominated government but also the most militarily powerful country in history.[19] Different analyses implied different ideas about how to persuade Americans to support peace.

Now, fifty years later, these conflicts in understanding the war remain, as the enormously varied responses to the Burns and Novick film demonstrate. It is no surprise that in the late sixties and early seventies, disagreements about how we got in led to harsh differences about how to get out. Running peace and freedom candidates or bringing the "war home" in disruptive acts? Encouraging GIs to refuse combat or teaching them to be tomorrow's Bolshevik agitators? Weapons training for civilian protestors or nonviolent civil disobedience actions? Larger peaceable marches or bigger homemade bombs? Or all? Contention within the movement matched the controversy in successive administrations: Bomb more? Inform Congress? Negotiate? Withdraw? Burglarize in Watergate? Military wisdom to the contrary notwithstanding, war is a chaotic system of conflict that dislocates everything it touches.

It's tempting to end this chapter with a high peroration about what we, as a movement, had accomplished during the sixties. How we had challenged gender norms, racial hierarchies, imperialist assumptions, the old social order, and a calamitous war. We did. We really did. Being realistic, however, I want only to speak of how the peace movement appears to me now, half a century later.

Pretty damn good.

Lookit: at the outset, we were, from the mainstream perspective, a few dozen weird folks who sat-in rather than join air-raid drills; some others who withheld their telephone taxes; a few dozen commie students and formerly commie women affiliated with Women Strike for Peace; and a bunch of religious types who testified for peace and did not, like proper Americans, carry guns. We ended up, hundreds of thousands of us, forcing the president to hide away while we were around, and ultimately to hightail it out of town on a chopper, like his brass would do a little later as Saigon fell around them. The Vietnamese did that, not us, though we helped and encouraged them.

And it was right to do so. Not because the United States is always an oppressor nation, though it often is. And not because the Vietnamese were the noble heirs to peaceable Asian civilization, though there's something in that. But because it was right for the Vietnamese people to determine their own futures. And it was wrong, as well as foolish, for the Americans to try through arrogance, violence, and fraud to impose our desires on a not-so-small country half a globe away. I continue to support what we peaceniks did, ill-informed, confused, and imperfect as it sometimes was. We made a difference and we have continued to do so as the movement (and the movements it helped spawn) continues the struggle for democracy, equality, and peace, for which the Vietnam antiwar movement has provided a model and an inspiration.[20]

Where we did not succeed was in translating a movement against that war in that time into a movement against all war in every time. Nor did we ignite a movement against the depredations that inevitably spring from the capitalist organization of society. Neither pacifism nor socialism emerged from the peace movement. American policies remain arrogant, violent, and chock-full of fraud. But we taught ourselves, and many others, to stand up—often by sitting down. We're still teaching, and thereby learning, the lessons of this movement.

Chapter Eleven

A MAN IN THE WOMEN'S MOVEMENT

At the 1969 national convention of the New University Conference in Iowa City, the women formed a separate caucus on the first day. They left the men in order to work out their own organizational demands. In 1969, everyone had "demands." Students made demands of their colleges, and sometimes their high schools; minorities made demands of mayors; wives made demands of their husbands; and children learned to make demands of baffled parents. Given this trend in the movement and the strong separatist tendencies already evident in nascent feminist groups, it was not altogether a surprise that the women would decide to meet separately—at least for a time.

The guys were not especially troubled; we sat around in the dormitory lounge, reading and arguing, and trying to make ourselves comfortable on the serviceable beige furniture. Some went for a beer and pizza. A certain impatience vexed the lounge—after all, we could be there only for two or three days, and obviously we couldn't move forward on organizational business with half the people off in another room. But we counted on the affiliations most of us had with one or another of the women. Sooner or later the demands, whatever they might be, would be revealed; discussions, more or less fraught, would begin; agreements would be reached; and we could then get on to the "real work" of the meeting.

Late in the evening, Florence Howe was dispatched by the women's caucus to meet with some of the men to discuss or perhaps to negotiate these demands. She came into the lounge where we were hanging out and said something to the effect of "here's what the women have decided we want." "Sharp struggle," in the Chinese phrase then popular, ensued, sharpest over the most obvious organizational mandate—equal numbers of women and men on the steering committee. Hardly a radical departure, we were made aware, since both the Republican and the Democratic Parties already had such an arrangement. Even so, we quickly heard every argument against "special group privileges" and the burden such "unnecessary," rigid measures presented to our radical organization. We were—were we not?—democratically committed as activists, socialists even: Why did we need such rules, which seemed to bring into question our basic commitment to equality? We should be electing those most qualified, regardless of gender or other forms of identity. Who else would come to demand representation in the future?

Given my relationship with Florence, I somehow came to feel a special burden to stand up to the demands she was conveying, though many of the arguments against them struck me as silly. Or was it something more aboriginal and personal I was trying to maintain? She and I certainly got heated, socialism or no socialism. Maybe we felt, indistinctly, that we were being played, somehow pressed into speaking out the bitterness between men and women, allowing others to thus evade confronting it. I'm sure some of the men enjoyed the performances.

When Florence and I finally retreated to our room in the wee hours of the morning, after the abrasive quarrel and a nascent settlement, we were both expecting to depart separately. That did not happen, perhaps out of exhaustion. I'm struck now how puerile most of the resistance, including my own, was to the women's quite modest demands: equal representation on NUC's committees and equal opportunities to chair and, of course, to speak. Mainly, I think, their stand had to do with being accorded recognition, which movement groups—not just the National Conference for New Politics (NCNP) and Students for a Democratic Society (SDS)—had too often effectively denied women. I could hardly forget the gross hooting of Marilyn Webb at the counter-inaugural in Washington in 1969, where a bunch of guys—who were they?—shouted out sexual remarks and yelled about screwing her out back. We flopped into our beds—separately, of course—still livid. But a day or two later, instead of separating, we got in the car and drove with a case of tequila to Robert Bly's farm in South Dakota. There, he taught me to plough up the grass choking the trees on his property. Carol Bly modeled the humor and patience necessary to deal with men like Robert.

I open my discussion of being a man in the women's movement here because the episode measures how much I had to learn. And how simple some of the lessons were. I began to see how closely aligned were my personal life and the politics we were learning to negotiate. One of the slogans of the early feminist consciousness-raising groups was "the personal is political." That meant that women's feelings of anomie, dissatisfaction with life, yearning for more—what Betty Friedan called "the problem that has no name"—were rooted not in psychological maladjustment but in the politics of gender arrangements. For me, the reverse seemed equally true: "The political is personal." Over a decade and a half, every political action in which I engaged was inflected, less or more, by the fact that I was, to any outer eye, married to one of the leaders of the academic women's movement, Florence Howe. Nothing I did—go to Mississippi, not go to North Vietnam; take a job at the Adams-Morgan Community School project, not take a job with NCNP; become a founder of The Feminist Press; lose the election for president of my union—nothing was unshaped by that personal *and* political fact.

That was not, I maintain, necessarily a bad thing, or a good thing. Two people in a conjugal relationship, closely bonded, working diligently together, must always be aware that they are not any longer independent free agents. Should they forget, others will soon enough in language and in gesture remind them that they constitute not two individuals but a twosome, or as I've said earlier, a little "caucus." I think it was John McDermott, during a savage conflict we would later have at SUNY College at Old Westbury, who snidely responded to something Florence said: "Florence is appalled, and Paul is aflorenced." Clever and hurtful, but suggestive about the strains common work and organizational involvement introduce into such a bonded relationship. What must a man surrender to maintain the bond?

Florence and I lived together for seventeen years, from December of 1965 to June of 1982. We never actually married, though that was largely irrelevant—except when we explored adopting a child and when we were charged with "nepotism." We wrote together, organized together, traveled together, spent school vacations with my children together, were often a nuisance to our friends together. One of the jokes about us was that the initials of The Feminist Press actually stood for Florence and Paul. Until 1982, when I left her.

Here's a paradox: throughout the 1960s and 1970s our work was extensively intertwined. Yet for all the togetherness, we lived significantly separate lives. In nothing was that more true than in my experience as a feminist. Sure, when we were starting The Feminist Press in a second-floor bedroom of our house in Baltimore, I sometimes served

as Florence's secretary, sometimes her ghostwriter, generally her partner in thinking about what the press might do. Certainly, The Feminist
Press provided for me, as it did for many others, a kind of cultural
laboratory in which we studied and tried out versions of that conflicted
creed, feminism. But finally, my feminism had less to do with my roles
in The Feminist Press, extensive as they were, than with how I tried
to carry out my slowly developing perceptions of women's liberation
in the many organizations in which I was active. How to be a "feminist" in Resist, in the American Studies Association, in my union—or
in my classrooms? How would I alter the texts we might read, especially
after my experience at Smith College with the all-male, all-white lineup
in the English Department's required course? How might I change
the questions I asked or the ways I responded to students, especially
women? How might I deploy *he* and *she*? Since I could not start out
from identity, being male and white, what perceptions would enable
me to respond to such questions? And how would I—could I?—come
to convincing answers? If you believe as I do that feminism is not out of
the reach of men, what is the route toward becoming a feminist?

That was for me a sluggish and often wobbling process. I wasn't
a male "heavy" who thought I automatically rated attention. In many
meetings I actually did not feel qualified to speak, much less to *interrupt* as more commanding figures could. I imagined myself sitting in
the gallery with the silenced women as William Lloyd Garrison had
done at the London women's rights convention of 1840. But as Adrienne Rich framed it in lines that became for many of us paradigmatic:

> No one ever told us we had to study our lives,
> make of our lives a study, as if learning natural history
> or music . . . .
>   ("Transcendental Etude")[1]

In time, I came to feel that my ability to analyze the current politics was as well-developed as that of my earlier mentors from the AFSC
and SDS. But that was later.

Initially, my problem was sheer ignorance. For example, my children attended what they called the "Katy Stanton School" in Seneca
Falls. But I had no idea who the school was named after or, until The
Feminist Press began the process of publishing a biography of Elizabeth Cady Stanton, why I really had to learn about her. Nor did I think
of myself, like some of my male comrades, as God's gift to the female

sex. I was a polite, enthusiastic, and sometimes failed lover who took quite a while to get it that women might be as turned on by political action in the street as I was. What did I know? What *could* I know?

So there was ignorance to start. Then, too, the women I knew intimately—my mother, my first wife Tris, Florence—played dominant roles in our family dramas. Only later did I begin to recognize how their lives had been limited. My mother had been an excellent actress in the flourishing days of amateur theater in New York of the late 1930s. I had actually seen this for myself watching what was for an impressionable child a terrifying rehearsal of *The Children's Hour*. Offered a screen test, she turned it down because she thought my father might not be happy if she were to go into the movies. She continued acting almost to the last of her 106 years; while it engaged and pleased her, it would never again fill her life. Tris earned her doctorate shortly after I did. But it surprised neither of us that she took a job as a historian only after we had long parted ways. Florence, early on in her career, developed swollen lips—hives of some sort—whenever she faced the prospect of giving a speech. But that passed; it didn't seem to me that serious.

I didn't really understand. I observed these women through the glasses of my own male life, and it took a long while to comprehend something of the difference their experiences fostered. Learning to see better, however imperfectly, was the invaluable gift I received from The Feminist Press, and especially from our reintroduction of "lost" or dismissed texts by earlier women writers like Rebecca Harding Davis. Adrienne Rich again seemed to express our experience:

> I came to explore the wreck.
> The words are purposes.
> The words are maps.
> I came to see the damage that was done
> and the treasures that prevail.
> ("Diving into the Wreck")[2]

Feminist activity, as I understood it in the years I helped found and grow The Feminist Press, seemed generated by two powerful engines: rage and creativity. The rage, as I perceived it and sometimes experienced it, came from the accumulation of abuse, belittlement, deprivation, and occasionally terror that have marked the lives of most women—as well as minority people—in American society. The creativity emerges from the need to develop the material support necessary for all marginalized groups to build better lives: meetings, organizations, magazines, books, pictures. The Feminist Press has been devoted in its publishing and its educational programs mainly to the problem of creativity. I will turn to that shortly. But before doing so I must try to lay out my understanding of the character and the sources of the anger that deeply affected our lives and our work.

Anger first, then:

I already knew how angry Florence could be over exclusion. When I had been asked to join the second delegation of Americans to visit North Vietnam in early 1966, she bridled: why had *I* been asked, and not her? I had no answer then that would satisfy her, though there were answers having to do with my working full time for a significant peace organization. In the end, I turned down the opportunity, something I have always regretted. More and more, we began to hear a ground tone of anger within the feminism of that moment, a tone that would amplify as the sixties slid into the Nixon years. Valerie Solanas gave expression to it in the *SCUM Manifesto*, published in the summer of 1967. Solanas might have been quite "mad"—she did shoot Andy Warhol the following year. Her rage, however, was directed not so much at individual men, but male domination, patriarchy, a word made prominent by the movement. In 1973, as part of *Diving into the Wreck*, Adrienne Rich published "The Phenomenology of Anger." It concludes:

> others plan rebellion:
> night after night
> awake in prison, my mind
> licked at the mattress like a flame
> till the cellblock went up roaring

> Thoreau setting fire to the woods

> Every act of becoming conscious
> (it says here in this book)
> is an unnatural act
>   (*Diving into the Wreck*, 31)

Rich's extraordinarily resonant lines link the impact of feminist consciousness raising to earlier rebellions, embodied in Thoreau, as well as to the unnamed captives imprisoned in the daily life of patriarchy. They powerfully illustrate how Rich's poetry provided a theory and images of feminist anger.

The attack on Florence in the Adams-Morgan Community School, most painfully, came in the main from women. In 1967 that was something of a surprise—sisterhood was still powerful. It would remain so, of course, even as "sisters" within the feminist movement devoted a great deal of energy to pulling one another down.[3] Tensions among women would in time play out at The Feminist Press and in other organizations, such as the National Women's Studies Association, in which we were both involved.

Internecine warfare wasn't the same kind of problem for me, however, partly because I had no overt authority within women's organizations. I could suggest, and I did. I could also be ignored. Since I wasn't aggressive, women found me, I think, unchallenging, even supportive. Surely some thought I could always be told to take my marbles and go play with the boys somewhere else. However, I cannot leave the Morgan story without acknowledging my own rage, mostly at the administrative honchos of Antioch College, which I only became conscious of many years after 1967. I've always been slow to burn, so I didn't fuss over how I'd been treated at the time. Instead, I took Antioch's salary and used it to subsidize my writing and movement work. Later, a friend became Antioch's acting president and my then spouse, Ann Fitzgerald, became director of their Women's Studies in Europe program. Only then did I begin to look back on 1967. I'd been suckered, I realized, into a position different from the one for which I'd been hired, one that I was equipped for in theory but quite ill-prepared for in practice. I'd been left without support staff or necessary resources, forced to carry both Antioch-Putney's ball and that of the school system: working as principal, telephone receptionist, and fundraiser too. And I'd been kicked out—twice—with no reasonable explanation. And told to smile and write fundraising appeals for administrators who would soon bring the college to bankruptcy. The miracle is that I didn't beat down their schoolhouse doorway. But I did discover my own capacity for rage, which perhaps made me empathize more with women who had lived with it as the norm of their entire lives.

To return for a moment to the Morgan Community School project itself: apart from the problem of gender friction, serious racial issues undercut our goals. Such tensions would continue to haunt the feminist movement in the following decades. They point to a fundamental reality: one cannot deal with the oppressive structure of patriarchy without from the beginning addressing race.

It took some time for that lesson to be fully taken up by the organizations in which we worked (some would say it hasn't yet been taken up in national politics). Friends active in the National Women's Studies Association were antiracist in outlook, but translating antiracist ideas into organizational practice involving active minority women turned out to be slow and difficult. For a while in the 1970s, it was not clear whether the organization would survive the stresses involved in making it useful to working-class women and women of color. Obviously, a white Jewish male was unlikely to play a beneficial role in organizational conflicts predicated on identity issues. Looking around, I noted a distressing level of ignorance among many colleagues about the creative accomplishments of women of color and working-class women. With bibliographies of the work of black women newly available, I called on my library training to create a bibliography, "Working-Class Women's Literature: An Introduction to Study."[4] Serve the people. In those pre-internet days, the bibliography designated as culturally and politically significant a vast area of female creativity.

In time, I would also examine women writers who were seen as marginal even within the women's studies community—for example, Amy Lowell[5] and Lydia Sigourney.[6] I think it useful to scrutinize the margins for there one discovers what defines and might also destabilize the "mainstream." Sigourney had been dismissed as merely sentimental, and a good deal of her work is. But I found many of her poems about Native Americans—for example, "Indian Names" and "The Indian's Welcome to the Pilgrim Fathers"—not only powerful and politically significant but also eminently teachable. And that led me on to reconsider other of her poems, like those on death.[7] Lowell was marginalized for quite different reasons. An antagonist of male modernist leaders, especially Ezra Pound, she was ridiculed in life for being rich and overweight and dissed after her death as much for her lesbian sexuality and her assertive leadership in the Imagist movement as for her poetry. Very little of either writer was generally available, and the only biography of Sigourney was outdated and mean. One of the functions of the 19th-Century American Women Writers Study Group, in which I participated since its beginning, and of the Society for the Study of American Women Writers has been to help carry forward the changes needed to reread such authors.

These seem to me some of the concrete ways of taking seriously women's work, so often marginalized or dismissed. That issue—taking people seriously—underlies many of the developments of the late sixties and early seventies: the separate caucuses, the formation of commissions on the status of women, women's studies as an independent discipline, the National Women's Studies Association, the founding of magazines like *Ms.* "Hear me," these said. "Hear and acknowledge the distinctiveness of my experience, my history, my art. See me, as I am, not in your shadow but in my own brightness and that of my sisters." At the American Studies Association meetings, which I began to attend around that time, I always showed up at the women's breakfast—at some ungodly early hour like 7 a.m.—along with John Stephens, the executive director, and Jay Mechling from the University of California, Davis. The talks, the interactions, the drawing together of academic and political concerns not only proved more interesting than most of the academic papers, but also helped set a pattern that, over time, would change the organization much for the better.

For me, however, The Feminist Press provided the most meaningful venue for taking women's work seriously.

The first open meeting of what would become The Feminist Press took place at our house in the fall of 1970. Someone had placed an announcement in the summer issue of *Women: A Journal of Liberation*, or its newsletter, which was produced by a Baltimore group. When we returned from our weeks at Cape Cod, we discovered a flood of mail. People *wanted* a feminist press. There was nothing to do then but have a meeting and launch one.

Our house on Greenspring Avenue, near the Pimlico racetrack, was a large, turn-of-the-twentieth-century affair, with three floors, a central staircase, and what had been intended as a formal dining room located immediately to the left of the entry hall. Since we didn't own anything related to dining-room furniture, we'd placed the ping-pong table that we had somehow acquired into the dining-room space, for which it was slightly too big. The ping-pong table was built with two large wings that could be lifted up so that the table didn't occupy so much room when you weren't playing on it. On the bottom of the wing closest to the entry, we'd affixed a three-foot by four-foot poster of Lenin. Most of the thirty or forty people attending the meeting understood the comic gesture of that ping-pong poster. We were hardly Leninists. But there were a few people, notably a middle-aged couple we'd never seen before, uncomfortable with Vladimir staring down at them. They kept glancing over at him as if to solve some puzzle at this quite un-Leninist get-together.

Nevertheless, it was a successful meeting, largely taken up, in the style of feminist gatherings of the time, with people introducing themselves and saying what their interests in a feminist press might be. We confirmed that people were attracted by nonsexist children's books and biographies of underappreciated women. Then or soon after—of particular concern to me—the idea emerged of doing reprints of lost or forgotten literary works by women writers. One of Florence's students, Barbara Danish, soon produced the first (and as it happened, one of the few) children's books, titled *The Dragon and the Doctor*. Its main feature, apart from Barbara's delightful drawings, especially of a dragon with a zippered tail, was that in imitation of its Chinese model the doctor was female and the nurse male.

The first two biographies we commissioned were of Stanton and Constance Markievicz, but the first actually to be published was Mary Jane Lupton's book on Elizabeth Barrett Browning. Where and how would we sell such volumes? None of us starting up the press knew much about that part of publishing. I devoted a great deal of time and energy over the next decade to hauling round copies of the biographies and other Feminist Press books, and displaying them at any gathering that would have us. My tasks included meeting and greeting, as well as selling. At the National Women's Studies Association (NWSA), a man working a book table was not out of place, though he might have been one of only two members of his sect (as Marietta Holley called it), and though he would not have been welcome at the evening's dancing or at other serious party moments. I learned my place.

I also learned a lot about what our browsers and buyers found interesting: curriculum material in particular. Our initial meeting had not pointed us in that direction, possibly because few of the participants were teachers. KNOW, Inc., one of the other indie feminist presses, had begun to publish collections of syllabi of women's studies courses in a series called Female Studies. We joined them in that endeavor, realizing that the advent of new courses left plenty of room for multiple volumes with various focuses: women's studies in foreign languages, in the sciences, in math, in history, in English and American literatures. The first of these, edited by Sheila Tobias and published by KNOW, Inc. in 1970, is accurately described in its subtitle as "a collection of college syllabi and reading lists."

The last subject, literature, particularly excited me. Many years later, I would collect and edit a volume called *Reconstructing American Literature* (1984)—Amazon still has a few at $117.58. I must be rich, because I have forty or fifty of them in boxes in my storage unit. I learned its value when, teaching at San Jose State, I was at the last minute given a course in modern American literature. "How can I figure this out in two days?" I wondered, panicking. Then I noticed the orange-covered volume on my small bookshelf, a book I myself had prepared, and in it I found a couple of models to work from. Many users of the Female Studies series had this experience—we didn't all have to reinvent the wheel. What we did need to do, though—and this was a major task of The Feminist Press—was to publish for teachers and students key works by women not otherwise available. Works like Rebecca Harding Davis's "Life in the Iron Mills," Charlotte Perkins Gilman's "The Yellow Wallpaper," and Agnes Smedley's *Daughter of Earth.* To lead that task, we organized a Reprints Committee. For a period of time, it was the most important part of The Feminist Press and a who's who of academic feminism in the 1970s.[8]

I served on the Reprints Committee and edited and wrote the afterword for the Smedley novel. But for me the most interesting moments associated with the press were working with Tillie Olsen on our edition of "Life in the Iron Mills." Florence and I first met Tillie at One Fifth Avenue, which was then a hotel. We waited for her in the silent lobby around mid-day; when a middle-aged white woman, who looked very much like my aunt Syd, arrived, we decided that she must be Tillie Olsen. She was. Tillie had a package containing a precious copy of the story as it was first printed in the *Atlantic* in 1861. "Don't read it late in the evening," she told us, "it will make you cry." I mentally pooh-poohed her warning. The three of us talked about other books we should consider reprinting, including *Daughter of Earth,* with which we were not at all familiar, though I vaguely recalled that Smedley had written about the "long march" of the Chinese Communist Eighth Route Army. After much conversation about books and the infant press, I took the copy of Davis's story and got on the train back to Baltimore while Florence went off to her appointments. Later that evening, alone in Baltimore, I sat down in the small dinette cubby and, for the first time, opened "Life in the Iron Mills." As Tillie had predicted, the tears began welling up as I got toward the end. I never wanted to examine my response too closely: Was it the power of the story, the power of Tillie's suggestion, the desire to find from such fragments of a forgotten past a "new" canon, as we would come to call it? Just loneliness? Whatever, the story gripped me as few ever had. It would not be long before we had decided to bring out a Feminist Press edition, released in 1972.

Of course, it made sense to ask Tillie Olsen to write the afterword. As the in-house editor for her remarkable essay, I realized that I had to carefully check all of Tillie's quotations and references. She had the tiniest handwriting, barely legible to the naked eye; she kept notes on tiny scraps of paper—a consequence of her earlier days of poverty when paper was precious. When she later stayed with us in our spare bedroom in New York, we would find these minute scraps for days afterward. At any rate, I did check her quotations, particularly from the Seneca Falls "Declaration of Sentiments." And like a good editor— so pedestrian!—I corrected her alterations of the original. When she returned the edited manuscript, she had changed them back to her version. So I called her to say that quotations from the "Declaration" needed to be accurate. "But mine is better," she insisted. That may well have been; I did not presume to argue and simply changed them to conform to the source when I prepared the manuscript for typesetting. I had learned working with coauthors that the person who last holds the manuscript before it goes off for printing has the final say about the text.

The other particularly intense experience at the press had to do with Agnes Smedley's *Daughter of Earth*. An unstated premise at the press asserted that prefaces, afterwords, and the like would be written by women. So it was only after considerable discussion, and some soul-searching, that I came to write the afterword for Smedley's novel. I found as many of her books as I could—a number at the Southern California Library for Social Studies and Research—read them all and found out whatever I could about her. Smedley, I discovered, was not only an excellent writer but also a significant activist on the Left for many years. Recent biographers have described her as a triple spy: for Indian nationalists, the Comintern, and the Chinese communists. So a good deal of her actual life was deeply hidden. I went with Jan MacKinnon, coauthor of the first biography about Smedley,[9] to open the trunk Smedley had left at Yaddo, the artists' colony in upstate New York, before she left the US for Britain, late in 1949, where she would soon die. I copied much of what the MacKinnons had accumulated by and about her in order to present the material to Chinese officials in 1974, when I was part of an early delegation to what was still being called "Red China." For the Chinese, Smedley remained an icon. I remain proud of my role in bringing the novel back into print.

My other enterprise within The Feminist Press had to do with writing, together with Alice Kessler-Harris, an introduction used for each of a group of novels from the thirties by Tess Slesinger, Fielding Burke (Olive Tilford Dargan), and Josephine Herbst. The introductions, cowritten by Kessler-Harris and me, were considered an acceptable exception to the rule that only women should write them. Later, though we were not consulted about it, the press added another novel, by Myra Page, to the series. This was an excellent initiative, part of the effort to rehabilitate 1930s left culture, and I wanted to add other books to it; my split with Florence in 1982 effectively terminated the effort.

At much the same time, a wave of hostilities within the feminist movement hit The Feminist Press. A number of its employees, perhaps six or eight, decided that they wanted to unionize. I was busy in my own union at SUNY, the United University Professions. In fact, I was running for president, and I was pressed, particularly by delegates from SUNY/Purchase College, to enable The Feminist Press union to happen. Florence seriously opposed the union. She seemed to regard the effort to unionize as a kind of attack on her, a feminist "mother." Perhaps it was. In any case, I knew that I'd get nowhere trying to persuade her to change her view of the controversy; whether by accident or design, the unionization struggle at The Feminist Press seemed to engage the whole history of conflict and division within the feminist movement. I was still, in theory, the treasurer of The Feminist Press, but in fact I had less and less to do with its actual operation and not much interest in it. That cut no ice with my voters in Purchase, New York. They let me know that they would not be voting for me as union president. I lost by two votes.

I had promised to throw a party if I won. Florence said that she would throw a party if I lost. I do not remember whether she did, but it really did not matter. Losing that vote marked a huge turning point in my life. Had I won, I would no doubt have continued down the path of union activism, perhaps becoming some sort of official or pie card in the national teachers' organization. As it was, I turned away from the union and rekindled my scholarly life. I worked more and more systematically on the *Reconstructing American Literature* project, which I had already begun at The Feminist Press, and on what would become the *Heath Anthology of American Literature*.

Rage and creativity. Where did these engines of feminism leave me? Then and thereafter? This book is a chronicle of uncertainty. And of betrayals.

Florence served a term as visiting professor of women's studies in 1979 at Denison University in Granville, Ohio. I came along and was asked to participate in what its members described as a male consciousness-raising group. The whole enterprise seemed to hinge on a single pair of questions: Why should any of us be in a relationship with a feminist? Do we have to be? It was never very clear to me whether the conversations were designed to open men to the difficult politics into which their significant others were launched, or to provide some of the men with exit visas. It had that effect in one or two cases. Men in the group regarded me both as a curiosity and an authority. I became a brother from another planet. One of the men approached me independently of the group: a friend of his, he said, claimed to be a feminist, yet he was harsh with his partner and had admitted to the guy I was talking with that he had occasionally been violent to her. His question was this: How could a man who described himself as a feminist assault a woman? Wasn't that contradictory? I tried to claim no special insights in that Granville group. It wasn't clear to me whether the person being discussed was a friend or a doppelgänger for the guy himself. I suggested mildly that some feminist men might feel their own kind of rage for having stepped back from the "norms" of male domination into less determinative positions. Feeling deprived, they became angry. And maybe they took out their submerged feelings on the women in their lives. Sounded plausible, and perhaps it did explain this particular instance of conflict.

But that was not usually my own experience. I never felt done to by feminism, if occasionally by feminists. Still, I must sometimes have found a yawning frustration because I could not claim or really think of our endeavors at The Feminist Press as my own. Let's face it: people need to feel good about their accomplishments, whether we're speaking, as Merle Travis's song has it, of mining sixteen tons, composing *The Prelude*, teaching an algebraic equation, or writing an afterword to *Daughter of Earth*. (The last was something I could no longer claim, as Florence replaced my afterword with one written by a friend of hers in the aftermath of our split.) There were moments when, yes, I felt used. But the experience of The Feminist Press over a decade was for me almost wholly positive, a lesson in the creative application of academic skills.

That period of my life came to an end there in Granville in 1979. The guys' discussions, however comic and weird, did provide me with a certain confidence that I was at a forward edge among feminist men. But the real life-changing event of my time in Granville was deeply unfeminist. I entered into a passionate affair with a woman who, a few years later, I would marry. In the meanwhile, she enabled me to feel better about myself than I had ever felt before, even in my too-brief time with Sue. It was unbecoming to enter this relationship, and hurtful. But it helped rescue me from a downward spiral, psychologically and physically, that emerged from the keen disappointment at the end of my union career, the disappearance of opportunities for direct action in the movement, and the disintegration of our educational aspirations at SUNY College at Old Westbury. And it opened out into an amazing expanse of confidence and sheer joy in my life.

In short order, I returned to writing and, fortuitously, those possibilities quickly multiplied. Joel Conarroe became for me a sort of magical patron by asking me to write an essay for the 1984 centennial edition of *PMLA*. The essay attempted to bring together the cultural and political concerns that I shared with my comrades at *Radical Teacher* magazine.[10] That, and a 1983 essay in *Feminist Studies*[11], helped me reenter the world of literary criticism, from which I had largely absented myself for a decade. That brings me to the final chapters in this chronicle, for which I must step back a few years.

Chapter Twelve

WHERE WE WENT AND WHAT WE DID
(AND DID NOT) LEARN THERE

The "sixties," as we know, did not end on December 31, 1969. The war in Southeast Asia continued. Racism didn't evaporate. Feminist organizations dedicated to combatting patriarchy were just being organized. And America was confronted by a corrupt and secretive presidency that attacked "enemies," domestic and foreign, and would end only with a resignation provoked by the threat of impeachment. There was plenty to keep activists busy.

Many different paths opened before me. In 1972, after a year at the United States Servicemen's Fund (USSF), I returned to full-time teaching at a college, the State University of New York's College at Old Westbury. I wondered: Could I apply some of the lessons learned in nearly a decade of movement activity? Would the teaching and scholarly work I had begun at the University of Maryland, Baltimore County and at The Feminist Press be politically relevant? This new SUNY campus was an untried experiment that hadn't existed ten years earlier. Now the college was under construction in opulent Old Westbury, where the zoning then required two acres to build a house—or, more accurately, a mansion. The new campus, once the F. Ambrose Clark family estate, included some five hundred wooded acres belonging to a network of fancy establishments that once upon a time graced Long Island's North Shore. In the beginning, the college had been located in another elegant domain, the Planting Fields Arboretum in Oyster Bay. The SUNY system had shut down that first version of the college, in part because it gave birth to the radical Puerto Rican Young Lords Party. But more troublesome, its students and faculty, oriented to 1960s beliefs, and its liberal president, Harris Wofford, were unable to agree on governance structures and central elements of the curriculum.

Now, SUNY College at Old Westbury was to reemerge as one among a number of experimental colleges—like Hampshire, Evergreen State, Governors State, Naropa University—across the country.

I asked myself: Could this innovative college become a movement outpost? Could a largely new faculty and student body pursue movement priorities: a commitment to social justice, open access for an unusually diverse student body, hiring an equally diverse faculty, and establishing a curriculum informed by freedom school values? Would taking a job there constitute a retreat from activist political commitments? Or an extension of those commitments into an ongoing work life? I had no easy answers to those questions.

No surprise. Even the most experienced, hardened revolutionaries, if their rebellion is successful, face the day on which they must translate insurrection into bureaucracy. Some can, like Che Guevara—always an "enemy of boredom"—move on to new fields of conquest, or loss. Most take up the unglamorous work of governing. Administration—a long, tedious word—replaces revolt. The daily grind of maintenance work, often vital to sustain progress, or even hope, can seem banal after the heady hours of combat. Despite my best efforts, I couldn't see myself as a hardened revolutionary—I'd not shot a bow and arrow since Boy Scouts camp and never so much as handled a gun. Besides, in 1971 and 1972 revolution wasn't really on any rational agenda, though we had made identifiable progress in getting the United States out of Vietnam. A couple of hundred people had gone "underground," but most of us needed to figure out how we might earn our daily bread—and maybe a few beers—and also sustain the variety of movement activities that gave meaning to our lives. Perhaps by joining the struggle for open admissions, women's and black studies, and other educational innovations that seemed possible at a college like Old Westbury.

Or getting active in the union of SUNY faculty and professional staff, United University Professions (UUP)? Initially, I turned in that direction. Most of my colleagues at Old Westbury, despite—or because of—their ostensibly radical politics, saw little attractive about union activism. The teachers' union, the American Federation of Teachers (AFT), was hardly a bastion of the movement's progressive politics. On the contrary, many officers supported the backward tendencies of Democratic Party conservatives: pro-war, suspicious of student activism (especially when it threatened faculty privilege), and indifferent to the need for change in the ranks of dominantly white and male faculty.

Meanwhile, people were needed who could implement the contract, including the local grievance procedures. I undertook that work as chapter chair or as grievance officer, and also became involved in the statewide union. That included helping start a Reform Caucus, which pushed UUP to undertake a wider range of progressive activities, from supporting the farm workers to developing SUNY's affirmative action plan. Before long, I was elected to the statewide executive board and, in time, became statewide vice president for academics.

I carried into the union the experience and the values of the movement. These commitments won me many friends in what was largely a progressive organization led by traditional social democrats. Occasionally, my movement values got me into trouble. I promoted women's advancement—even though I would run against a woman for union president. I spoke for student causes—even though they sometimes involved claims of bad conduct by faculty that the union represented. I wrote for union papers and also for the "suspiciously" named *Radical Teacher* on retrenchment, the exploitation of adjunct faculty, and what I described as the "assault on the public sector."[1] The leadership of the statewide union, New York State United Teachers (NYSUT), regarded me distrustfully, especially when I passed out announcements of new *Radical Teacher* issues at meetings. At the 1980 national convention I spoke from the floor to urge the AFT to support Jimmy Carter against Ronald Reagan. If Carter is beaten, I maintained, the woman from whom we are renting our New York apartment would lose her job in the administration, return to the city to reclaim her space—and we would be out of an apartment, a disaster then in New York.

Generally, I took union business more seriously. Unions were among the very few progressive institutions that might be able to contest neoliberalism. Undermining union power is why Reagan, early in his regime, came down hard on the air traffic controllers union (PATCO), initiating a downward spiral in union membership and political clout. It was one thing to thumb your nose at the public, as PATCO seemed to do, when you had significant power; it was quite another when you were losing strength and needed friends. Very few unions sought, as nurses do today, to make common cause with the people they served—increase wages, yes, but also provide healthier care for patients. Instead, like my own union, they tend to be defensive and hold on to hard-won rights, which the general public often sees as privileges. The question, seldom adequately posed in UUP, was how could a union form alliances with students, parents, and other members of the communities we served, as well as with unions like those representing groundskeepers and secretaries? We were sometimes aware of other union struggles; on rare occasions we made a financial contribution to a strike fund, like one for the United Farm Workers. But coming out of the sixties—in which most unions, if they did not support the war, did little to oppose it—few movement people understood how unions and communities could create progressive coalitions, especially to combat a resurgent capitalism. I certainly did not. And that was never the subject of AFT president Al Shanker's always interesting but hardly liberal speeches.

More recently, some activists, such as Staughton Lynd, have questioned the whole structure of unionization, with its commitment to avoid strikes and emphasis on contracts and formalized procedures for resolving conflicts.[2] Union contracts generally place authority in the hands of bureaucrats, who are not inclined to rock the boat. Staughton, on the other hand, like the Industrial Workers of the World (IWW) of the late nineteenth century, advocated direct actions—strikes and other job actions—as the means to return power to rank-and-file actors. That strategy paralleled the sit-ins and freedom rides of early civil rights movement activists, central to producing change in the face of segregationist intransigence.

I enjoyed the union work, especially the organizing efforts of effective caucus members like the late Mac Nelson (from SUNY Fredonia) and Susan Puretz (from SUNY New Paltz). We helped elect thoughtful people to the executive board and put forward sensible policy proposals. Our effort to resist the exploitation of adjunct faculty, which had only recently begun, offered an early model for contesting the growing exploitation of untenured faculty. And we had a good time, even in Albany, where I remember running one morning with Mac and Susan in five-below weather and returning with sweat icicles hanging from my hat. I always looked forward to at least one special meal in an old Albany deli in the neighborhood where my uncle long ago had his butcher shop; that deli continued to serve sweetbreads, as well as brains and eggs. I even relished spending long hours as grievance officer on the case of a former Old Westbury vice president, with whom I had struggled for over a year about formalizing the rules for faculty governance. A new president demoted him; now he was set up to be fired. Supporting him was a bore, but the right thing to do.

Still, more and more, we seemed focused on implementing the contract and very little beyond it, like affirmative action, the rights of students, and carrying out Title IX, much less opposing the continuation, post-Vietnam, of American imperialism. Such progressive policies, it seemed to me, ought to be objectives for our union, along with better pay and working conditions. The contract itself did not seem very forward-looking with regard to salaries for ordinary faculty, much less for part-timers. So I ran for president. I began my election speech saying "I stand for change."

What change would I have been able to accomplish had I won? I would certainly have pressed the issue of exploiting adjunct faculty. Hiring adjuncts and paying them poverty wages with no benefits always seemed to me part of a neoliberal recipe for speeding up and controlling educational workers.[3] It's often said that higher education imitated corporations in developing a part-time, temporary, and vulnerable workforce. Looked at more closely, I would argue, the history of adjunct employment reverses the sequence: higher education tested out such exploitative hiring, which was then used by other kinds of businesses to produce today's "gig" economy. Resisting the growing abuse of adjuncts in the 1970s would have been difficult: the stakes were higher and more complicated than we realized, and the path to change was strewn with explosive problems. For example, many full-time faculty, even those who deplored adjunct employment in theory, found the practice useful: they could accept grants and replace themselves cheaply. As full-time lines were not filled due to cutbacks in state funding, departments could employ adjuncts at minimal wages to cover their courses. Finally, few full-timers were willing to commit to job actions to support their part-time colleagues—indeed, some failed to see them as "colleagues."

To challenge the adjunct system required mobilizing students and parents, as well as full-timers, to oppose what had to be designated as the depreciation of educational values. But to make that argument suggested, incorrectly, that adjuncts were less capable teachers. In fact, many adjuncts were—and are—as credentialed and creative as the "regular" faculty. The issue was not the competence of adjunct instructors. However, the system was calculated to keep adjuncts marginalized. They often had no offices, held other jobs that hurried them away, and suffered from great uncertainty about future employment. In other words, the adjunct system was designed to establish a "reserve army" of potential employees whose very vulnerability made them easier to hire, fire, and generally to control. In the mid-seventies, very few activists understood how the adjunct structure would metastasize; we couldn't imagine the current scenario: a vast majority of college and university courses taught by contingent faculty, who now constitute a preponderance of the teaching staff at many institutions.[4] Had we known in 1975 what we know today, we might have been even more highly motivated to strangle this baby horror in its cradle. We didn't, and very likely we wouldn't have succeeded, given the conflicts I have enumerated and the transformative character of capitalism we faced.

Also, union bureaucratic work wasn't as exciting, and seemed much less productive, than climbing into a building to support a student takeover. And our students continued to live as if the political forms of sixties activism had never altered. Being involved in the union resembled trying to work within other mainstream institutions, like the Democratic Party—same frustrations, same doubts about results, same sense that one's time might better be spent elsewhere. But where?

After I lost the election for president (by two votes), I answered that question by renewing my academic commitments at SUNY College at Old Westbury, especially those connected to the developing Feminist Press. But Old Westbury presented a person interested in scholarship, and even certain forms of experimental teaching, with difficulties. First, the college's "mission" statement—to address "the riddle of human justice." That mission was embedded in our affirmative action goal: as we described it, "30, 30, 30, 10"—that is, 30 percent white, 30 percent black, 30 percent Latino/a, and 10 percent "other." Half men and half women. That goal would, we hoped, shape an unusually diverse student body, as well as a distinctively integrated teaching force. We never reached those goals, though in 1972 I was the last white man hired to a full-time appointment for a number of years. In hiring both faculty of color and white women, and enrolling "historically bypassed" minority and female students, Old Westbury placed itself and its faculty in the vanguard of what came to be called "open admissions." That had implications for which students we enrolled, which faculty we hired, and what we, as faculty, actually taught.

Our open admissions program brought to campus some remarkable students—as well as some who really did not belong there. One enterprising young black student discovered an unwritten North Shore compact that allowed equestrians to gallop over adjacent properties; he organized a kind of cavalry of black riders, taught them horsemanship, maintained the estate's horse barn, and proceeded to engage some of the college's neighbors. Others like Craig Harris became and remain important in the New York music scene. A few older women students, returning to school after years in offices and raising families, became staff members for The Feminist Press, which had been given a small building deep in the campus's woods as its headquarters. They were essential to the development of the press, and their help enabled me to start the *Reconstructing American Literature* project, which took up the next few decades of my life.

On the other hand, some of our students—younger ones in particular—arrived with few of the skills, including reading and writing, necessary for college work. A skills program led by the indomitable Onita Estes Hicks aimed to move such students, many of them young people of color, from functional illiteracy to some degree of competence. One term, I decided to do a course for students with weak skills on reading a newspaper. The first day I asked the group of thirteen or fourteen where one would find the sports sections of tabloids like the *New York Daily News* or the *New York Post.* They looked at me, baffled. None of them, I soon realized, normally read any newspaper. I made the newspaper into our textbook. Later in the term, I noticed that most of the students were busy scribbling during class period. Since it was not a course designed for taking notes, I asked what they were doing. They hemmed and hawed, but finally one blurted out that she was doing the homework.

The others nodded. "Homework," I said, "is for doing at home."

Another student replied, "Nah, they always said that in school, but they never collected anything."

Another chimed in, "Anyway, they never let us take books home."

"Well, in my class, you do the homework at home and come ready to hand it in at the beginning of the next class. Got it?" They nodded.

When the next class was scheduled to meet, only two students were present. It took me a week to reassemble the group. "What was that about?"

"You said to have the homework ready to hand in at the beginning of class. We didn't have it done, so we didn't come to class." QED.

In a course titled American Voices, only one of the twenty-five students enrolled attended all the classes, always sitting in the first row in the seat nearest the sealed-up windows. She never willingly entered conversation and spent much of the period rummaging in the two large paper bags she kept. I came to realize, much to my surprise, that she might have been homeless. Many of the other students dropped in periodically; some even wrote an occasional paper. Only our credit/no credit grading system saved over half the class from flunking.

By the late seventies, very little at Old Westbury seemed to function. Rumors of corruption in student services preceded a number of firings. The dorms were awash in drugs. I once said to a student, "I hear there's a drug problem." "Oh no," he replied, "you can get anything you want." The battles within our own program escalated, with former friends and comrades at each other's throats. One colleague began putting up what the Chinese called "big character posters" attacking Florence and me. To sustain the intensity of our educational program and respond to the students' massive needs required the kind of energy one brought to an ardent demonstration for brief periods. Ditto for supporting each other through thick and thin—mostly thin—and upholding the college's conflicted "mission."

Open admissions required political commitment more than empathy, and a degree of creative energy few faculty could maintain over the years. One pulled back, played out. I recognized the symptoms of burnout in teachers, about which I'd heard from innovators like Herb Kohl and Zelda Wirtschafter: self-doubt, easy distraction, things hanging in the winds of change. Many of the faculty, Florence included and I sometimes in her wake, grasped opportunities to teach elsewhere or simply to take leave. That was, of course, no way to run a railroad, much less a fragile undergraduate college. A new president began to insist that we stay at home.

Staying put at Old Westbury was not, for me, a solution. I fretted, then worried about my skills and emotional resources. My movement education, which had long empowered me, seemed to be dissipating. Here I was in my forties, and where was I? A big frog on the verge of drowning in a very little collegiate pond? Second fiddle in a publishing enterprise I could never call my own? During this period I wrote about how abstinence was the new, hot frontier of sexuality. Uh huh.

Still, all was not grim: affirmative action provided us not only with goals that informed our searches for new faculty and student admissions; it also shaped our organization, primarily into interdisciplinary programs like American Studies and Politics, Economics, and Society, rather than traditional academic departments. Our music program focused almost entirely on African American composition and performance. Ken McIntyre, who directed it, rejected the term "jazz," which he said only meant having sex (as in Gwendolyn Brooks's "We / Jazz June"). Dedicated and creative faculty members, although frequently contentious, were always ready to climb into a building to join students who had seized it. We held two minutes of silence to mark that first September 11, in 1973, when future dictator Augusto Pinochet, with help from the American CIA, overthrew and murdered President

Salvador Allende in Chile. I noticed that almost all the white, male faculty wore jeans and often t-shirts, whereas the black men wore jackets and ties and the women wore dresses. I asked one of the black chemists, Samuel von Wimbush: "Bush, why does the black faculty wear such formal clothing?" "It's out of respect for our students," he said. Thereafter, and for most of my career, I wore a jacket and an often conspicuous tie.

American Studies, which I would join full-time when I left USSF in 1972, was equally untraditional. We had tracks in women's studies; labor studies; literature, editing, and publishing; and US history—all with a faculty of about ten. Our high-powered group included Barbara and John Ehrenreich, whose formulation of the "professional-managerial class" played an important role in left thinking for the following decades—though Barbara would become famous for *Nickel and Dimed: On (Not) Getting By in America*.[5] Ros Baxandall brought her degree in social work, along with her activism in Redstockings and other early feminist groups in New York. John McDermott had written an important essay on culture and class, "The Laying on of Culture,"[6] the significance of which still hasn't been grasped by many liberal Democrats. Naomi Rosenthal wrote about spinsters; Liz Ewen did groundbreaking work on suburban women; Dierdre English, with Barbara, wrote about "witches," midwives, and the roles of women in health care. Florence and I were rapidly pushed into chairing the program.

The internecine warfare that I had evaded during the previous decade caught up with me at Old Westbury. I will spare my readers the stultifying details of our internal conflicts. Direct actions, a mark of university life in the chronological sixties, continued apace: students seized buildings; faculty fought with administrators—and with each other; experimental courses flourished, or flopped, or both. Precisely because our students were not from traditional backgrounds, indeed had been failed by traditional approaches, we were free to pursue many of the educational experiments that marked the sixties. The questions that freedom schools had raised about content and process remained. I had a better understanding of what was required to change classrooms so that they spoke to the needs of the nontraditional, often minority and older female students, who were coming to Old Westbury and increasingly to other public universities. Still, many of us exited Old Westbury hating one another.

క్రి క్రి క్రి

I had concluded that I could pursue the values embodied in freedom schools more effectively in my classes and in writing than in union meetings. I began thinking back to the one vote we had lost at the 1968 Modern Language Association convention: a motion to divert to other uses government funds directed to the Center for Editions of American Authors (CEAA), which published massive new compilations of the traditional white, male writers. We wanted to use those funds to uncover the work of lost and forgotten women and men, writers of color, and others marginalized by traditional scholarship and thinking. While we lost that vote, the idea remained alive, especially for me in the form of The Feminist Press reprints series. I began devoting myself to changing what we soon would call the "canon" of American literature.

But I worried whether, as some thought, focusing on altering what students read in classrooms and maybe what adults read outside of them constituted a trivial exercise. Did it matter, given police violence in black communities? Or American bombing in Vietnam, Cambodia, and Laos? For someone who had courted arrest and danger to challenge racism, who continued helping organize rallies against the war, who had put the time colleagues devoted to building careers into organizing a feminist press, why this turn? Was all this canon business simply an academic matter? Weren't the real goals the cultural capital of ambitious professors rather than serious change in an increasingly unequal and violent society? Perhaps I should be spending more time in the street and on the picket line than in the library. Isn't reality constituted by what we *do* rather than what we talk or read about? Would it matter if the movement took over the study of literature or art while fascists began to dominate the political landscape? Those early seventies questions—still so relevant—have ambiguous answers about which I wrote at length.[7]

My response begins as follows: who and what you read about, who and what you see on screens large and small helps shape what you find important or even visible. Consider the conjunction of the March on Washington for Jobs and Freedom and James Baldwin's *The Fire Next Time* (1963); or that of school integration (1957) and Gwendolyn Brooks's "The Chicago Defender Sends a Man to Little Rock," with its compelling final lines: "I saw a bleeding brownish boy. . . . / The lariat lynch-wish I deplored. / The loveliest lynchee was our Lord." Black civil rights activism, black rebellions all over America in the sixties, *and* the work, new and old, of black writers were reshaping consciousness, especially among whites. I could see the impact of older works like those of Claude McKay:

If we must die, let it not be like hogs
Hunted and penned in an inglorious spot,
While round us bark the mad and hungry dogs,
Making their mock at our accursèd lot.
If we must die, O let us nobly die, . . .
                    ("If We Must Die," 1919)

Rather than McKay's militant and angry poem to illustrate my point, I could have chosen a work from the century before I started teaching it, like Frances Harper's "Aunt Chloe's Politics" (1872):

Of course, I don't know very much
About these politics,
But I think that some who run 'em,
Do mighty ugly tricks.

For many of my students at Old Westbury and elsewhere, such work provided a view of African American experience quite different from what they had encountered in the classroom, the church, or the street. That was true for white as well as black students, for women as well as men. Action and art do—both—change consciousness. Why, otherwise, make films like *Do the Right Thing, If Beale Street Could Talk*, or even *Detroit*, whatever their limitations?

Turn the equation around: to designate a group's cultural practices as trivial or worse—as not really "culture"—is to consign members of the group to the fringes of society, or outside its borders in camps. The Nazis used the term *Entartete Kunst* (degenerate art) to characterize modernist work that, according to them, displayed "Jewish" traits.[8] African American music, especially "jazz," was for many years regarded—and not just by Nazis—as "jungle" music, and those who produced it as not far removed from "jungle" creatures. For a long period the term "women's writing" suggested—even among otherwise sensible critics—the banal and sentimental; clearly, its creators were people of lesser capacity who had no business claiming cultural space. Was that the point of Americans designating Vietnamese as "gooks, chinks, slopes, dinks, and zipperheads"?[9] Such judgments underwrote forms of social marginalization from derision to imprisonment to bombs and death camps. What we teach, as I have argued throughout this book, is not trivial nor is it a neutral matter.

Obviously, culture does not totally determine how we see the world. On the contrary, the conditions of life—poverty and wealth, disease and health, opportunity and work, or their absence—shape our perceptions, our understanding. H. H. Lewis makes the point with gross hilarity:

> Here I am
> Hunkered over the cow-donick,
> *Earning* my one dollar per
> And *realizing*,
> With the goo upon overalls,
> How environment works up a feller's pants legs
> to govern his thought.[10]

Yes, but culture—in the sense of what we read, hear, and see—also makes a significant and *changing* impact on one's "thought." Or as Charles W. Leslie, co-curator of the Leslie-Lohman Museum of Gay and Lesbian Art, straightforwardly put it, "When people are confronted with imagery, it finally helps them overcome biases and prejudices."[11] I needed to put what I could do best—write and teach about literature—into the effort to bring about progressive change. But *how?*

My introductory literature course, American Voices, included work such as blues lyrics, poems by then little-known writers like Frances Harper, and autobiographical narratives by ordinary Americans, in addition to those by Benjamin Franklin and Henry David Thoreau. The syllabus featured writers of color and white women, authors who had largely been marginalized in traditional introductions and anthologies. I kept before me the ironic words of Dudley Randall's wonderful 1968 poem, "Black Poet, White Critic":

> A critic advises
> not to write on controversial subjects
> like freedom or murder,
> but to treat universal themes
> and timeless symbols
> like the white unicorn
> A white unicorn?

Widening the scope of my students' awareness of "others" and their lives was a key objective. Easier said than done. First of all, many of the texts I might have used were not readily available in those pre-internet days. Like many colleagues, I spent hours Xeroxing handouts for my students or turning my fingers purple at the ditto machine.

Predictably, colleges began to claim they were running out of money for reproduction, so we had to devise all sorts of work-arounds to make texts available—assuming that we knew well enough what works we wanted to teach. But it was clear from the early successes of The Feminist Press, with stories like Gilman's "The Yellow Wall-Paper" and Davis's "Life in the Iron Mills," that in the early 1970s relatively few faculty members were familiar with such fiction. Fewer still knew about the two centuries of African American poetry, songs, stories, and slave narratives, much less work in Spanish or other languages of the Americas. It would be some time before many teachers of American literature came to see slave narratives as constituting a *literary* genre, as distinct from pieces of historical interest, or work in Spanish as *American* literature.

Such restrictions raised the problem of the canon both in theory and in practice: What were we willing to include under the rubrics of "literature" or "American"? What was appropriate to be taught in English courses? I remember a senior member of the faculty at the University of Pennsylvania disparaging Frederick Douglass's *Narrative* as being of "merely rhetorical interest." How then to fit such texts into an introductory American literature course, even one more conventional than my American Voices? Oh, the agony over the decision to omit Henry James and include Douglass on a syllabus. Who else would we radicals eject from our reading lists? And what creatures of some lesser cultural god would we import?

We radicals were hardly innocent bystanders in the culture wars of the 1980s. In fact, we began them by insisting that the received literary canon—the work of my graduate school peer, Harold Bloom, notwithstanding[12]—was far too narrow: it did not reflect the range of human experience, and omitted excellent work by most artists and thinkers who looked different from the people defining what was significant to read or learn about. Similar problems affected the canons of history, visual art, film, politics, and the like. As colleagues began challenging these exclusionary canons in articles, books, syllabi, and collections, I proposed a new kind of anthology of American literature.

An anthology? Bad enough to worry over something we called the "canon." Now to become an anthologist? I couldn't forget E. E. Cummings's mean takedown of Louis Untermeyer:

mr u will not be missed
who as an anthologist

sold the many on the few
not excluding mr u

Unlike "mr u," I certainly didn't need to worry about my own poetry gracing the pages of any collection—it remains unpublished. But I did find it necessary to write at length about the theory underlying the anthology.[13] The volumes that finally emerged as *The Heath Anthology of American Literature*, I wrote, embodied the values and priorities of the movements of the time. This translation of movement priorities into literary study became my main concern for the next two decades.

The changed forms of cultural study embodied in *The Heath Anthology* emerged from discussions among a big group of people with somewhat different experiences and understandings of what we meant by "literature" and "American."[14] While I largely chose and organized the initial editorial group, my choices were determined by movement values: equal numbers of women and men, and of whites and minorities. The group represented the range of identities, experiences, and creativity that constituted "America." It was clear that no one person or even a small group—like those staffing all existing American literature anthology editorial boards—was sufficiently knowledgeable to implement the changes to which we aspired. Few whites were more than tolerably familiar with the histories and creative productions of minority writers. Likewise, few men had adequately examined the writing of women. To make *The Heath Anthology* inclusive—as no anthology had ever been before—required a large, fully diverse and representative editorial board.[15] A buddy from graduate school who had moved into publishing, Phillip Leininger, warned that every addition to the editorial board beyond five would add a year to the time between conception and publication. He wasn't far off.

The difficulty in bringing significant work by minority writers and white women into the anthology and the syllabus had everything to do with the operations of "tradition" in canon formation. Tradition functions in two largely separate domains. First, there are the works of art that constitute what T. S. Eliot, who in the mid-twentieth century was still among the most consequential of critics, described as being shaped by "the whole of the literature of Europe from Homer." That remark resonated as much in the academic world of the 1980s as it did half a century before when it was written. In constructing an inclusive anthology, we needed to look not only at an expanded (especially by gender and race) idea of the "literature of Europe," brilliant as it was. That was particularly true of writing in these United States, whose traditions—customs, behaviors, and forms of creativity—were often distinct from those of European origin. Think about "There's a Man Goin' Roun' Takin' Names"—Paul Robeson's way of singing that traditional song, and Margaret Walker's use of the title in "A Poem for Farish Street." The song initially alludes to a New Testament account of judgment day, but Robeson makes it also denote the anti-communist crusade in the post–World War II United States and the insistence of the period's inquisitors on forcing witnesses to name names. Walker incorporates the line into the "Patchwork Quilt" section of her long poem: "This patchwork quilt is stitched with blood and tears. / This street is paved with martyred Black men's flesh and bones." These artists intended their work not only to evoke the Bible and to be appreciated, but also to be a part of ongoing political struggles in which "the whole of the literature of Europe" turns out to be marginal. So our first task, still underway, was to begin comprehending the multiple traditions that have constituted the literatures of America.[16]

Selection was only one of our challenges. The other problem embedded in "tradition" had to do not only with *what* we studied but *how*. Changing the canon was necessarily the primary goal of an anthology. We also had to consider why we and our students read and how our choices shaped what we did together in and out of class. To fulfill the movement's objective of reconstructing what and who we see when we talk of American literature—what and who are important to see, who "matters"—demands reconsidering how we do our work. A reconstructed canon required a fresh appreciation of the worlds out of which a literary work emerged and to which it speaks, then and now.

All this may seem obvious now. It was not in the 1970s. Putting it into practice was a difficult, joyous task for teachers, and at its best for students too. The primary cry of the movement then was for representation, that is, for being *heard*, not as the inheritors of the "whole of the literature of Europe from Homer," but as those who had in practice been marginalized by that very formulation. Being heard, that is, as black women or men, whose experience of slavery and its racist sequels were seldom if ever addressed in that literature. Being heard involved artistic forms, like sorrow and work songs, call-and-response, or even hip-hop, which were seldom accounted as part of literature. Being heard as women writers, who composed out of their particular experiences of relationships, law, and sex, rather than as muses for male creativity. Identity, its celebration and display, became our mantra. Our anthologies, syllabi, and our methods of work responded to the need to end the exclusions that were central features of literary and cultural study. The creation, revision, and distribution of this transformative anthology turned out to be marvelously absorbing, as well as one extension of the culture of the sixties into the future.

Of course, our anthology was incomplete. We did not succeed in including working-class culture and art. Any anthology has to fit within the boundaries of introductory, mainly college-level American literature courses. Working-class culture, with its emphasis on songs, involvement in historical struggles, and lesser-known, often anonymous authors beat against the constraints of literary courses. Most cultural courses and anthologies that functioned in them were not calculated to introduce the concerns of working-class people, like Lowell mill girls, Kentucky miners, Philadelphia domestics, emergency room nurses, Warren Buffett's clerks, San Francisco Uber drivers—or portray the power of economic elites. Strikes and steel mills, wage slavery or wage theft, spinning wheels and shuttles, operating rooms, or the many iterations of today's "gig" economy are not the subjects of "The Love Song of J. Alfred Prufrock" or "Daisy Miller," nor yet of McKay's "If We Must Die" or Harper's "Aunt Chloe's Politics." In short, during the sixties, seventies, and eighties, issues of racial, gender, and sexual *identity* overwhelmed those rooted in the experience of class anxiety or pride.

Apart from selection of texts, which helps determine who and what matters, the functions of literary study—at least as it exists in the formal settings of schools—haunted our efforts. A major part of working-class art also serves to put working-class people in motion toward goals of solidarity and power.[17] "Which Side Are You On?" is a vivid song, adaptable to many situations of conflict. Its significance lies less in its formal properties as poetry and song—though these remain important to its success—than in its usefulness in building and maintaining an active social movement. That is, the aesthetic criteria we use to select works for a literary anthology or a syllabus differ from how we choose a work to sing on a picket line, in a cotton field, at an organizing meeting—or even print in a union newspaper. The former sets a song in relationship to, say, an intensely metaphorical poem like "A Valediction Forbidding Mourning." The latter sets a song in relationship to maintaining a sit-in or picket line in the face of attack or arrest, or as a gesture of solidarity.

The distinction I am drawing here is, of course, not absolute. Gwendolyn Brooks's "The Chicago Defender Sends a Man to Little

Rock" is as much a stunning aesthetic achievement as an evocation of African American values and a means for nourishing them. Similarly, James Oppenheim's "Bread and Roses," especially set as song, enables working-class feminist inspiration and action even as it stands as a striking poem:

> As we come marching, marching, in the beauty of the day,
> A million darkened kitchens, a thousand mill-lofts gray
> Are touched with all the radiance that a sudden sun discloses,
> For the people hear us singing, "Bread and Roses, Bread and Roses."

Underlying this problem are the functions of university education, with their calculated goals of inducting college students into the economic, political, and—most important—cultural "common sense" of bourgeois society. Working-class art, on the other hand, is an art of combat. Because working-class life remains an act of combat. Not only. Not always. But sufficiently to mark it.

That combat remains between divergent social forces and differing cultural formations. Many there are who shout "peace, peace" when there is no peace. In the United States, the working class and the employing class have much, perhaps too much, in common now. Yet there is no peace. There is more hunger and want, both literal and metaphorical, than most Americans care to acknowledge. Want of health care[18] and a sustainable future, hunger for a decent job at a livable wage.[19]

As I pointed out in chapter nine, Raymond Williams explores the cultural dimensions of this divide, characterizing bourgeois aspirations as individualistic and working-class hopes as collective. This dichotomy, however simplified, remains useful, especially in a country like the United States, where self-realization is all. Our students tend to doubt any form of collective success—everything in their schooling tells them the contrary. They flee the collective for the private in their ways of thinking as well, too often, as in voting.

Not surprisingly, teaching writing by, about, or even for working-class people often does not find a ready audience. At professional conferences after the 1970s, I found little sustained interest in working-class literary culture (though somewhat more in the literature of social protest). When I assigned stories by Alice Cary[20]—many about ordinary working people, often rural—my younger students hated them; however, my older students, especially middle-aged women, found them moving. These are not stories about aspiration and the future, but often about desire forgone and hope run out—conditions that mark too much of working-class life, as contemporary political arguments tell us. However, a syllabus filled with fiction about such lives—"The Tartarus of Maids," "Life in the Iron Mills," "Up the Coulee," Theodore Dreiser, Agnes Smedley, Harriet Arnow—wore my younger students down.

Initially, I had no adequate theory of how, as a teacher, I could change that wearying dynamic. It helped to construct comparative studies courses for the late nineteenth century and the modernist period. In such a context, I could compare Meridel Le Sueur's *The Girl* with F. Scott Fitzgerald's *The Great Gatsby*—both, in part, books about gangsters, sex, death, and class in middle America. But discussion insistently verged into gender. No surprise, since the students had virtually no experience examining or even talking about class. They tended to think about class as yet another form of identity, embraced, perhaps, or scorned—what people "were," rather than how they experienced autonomy or control. I had no helpful account to give them of how class experience differed from gender identity.

But then two strange bedfellows, T. S. Eliot and Toni Morrison, led me toward a useful model. In "Tradition and the Individual Talent" Eliot writes: "The existing monuments form an ideal order among themselves, which is modified by the introduction of the new (the really new) work of art among them. The existing order is complete before the new work arrives; for order to persist after the supervention of novelty, the whole existing order must be, if ever so slightly, altered; and so the relations, proportions, values of each work of art toward the whole are readjusted; and this is conformity between the old and the new." I had never adequately thought through what happens to Eliot's "Prufrock" when a "really new" poem like Sterling Brown's "Ma Rainey" arrives beside it a decade later. How could the literary theory embedded in "Ma Rainey"[21] alter the "relations, proportions, values" of Eliot's poem, as well as challenging his allusive strategy and the very range of his allusions? How does this strategy help shape the experience of a reader who has been asked to join the speaker passing "through certain half-deserted streets, / The muttering retreats / Of restless nights in one-night cheap hotels / And sawdust restaurants with oyster-shells"? What dominative fantasy is being played out here between the poet and his reader? And what do the differences in our experience of engaging Brown's speaker illuminate about art, race, and class?

Toni Morrison offered powerful answers to these questions. I'd often taught *The Bluest Eye* and even, strange experience, *Sula* in Berlin in 1978. *Playing in the Dark* was new; she writes, "The contemplation of this black presence is central to any understanding of our national literature and should not be permitted to hover at the margins of the literary imagination."[22] I was arguing that we must open the received canon—"the whole of the literature of Europe from Homer"—to marginalized writers. Morrison makes clear that the work of black and other minority writers in fact *transforms* that tradition itself, altering the European paradigms that had initially molded American culture. To say this another way, the "Africanist" existence in what became the United States was critical to giving all the literary, musical, and visual cultures of America their distinctive forms.

Morrison's argument suggested a strategy different from those I'd mainly pursued with respect to the class content of literary texts. I wanted to insist on the *value* of such texts. And would do so.[23] However, I did not generally use the working-class lives these texts embodied and expressed to uncover the class content of the mainstream works that have dominated literary study. Yes, it was essential to bring "Life in the Iron Mills" or Harriet Jacobs's *Incidents in the Life of a Slave Girl* to a wide readership; but also, what did they change in how, as American scholars, we answered Emerson's vivid question: "What would we really know the meaning of? The meal in the firkin; the milk in the pan; the ballad in the street; the news of the boat; the glance of the eye; the form and the gait of the body . . . ." ("The American Scholar")? How differently do we experience Emerson, depending on the class grounds from which we read? What do such marginalized works reveal to us about other canonical texts like "Self-Reliance," *The House of the Seven Gables,* or "The Birthmark"?[24]

Old Westbury, with its significant constituency of working-class students, had provoked me to think about both theories on and the practice of working-class culture. But such concerns competed for my attention with others. In the 1970s and 1980s, especially after my union aspirations collapsed, I was occupied with the project—modestly titled *Reconstructing American Literature*—that led to the anthology I have been discussing, *The Heath Anthology of American Literature.* The *Heath* succeeded in provoking many friends and foes to change what they meant when they used the phrase "American literature"— both words in that phrase. It forced me to take on that icon of conservative culture, the literary canon. And it enabled me to become an agitator on the academic circuit and, in fact, to gain a certain happy recognition from colleagues in my field. I left Old Westbury in 1988 for an appointment as the new Allan K. and Gwendolyn Miles Smith Chair at Trinity College, where I spent twenty-six agreeable years. *Mirabile dictu,* I was also well-rewarded for my radical activities. Mine is a not-unfamiliar story of yesterday's insurrectionists becoming today's privileged, the "tenured radicals" jealous reactionaries complain about.

ଓଃ   ଓଃ   ଓଃ

Paul at Trinity is also a story of the sixties. I invented a course, I set up an archive, and I began to work seriously on this book, *Our Sixties.*

The structure of the course on the sixties was simple if demanding.[25] A graduate course open to advanced undergraduates, it required that we read a novel or some stories or poems every week and see and talk about a movie that paired well with the reading. I tried to stay within the framework of the chronological 1960s. For example, I combined Anne Moody's *Coming of Age in Mississippi* and Phil Alden Robinson's film *Freedom Song;* Kurt Vonnegut's *Slaughterhouse 5* and Stanley Kubrick's *Dr. Strangelove;* Amiri Baraka's *Dutchman* and Spike Lee's *Malcolm X;* poetry by Denise Levertov, Robert Bly, and Galway Kinnell, as well as work by Vietnam vets such as John Balaban, Bruce Weigl, and W. D. Ehrhart, and Haskell Wexler's *Medium Cool.* From year to year I changed some of the readings and the films; for example, I began to use *The Heretics* (2009) about the feminist art collective Heresies, and *I Had an Abortion* (2005). Very few of the students—none of the undergraduates—had been alive during the sixties. As a result, the discussions grew out of the readings and the movies, what students' curiosity led them to look into, mainly online, and what discussion leaders proposed about the films. I liked the course. So did the students, though most of them never quite got why I found *Dr. Strangelove*—"Mine führer I can valk"—such a gas.

The course seemed to me an educationally valid way of supporting the claim I made back in the first chapter of this book: "The Sixties were good for the country, and healthy for people, cats, and other slightly domesticated species." I wanted to contest the negative ideas about the sixties that I occasionally heard students express; a few of my grandchildren's generation got in touch with the sixties history that, in my view, reshaped American culture and politics before they came on the scene. All the same, when I found myself teaching a course on my own life, I figured it was time to retire. And so I did.

Meanwhile, I had begun assembling, on paper and online, materials that might be useful not only for such a course but also for a book—actually many books. Those papers now reside mainly in a sixties archive I created at Trinity's Watkinson Library, on which, as my notes indicate, I've drawn extensively. What's online threatens to overwhelm even the considerable resources available to me as an emeritus professor. In any event, the archive gave me some roots, and the foliage is what has preceded this chapter.

The story of this book, *Our Sixties*, is more complex, and I will turn to it in a moment. But first, I need to acknowledge the many women and men I encountered in writing this book, people of color and whites, gay and straight, peers and students. Like me, they conceived organizations—for example, the 19th-Century American Women Writers Study Group and the Society for the Study of American Women Writers. In such groups I could play a not-at-all ambivalent, even avuncular role. I could deploy what I knew from an earlier literary and political education, drawing on the Indiana School of Letters, Yale, the SANE Nuclear Policy Committee, Student Nonviolent Coordinating Committee, and Students for a Democratic Society. I brought not so much Eliot's tradition—"the whole of the literature of Europe from Homer"—as, for example, contrasts between the female subjects being rediscovered and the largely male and white catalog my fifties doctorate had once forced me to internalize: Washington Irving or Emerson or Whitman. Trotting out my "knowledge" from those earlier venues amused me; maybe it also helped us be grateful for the cultural feats performed by the women writers we were now studying.

All the same, I realized, balancing along the margins of cultural studies does not necessarily lead to some kind of triumph, if only you do it long enough. In fact, you will often lose. Patriarchy and capitalism will not dry up and blow away like salted fungi. The movement has taught me, again and again, that preparing for loss belongs to the process of learning to win. And yet, we will not go back to segregation, though there's far too much of it returning to schools today. We will not reenter the closet, however slickly fitted out it might now be with cheerful apps. And working-class institutions like unions, however reduced in this moment, will not be ground under the "iron heel" that Jack London warned against. For these optimistic conclusions

I am indebted to my comrades on the margins, aka departments of English and history and the other humanities. Yes, we no longer command dominant positions within university education. But the issues addressed by the writers and thinkers we teach remain central to defining social and intellectual values, even within the realms of Facebook and Twitter. Morrison will last; Zuckerberg will deliquesce.

Chapter Thirteen

AUTHORITY AND OUR DISCONTENTS

Edward Norton's 2019 film *Motherless Brooklyn* presents a character, Moses Randolph, largely based on Robert Moses, who—more than any other person—shaped the built environment of twentieth-century New York. The Moses Randolph character isn't particularly interested in wealth, though he uses it, but in power, authority. His goal, he insists, is to reshape the city for those millions who will live in it in the future. Central Park serves as a living model for his work; he is more than willing to dislocate those—mainly black—now living in Brooklyn and Manhattan to bring about that future. In the past, he imposed himself on a black woman and fathered a mixed-race daughter; she now works with preservationists to oppose Randolph's effort to destroy thriving communities in the name of "slum clearance"—aka "Negro removal," as one of the film's characters comments.

While the film is set in the 1950s, Randolph's outlook models the characteristic form of twenty-first-century capitalism: Silicon Valley disruption. Amazon will displace the bookstore and the mall; Uber will displace the taxi driver and the bus; charters and computers will displace public schools and teachers. Randolph will, in the imagery of the movie, displace the communities that provide nourishment for jazz musicians and the local black society. Of course, much money will be made by "developers" who will build on newly opened grounds. But that isn't Randolph's object in organizing a base for his operation, referred to in the film as the Borough Bridge Authority. The name is a neat substitute for its models, the Port of New York Authority, the Triborough Bridge and Tunnel Authority, the Metropolitan Transit Authority. "Authority," the key term here, designates the unelected power of those who run the organizations in the name of the citizens of New York and New Jersey. And generally for the benefit of future generations. Generally.

I remember a student at SUNY Old Westbury who worked as a conductor on the New Jersey Transit railroad. He always spoke of the "Port of Authority," which I took as a humorous jab at his employer. But I've now rethought his phrase. Not because these authorities create the disruptive troubles Moses Randolph produces in *Motherless Brooklyn*. Generally, they do not. But because twenty-first-century capitalism and especially real-estate developers, while never, ever indifferent to profit, seem more and more to be about exercising power over those they are determined to control. Who is to have power becomes the question.

As a somewhat rebellious kid, I always found the idea of "authority" troubling. I did not like being told what I should do or be, particularly by the powers that were, whether the junior high school vice principal, some dean, the cops, or other "authorities." The word took on new life for me when we issued the "Call to Resist Illegitimate Authority" in 1967 (see chapter 8 and appendix A). I struggled with my impulse to think of all authority as illegitimate and, working with Resist, focused on Lyndon Johnson's and then Richard Nixon's war policies. What right had they to draft young men to kill and be killed in faraway Vietnam, where neither American lives nor legitimate national objectives were really at stake? That war, I felt deeply, exemplified the operation of "illegitimate authority." We pledged our support, our assets, and our "sacred honor"—as the end of the Declaration of Independence put it—to the young men who were resisting such authorities.

We learned a lot from that resistance during the sixties. First, all change in the United States begins by confronting racism. Racism is not just the "original sin" of American history; it has been and remains still the main wall blocking progressive change in our society. The underlying story of the sixties I've tried to tell is the not yet fulfilled struggle against the institutions of racial prejudice. That effort, first of all, shaped the personal experience of the young leaders of the movement. But also SNCC, SDS, CORE, the Fellowship of Reconciliation, the Southern Christian Leadership Conference, and other activist groups—these provided the shock troops to force change in institutions across the country, and to draw more and more ordinary citizens into the movement. The fight against racism provided a model for activists, as well as a stimulus for seeking change in other political and social domains. Nowhere is that better illustrated than by the 1965 antiwar slogan "No Viet Cong never called me nigger."

A second major lesson remains that under the veneer of moderation an ally can turn out to be a hideous wolf. Many of us who subscribed to liberalism discovered with horror that those with whom we shared many social and cultural values were the very people carrying out an illegal and repulsive war in Southeast Asia. Often individuals with whom some of us had studied or even gone to college, these liberals would strongly oppose George Wallace or "Bull" Connor. But they would also napalm farm girls in Vietnam. Change in one area of American politics—voting rights, say—did not at all guarantee alteration in other areas, like foreign policy or protection of the environment.

I learned from this contradiction between progressive racial accords and violent international coercion not to narrow the definition of change to one policy domain. In Resist, the organization that emerged from the "Call to Resist Illegitimate Authority," we soon extended our work beyond the issue of war and carnage. We began to support antiracist, feminist, and a variety of other progressive activities. Resist provided modest but meaningful funding to groups like the Boston Draft Resistance Group, the Black Panther Party for Self-Defense, 9 to 5: National Organization for Working Women, the Gay Liberation Front, Jobs with Justice, Rethinking Schools, and Unidos, among many others. My point is not to applaud an organization I directed for many years, though that's not a bad idea. Resisting "illegitimate authority," I discovered, meant supporting not any single organizational agenda but many and varied changes in American society.

In the first chapter, I argued that these forms of change are designated by many of today's activists as "socialism." I want to reiterate that claim here. American capitalism in the twenty-first century has emerged more clearly for much of the middle class as an anti-democratic, indeed dangerous form of economic organization. "Profit before people" might be its slogan. In education, for example, that slogan has translated into the efforts of billionaires to privatize education and to dramatically reduce taxes that support public schools. Charter schools, often operated for profit, and vouchers, especially those for religious schools, suck up public funds to pay investors and managers exorbitant sums, despite their failure to produce positive educational outcomes. Privatizing public resources has always been a feature of American capitalism, as in huge nineteenth-century land grants to transcontinental railroads. But only in the recent decades have the mavens of the "free market" tapped into public educational assets that properly belong to parents, students, and their teachers.

While profit is an inevitable component of the disruptions fostered most notoriously by Silicon Valley, the control over people and policies manifest in Moses Randolph of *Motherless Brooklyn* troubles me more deeply. The educational world provides a relatively quiet and generally less obvious instance of the menace I've been calling "illegitimate authority." More visible and dangerous to the planet's future is the continuing operation of polluting industries, like coal-fired plants, in the face of the clear threat of climate change to life on earth. The same forces, we know, oppose reasonable controls over weapons responsible for mass murder in schools, theaters, and places of worship. We see a dangerous, widening gulf between the 1 percent and everyone else, made evident by the demonstrations of Occupy Wall Street. We know that capitalism has brought great wealth to a few nations and some small number of individuals. The question now on the agenda is: At what price?

More and more, Americans see the cost of maintaining naked capitalism as far too high—that's a third lesson. In response, they have sought other forms of organization to replace the burdens it imposes everywhere on our planet.[1] The name many now give to that alternative is "socialism," even if there is wide disagreement about what this term might mean. The most elaborate argument promoting the idea that interest in socialism is growing in the United States was provided, oddly enough, by a report issued in 2018 from the Trump White House's Council of Economic Advisers. The report asserts that "socialism is making a comeback in American political discourse." Indeed, according to the *New York Times*, "the word 'socialism' appears 144 times—on average, twice a page" in this seventy-two-page pamphlet.[2] While apparently meant as an attack on left-leaning Democrats, the report assumes that "socialism" remains, as it was fifty years ago, a Cold War scare word with entirely negative resonance among Americans. But the council itself makes clear that sentiments about "socialism" in the United States, especially those of the young, have significantly changed.

I reintroduce socialism here also to compensate for the absence of political parties challenging fundamental "free market" power in America's partisan landscape. More than a century separates us from the time when specifically socialist parties made a significant impact in elections. But the issue is not solely voting for representatives—from local school boards to mayors, as well as the Congress and president. Most elections have until recently lacked real debate over progressive alternatives to capitalist priorities, which include financializing education, enabling pollution, and undercutting working-class organizations like unions. That absence has obscured what links the variety of reforms directed against the operations of power in our society—for example, Black Lives Matter, #MeToo, gun control, opposition to an intolerable military budget, Red for Ed, and similar forms of protest. All these issues turn on power: Who maintains it? Who is subjected to it? Who profits from it? The opposition to illegitimate authority is put forward by those claiming that "socialism" entails a redistribution of power; it calls for a shift away from the mainstream American assumption that money equals power, and that it should.

No! As I write, white power, male power, National Rifle Association power, military "warrior" power, "conservative" austerity power are being brought into question, together with the power of the billionaire's purse. The political struggle in education, to which I have alluded, suggests something different. Changes promoted by billionaire "reformers" are petering out. Does this scenario offer a model for change in other areas of the American political economy? A transformation that brings into question the power of capitalism itself?

I believe so. Police killings of unarmed black men and women and the sexual domination rich males have maintained over women belong to a continuum of practices I've been designating as "illegitimate authority." Such practices have a long history in the United States, from the abduction and rape of slavery, through the savagery of lynching under segregation, to the contemporary violence of blue-uniformed "authorities" today. Called by different names, they describe excesses of power that have been exercised primarily by, or on behalf of, rich, white males. We've seen similar excesses named by places like My Lai fifty years ago and Abu Ghraib a decade back in time. We've seen the practices of the NRA, for example, designed to maintain the profits of the gun trade, spelled out in the sacrifice of the lives of students at Marjory Stoneman Douglas High School, concertgoers at the Route 91 Harvest music festival in Las Vegas, and worshippers at the Tree of Life Synagogue in the Squirrel Hill neighborhood of Pittsburgh, Pennsylvania. Profit before people.

Putting forward an idea of socialism constitutes an effort to change that formula. In our time it echoes the effort contained in documents like the "Port Huron Statement" of SDS in the sixties. That statement and the organization it helped to generate proposed deep changes in the ways of looking at education, society, and the economy. But a question remains: Is it also following a will-o'-the-wisp, a ghostly light that would lead us into swamps of imaginary revolution? I think back to those early sixties. Fifty plus years ago, we were a small band opposing the emerging American war on Vietnam. We were inspired by a larger group, mainly of young people, who stood—or more often sat—against the power of racism in lunch counters, busses, schools, and pools. We persisted. We marched. We took to the streets and sometimes went to jail. We also spoke and wrote. So I have done here.

In this book I have tried to illuminate that earlier period of upheaval we call "the sixties" for 2020. Almost twenty years ago, when I started writing, I was puzzled by how I might begin exploring my own experiences (memoir) and the world I inhabited (social history). What would constitute that first step, which is always the toughest step, as I discovered in leafleting at the Amherst showing of *On the Beach* almost sixty years back? I wondered, since mine is in some sense an American success story, is it poor form to register unhappiness with the nation that enabled my success, as I have done in this book? Probably not. Americans think we're entitled to our contradictions. In fact, the book I initially planned to write concerned American values in times of war, segregation, and patriarchy; it might have been called "Entitled." But war, segregation, and patriarchy were "too much with us." I needed to know whether I, like the speaker in Wordsworth's poem ("The world is too much with us"), had given my heart away "getting and spending." Memoir promised self-discovery.

But self-discovery turned out to be just one trajectory of memoir. Yes, I needed to fathom the sources of the rage I felt about our war on Vietnam. I needed to comprehend how the modest comforts of my life had emerged from the subjugation, barely visible to me growing up in New York City's Washington Heights, of others not many blocks south in Harlem. I needed to grasp the ways my ambiguous sexual desires at once enfeebled and charged a hopeful voice. But if memoir were to be more than "the Inclination so natural in old Men, to be talking of themselves and their own past Actions"—as Franklin put it—it would have to resonate with my readers, as well as my friends and relations. This memoir, I understood, had to explore a common ground for us to act together for change. My own story could become consequential only if it suggested ways for us to embrace and travel forward, as many of you "holding me now in hand" have done. To do that required not only personal stories but the work of history: "So, then what happened?" as an uncle always asked (before he added, "and is it good for the Jews?"). And also, insofar as I could speculate, why? Increasingly, I turned to the hybrid form, strongly influenced by Birmingham social historians, that I'd learned to use in *From Walden Pond to Jurassic Park*.

That history, I have to acknowledge, was always shaped by an inveterate optimism. Almost every disaster in my life—and there were plenty—led to a new job, new relationships, and unimagined possibilities. I know this sounds like a self-help book or a fortune cookie: "In life, there is no security, only opportunities." Still, being dumped by my first wife threw me off the established academic road and into new work with the AFSC; that, in turn, led me into the civil rights and peace movements—and, not incidentally, into a loving relationship. Perhaps I was simply lucky; perhaps class and gender privilege helped me in an advantageous historical moment. Recognizing that privilege has its privileges, I have tried to make good use of mine, even if I often found myself on the margins.

Actually, I liked what I found exploring the margins of the road— rose hips, purslane, and arugula, plants like those my older son used to bring home after reading *Stalking the Wild Asparagus*.[3] Getting fired so often turned the periphery into my own stalking ground. The margins became for me, by slow, mostly invisible steps, a new inside path. I realized that change when first I read on a job application how using *The Heath Anthology of American Literature* marked the candidate as culturally in the know.

Coming to the end of this book about a time long past, I remain optimistic. Not because I am unaware of the threats of despotism; I was born in 1932, just as the Nazis were coming to power. I came of age in the midst of Cold War McCarthyism and the protracted ugliness of Roy Cohn and G. David Schine. I have observed close up some of the horrors of segregation and American war-making in Vietnam. I have seen the movement's own discord, our aspirations diminished, our hopes forgone. But I have also seen people rising up, again and again, like sunflowers in a great field. The end to the war on Vietnam stands for me as a symbol and inspiration. *Our Sixties*, this book, does not name a revolution, yet. It is an effort to mobilize for the future what we in the movement have learned from an often frustrating yet hopeful past— compost, perhaps, in nourishing the seeds of humanity's struggle for equality, life, and peace.

Appendix A

A CALL TO RESIST
ILLEGITIMATE AUTHORITY

A number of intellectuals came together to create the "Call to Resist Illegiti-mate Authority." These included Marc Raskin and Arthur Waskow at the Institute for Policy Studies in Washington, DC, Noam Chomsky and others in Cambridge, MA, Donald Kalish at UCLA, and in New York, a group led by Robert Zevin, then a professor of economics at Columbia. It was Zevin who opened an office and hired the first staff person for the organization, Resist, that would attempt to implement the call. These individuals and others circulated the call, mostly by mail, to colleagues and friends.

To the young men of America, to the whole of the American people, and to all men of goodwill everywhere:

1. An ever growing number of young American men are finding that the American war in Vietnam so outrages their deepest moral and religious sense that they cannot contribute to it in any way. We share their moral outrage.

2. We further believe that the war is unconstitutional and illegal. Congress has not declared a war as required by the Constitution. Moreover, under the Constitution, treaties signed by the President and ratified by the Senate have the same force as the Constitution itself. The Charter of the United Nations is such a treaty. The Charter specifically obligates the United States to refrain from force or the threat of force in international relations. It requires member states to exhaust every peaceful means of settling disputes and to submit disputes which cannot be settled peacefully to the Security Council. The United

States has systematically violated all of these Charter provisions for thirteen years.

3. Moreover, this war violates international agreements, treaties and principles of law which the United States Government has solemnly endorsed. The combat role of the United States troops in Vietnam violates the Geneva Accords of 1954 which our government pledged to support but has since subverted. The destruction of rice crops and livestock; the burning and bulldozing of entire villages consisting exclusively of civilian structures; the interning of civilian non-combatants in concentration camps; the summary executions of civilians in captured villages who could not produce satisfactory evidence of their loyalties or did not wish to be removed to concentration camps; the slaughter of peasants who dared to stand up in their fields and shake their fists at American helicopters—these are all actions of the kind which the United States and the other victorious powers of World War II declared to be crimes against humanity for which individuals were to be held personally responsible even when acting under the orders of their governments and for which Germans were sentenced at Nuremberg to long prison terms and death. The prohibition of such acts as war crimes was incorporated in treaty law by the Geneva Conventions of 1949, ratified by the United States. These are commitments to other countries and to Mankind, and they would claim our allegiance even if Congress should declare war.

4. We also believe it is an unconstitutional denial of religious liberty and equal protection of the laws to withhold draft exemption from men whose religious or profound philosophical beliefs are opposed to what in the Western religious tradition have been long known as unjust wars.

5. Therefore, we believe on all these grounds that every free man has a legal right and a moral duty to exert every effort to end this war, to avoid collusion with it, and to encourage others to do the same. Young men in the armed forces or threatened with the draft face the most excruciating choices. For them various forms of resistance risk separation from their families and their country, destruction of their careers, loss of their freedom and loss of their lives. Each must choose the course of resistance dictated by his conscience and circumstances.

Among those already in the armed forces some are refusing to obey specific illegal and immoral orders, some are attempting to educate their fellow servicemen on the murderous and barbarous nature of the war, some are absenting themselves without official leave. Among those not in the armed forces some are applying for status as conscientious objectors to American aggression in Vietnam, some are refusing to be inducted. Among both groups some are resisting openly and paying a heavy penalty, some are organizing more resistance within the United States and some have sought sanctuary in other countries.

6. We believe that each of these forms of resistance against illegitimate authority is courageous and justified. Many of us believe that open resistance to the war and the draft is the course of action most likely to strengthen the moral resolve with which all of us can oppose the war and most likely to bring an end to the war.

7. We will continue to lend our support to those who undertake resistance to this war. We will raise funds to organize draft resistance unions, to supply legal defense and bail, to support families and otherwise aid resistance to the war in whatever ways may seem appropriate.

8. We firmly believe that our statement is the sort of speech that under the First Amendment must be free, and that the actions we will undertake are as legal as is the war resistance of the young men themselves. But we recognize that the courts may find otherwise, and that if so we might all be liable to prosecution and severe punishment. In any case, we feel that we cannot shrink from fulfilling our responsibilities to the youth whom many of us teach, to the country whose freedom we cherish, and to the ancient traditions of religion and philosophy which we strive to preserve in this generation.

9. We call upon all men of good will to join us in this confrontation with immoral authority. Especially we call upon the universities to fulfill their mission of enlightenment and religious organizations to honor their heritage of brotherhood. Now is the time to resist.

Appendix B

SYLLABUS FOR A COURSE ON THE SIXTIES

Date	Reading	Film
Sept. 20	Anne Moody, *Coming of Age in Mississippi*	*Freedom Song*
Sept. 27	Kurt Vonnegut, *Slaughterhouse 5*	*Dr. Strangelove*
Oct. 4	James Baldwin, *The Fire Next Time*	*Berkeley in the Sixties*
	Martin Luther King, Jr., *Letter from a Birmingham Jail*	*Rosa Parks Story* or *King*
Oct. 11	Toni Morrison, *The Bluest Eye*	*Nothing But a Man*
Oct. 18	Amiri Baraka, *Dutchman*	*Malcolm X*
Oct. 25	Poetry from the Civil Rights and Black Arts movements	*Boycott*
Nov. 1	Stories from the Civil Rights movement	*The War at Home* or *Rebels With a Cause*
Nov. 8	Stories from the Vietnam War era	*Platoon*
Nov. 15	Poetry from the Vietnam War era	*Medium Cool*
Nov. 22	Tim O'Brien, *The Things They Carried*	*Sir, No Sir*
Nov. 29	Betty Friedan, "The Problem That Has No Name"	*Growing Up Female*
		Joyce at 34 or *The Heretics*
	Adrienne Rich, "When We Dead Awaken"	
	Linda Nochlin, "Why Have There Been No Great Women Artists?"	
	Kate Millett, from *Sexual Politics*	
	Megan Terry, "Calm Down Mother"	

(continued)

Date	Reading	Film
Dec. 6	Poems by Rich, Sexton, Plath, Lorde, Ginsberg	*Bob & Carol & Ted & Alice*
	Toni Cade Bambara, "The Lesson"	
	Grace Paley, "The Expensive Moment"	
	Lanford Wilson, *The Madness of Lady Bright*	
Dec. 13	Rita Mae Brown, *Rubyfruit Jungle*	*Easy Rider*

NOTES

Chapter One

1. "An unprecedented 67 members of Democratic Socialists of America were elected to municipal and state legislative offices, while two—Alexandria Ocasio-Cortez, from the Bronx, and Rashida Tlaib from Detroit—were elected to Congress." Kurt Stand, "The Election Within the Election," *The Stansbury Forum*, November 13, 2018, https://stansburyforum.com/2018/11/13/the-election-within-the-election. Accessed April 25, 2019.

2. "The New Socialists," *New York Times*, Aug. 24, 2018. https://www.nytimes.com/2018/08/24/opinion/sunday/what-socialism-looks-like-in-2018.html?searchResultPosition=2. Accessed Aug. 24, 2018.

3. Bob Dylan, "Ballad of a Thin Man." *Highway 61 Revisited*, 1965.

4. Jamelle Bouie, "Why Bernie Sanders Isn't Afraid of 'Socialism.'" *New York Times*, June 17, 2019, https://www.nytimes.com/2019/06/17/opinion/bernie-sanders-socialism.html. Accessed June 26, 2019. Bouie points to the contrast with Eugene Debs's 1904 definition of socialism as "first of all a political movement of the working class, clearly defined and uncompromising, which aims at the overthrow of the prevailing capitalist system by securing control of the national government and by the exercise of the public powers, supplanting the existing capitalist class government with socialist administration."

5. Lara Putnam and Theda Skocpol, "Middle America Reboots Democracy," *Democracy, A Journal of Idea*, February 20, 2018, https://democracyjournal.org/arguments/middle-america-reboots-democracy/. Accessed Dec. 29, 2018.

6. Andrew Kopkind, "Doctor's Plot," *New York Review of Books*, June 29, 1967, https://www.nybooks.com/articles/1967/06/29/doctors-plot/. Accessed Sept. 28, 2019. Also, Robert N. Strassfeld, "Vietnam War on Trial: The Court-Martial of Dr. Howard B. Levy," https://scholarlycommons.law.case.edu/cgi/viewcontent.cgi?article=1550&context=faculty_publications. Accessed Sept. 28, 2019. Levy had served as an army doctor for two years before the military tried, as he saw it, to force him to participate in its war on Vietnam by helping train Green Berets. Refusing orders meant he

faced up to eight years in prison; he was sentenced to three years, which he mostly served in Leavenworth.

7. A favorite quote from him was "America's disparity of income is the single most significant and sinister social fact in the nation. Everything comes back to that."

8. "Reflections of a Jewish Activist," *Conservative Judaism* 19 (Summer 1965): 12–21. "Strange Identities and Jewish Politics," *Reconfiguring Jewish-American Identity: Literary and Cultural Essays in an Autobiographical Mode*, Shelley Fisher Fishkin and Jeffrey Rubin-Dorsky, eds. (Madison: University of Wisconsin Press, 1996), 37–46.

9. Sara Germano, "Glory Days: The Unique Legacy of Brooklyn College Newspaper the *Vanguard*," *Columbia Journalism Review*, Sept.-Oct., 2010, https://archives.cjr.org/currents/glory_days.php. Accessed May 6, 2019.

10. The bulk of it was, without my knowing it, published as "Walt Whitman: Lover and Comrade," *The American Imago* 16 (Winter 1959): 407–35. It was reprinted in *The Literary Imagination, Psychoanalysis and the Genius of the Writer*, ed. H. M. Ruitenbeek (Chicago: Quadrangle, 1965).

11. The School of Letters is a whole other book, which no one has yet written.

12. *William C. Bullitt and the Soviet Union* (Bloomington: Indiana University Press, 1967).

13. Her primary work was a well-received book, *Aleksandra Kollontai: Socialism, Feminism and the Bolshevik Revolution* (Palo Alto: Stanford University Press, 1980).

14. Allan R. Brick, *Up From Chester: Hiroshima, Haverford and Beyond* (Bloomington IN: XLibris, 2009).

15. One–fifth of one-forty-second of my year's pay. An absurdity, since I taught six days a week and was involved for far more than forty-two weeks. I should have realized right then what university managers were about.

16. *Massachusetts Collegian* 89, no. 36 (Dec. 14, 1959). The articles were in the *Nation* of Nov. 28, 1959, and Oct. 24, 1959, respectively.

17. Nicole's comment is from the final paragraph of *Tender Is the Night* (1933).

18. Gilbert King, *Devil in the Grove: Thurgood Marshall, the Groveland Boys, and the Dawn of a New America* (New York: Harper Collins, 2012).

19. Robin D. G. Kelley, *Boston Review*, March 7, 2016. On *Portside*, https://portside.org/2016-03-16/black-study-black-struggle. Accessed March 17, 2016. The book he cites is *Lessons from the Damned: Class Struggle in the Black Community* (New York: Times Change Press [distributed by Monthly Review Press], 1973).

20. Benjamin Franklin, from *The Autobiography*, ed. Leonard W. Labaree, in *The Heath Anthology of American Literature*, 7th edition (Boston: Cengage, 2014), Vol. A, 935.

Chapter Two

1. Mickey Flacks and Dick Flacks, *Making History / Making Blintzes; How Two Red Diaper Babies Found Each Other and Discovered America* (New Brunswick: Rutgers University Press, 2018).

2. See a useful contemporary account, Richard Rothstein, "A Short History of ERAP," http://content.cdlib.org/view?docId=kt4k4003k7. Accessed September 27, 2018.

3. Martin Oppenheimer, "Pages from a Journal of the Middle Left," *Radical Sociologists and the Movement: Experiences, Lessons, and Legacies,* ed. Martin Oppenheimer, Martin J. Murray, Rhonda F. Levine (Philadelphia: Temple University Press. 1991), 120.

4. Martin Oppenheimer and George Lakey, *A Manual for Direct Action* (New York: Quadrangle, 1965).

5. Much of the manuscript resides in the sixties archive I set up at the Watkinson Library at Trinity College. It would, I think, have been an impressive volume. The table of contents, as it stood in fall 1963 (I think), was as follows:

Preface: Henry J. Cadbury

Part I: Some History of Nonviolence in America

1. The Social and Political Origins of Nonviolence in America
Mulford Q. Sibley (University of Minnesota)

2. The Quakers and Nonviolence in Pennsylvania
Edwin B. Bronner (Haverford College)

3. Nonviolence and Abolitionism
Louis Filler (Antioch College)

4. Nonviolence and American Foreign Policy in the Ante-Bellum Period
Staughton Lynd (Yale University)

5. Nonviolence in Negro Rights Movements of the Ante-Bellum North
Leon Litwack (University of California, Berkeley)

6. Nonviolence and the Peace Societies in America after 1860
John Swomley (St. Paul School of Theology)

7. Nonviolence and American Labor
Michael Harrington and David C. Smith

8. Conscientious Objection in the United States
Guy Hershberger (Goshen College)

9. The Peace Movement and the Manchurian Crisis
Justus Doenecke (Princeton University)

10. Nonviolence and/or Social Change: The Crisis of the 30s
Charles Chatfield (Wittenberg University)

11. The Sit-In Movement: Origins of a Revolution
Martin Oppenheimer (Bryn Mawr College)

12. The Sit-In Movement
Howard Zinn (Boston University)
Part II: Prospects and Theories of Nonviolence in America
13. The Case of Thoreau: Nonviolence as Means or End
Paul Lauter (American Friends Service Committee)
14. The Violent World of Nonviolence
Irving Louis Horowitz (Washington University)
15. Nonviolence and American Foreign Policy
David McReynolds (War Resisters League)
16. Nonviolence and Social Reconciliation
James Farmer (CORE)
17. The Nonviolence Society and the Nonviolent World
James Bevel (Southern Christian Leadership Conference)

6. F. Hilary Conroy, "The Conference on Peace Research in History: A Memoir," *Journal of Peace Research* 6, No. 4, Special Issue on Peace Research in History (1969): 385–88.

7. "Emerson Through Tillich," *Emerson Society Quarterly* 31 (1962): 49–55.

8. R. W. Emerson, "Self Reliance," in *Heath Anthology*, Vol. B, pp. 1869, 1870.

9. Arthur M. Eckstein, *Bad Moon Rising: How the Weather Underground Beat the FBI and Lost the Revolution* (New Haven: Yale, 2016), 242.

10. See in particular chapter 7, "A Veteran Against War," and chapter 13, "Growing Up Class-Conscious," *You Can't Be Neutral on a Moving Train—A Personal History of Our Times* (Boston: Beacon, 1994), 85–102, 163–82.

11. *A People's History of the United States* (New York: Harper & Row, 1980); *The Indispensable Zinn: The Essential Writings of the "People's Historian,"* ed. Timothy Patrick McCarthy (New York: New Press, 2012).

12. See chapter 11, "In Jail, 'The World Is Topsy-Turvy,'" *You Can't be Neutral*, 141–50.

13. The sharing of syllabi for potentially controversial and often ground-breaking curricula was a particularly effective way of fending off possible complaints from deans or right-wing commentators about such courses. Later such collections of syllabi would become important to the growth of academic women's studies.

14. The History of Non-Violence in America, Staughton Lynd, Spelman College; Seminar on Problems of Peace and Law, Robert Hirschfield, Hunter College; Formulation of International Conflict Issues, Roger Fisher, Harvard University; Psychology of International Relations, Joseph de Rivera, New York University; Social Psychology of Disarmament, Marc Pilisuk, University of Michigan; Problems of Disarmament, Otto Feinstein, Wayne State University; Dynamics of War and Peace, Richard Hathaway, Cambridge Center for Adult Education.

15. The conference also featured a series of disciplinary workshops on research and teaching in economics, geography, education, the

humanities, ethics, history, political science and law, psychology, sociology and anthropology, and the natural sciences. A series of panels dealt with multidisciplinary approaches to peace study, peace study courses and the community, teaching and research, and introducing peace study into the curriculum. A collection of the syllabi and summaries of the workshops and panels was published and distributed by AFSC. Copies of the collection, "Teaching About Peace Issues," and other information about the conference are available in the sixties archive at the Watkinson Library at Trinity College.

16. E.g., Derek Charles Catsam, *Freedom's Main Line: The Journey of Reconciliation and the Freedom Rides* (Lexington, Kentucky: University of Kentucky Press, 2009).

17. Henry David Thoreau, "Civil Disobedience," in *Heath Anthology of American Literature*, B, 1985.

18. See Betty Medsger, *The Burglary: The Discovery of J. Edgar Hoover's Secret FBI* (New York: Vintage, 2014).

19. *The Conspiracy of the Young* (with Florence Howe) (New York & Cleveland: World, 1970).

20. But not together. Though the passion remained, distance prevailed. A few years later, Sue would spend some years in New York working with The Feminist Press. It proved not to be an easy time, and after, we fell out of touch. I wish only that I had written this chapter, and been able to talk about it with her, before she passed away at age 91 in September 2016.

21. "Chester Report, Submitted by the Swarthmore College Chapter of Students for a Democratic Society," http://www.educationanddemocracy. org/FSCfiles/C_CC2b_ChesterPA.htm. Accessed Feb. 13, 2016.

Chapter Three

1. The film was written and directed by Phil Alden Robinson and co-written by Stanley Weiser. It is particularly good in presenting characters who embody recognizable leaders in the Mississippi freedom movement, like Bob Moses. I regularly used it in teaching a course for students at Trinity on the 1960s.

2. Perhaps the best single book about living black in Mississippi is Anne Moody's *Coming of Age in Mississippi* (New York: Dell, 1972; original, 1968). The richest historical account of Mississippi and the movement that I know of is John Dittmer, *Local People: The Struggle for Civil Rights in Mississippi* (Urbana: University of Illinois Press, 1994). Also excellent is Bruce Watson, *Freedom Summer: The Savage Season That Made Mississippi Burn and Made America a Democracy* (New York: Viking, 2010).

3. "Negro Voters by District and County, 1963." COFO leaflet in possession of the author. Now in sixties archive at Watkinson Library, Trinity College. The statistics are drawn from the *Congressional Quarterly*, week ending

July 5, 1963, 1,091–1,093. The leaflet is reproduced in *Risking Everything*, 113–15.

4. See, for example, https://www.aclu.org/issues/voting-rights/fighting-voter-suppression.

5. Jerry DeMuth, "'A Guide to Mississippi,' Spring 1964," in *Risking Everything*, ed. Michael Edmonds (Madison, WI: Wisconsin Historical Society Press, 2014), 5.

6. Ibid., 13.

7. See Charles E. Cobb Jr., *On the Road to Freedom: A Guided Tour of the Civil Rights Train* (Chapel Hill: Algonquin Books, 2008). Cobb's discussion of the hideous violence (and absurdity) of McComb is on 282–91.

8. See particularly Akinyele K. Umoja, "1964: The Beginning of the End of Nonviolence in the Mississippi Freedom Movement," *Radical History Review* 85 (Winter 2003): 201–26.

9. Dittmer, *Local People*; Charles M. Payne, *I've Got the Light of Freedom: The Organizing Tradition and the Mississippi Freedom Struggle* (Berkeley: University of California Press, 1995); Taylor Branch, *Pillar of Fire: America in the King Years*, 1963–1964 (New York: Simon & Schuster Inc., 1998).

10. "Overview of the Freedom Schools," summer 1964, mimeographed leaflet in possession of the author. Now in the sixties archive at Watkinson Library, Trinity College.

11. Much of the freedom school curriculum is reproduced in issue 40 of *Radical Teacher* (Fall 1991) and is therefore available through JSTOR and other online databases.

12. "Freedom School Workshop, Interim Report," November 16 [1964], mimeographed leaflet in possession of author. Now in sixties archive at Watkinson Library, Trinity College.

13. The phrase is Jay Gillen's and constitutes part of the title of his book about the Baltimore Algebra Project, *Educating for Insurgency: The Roles of Young People in Schools of Poverty* (Oakland: AK Press, 2014). The Algebra Projects in Baltimore, Boston, and elsewhere were initially organized by Bob Moses, who as a SNCC staff person was instrumental in starting the Mississippi project, including the freedom schools. My own review of Gillen's book appeared in *Radical Teacher* 102 (2015), http://radicalteacher.library.pitt.edu/ojs/index.php/radicalteacher/article/view/216; and also in a slightly different form in Diane Ravitch's blog, http://dianeravitch.net/2015/06/30/paul-lauter-reviews-jay-gillens-educating-for-insurgency-note-live-by-tests-die-by-tests/.

14. J. Saunders Redding, *Lonesome Road: The Story of the Negro's Part in America* (New York: Doubleday, 1958).

15. Phil Ochs, "Ballad of William Worthy" (1964): "William Worthy isn't worthy to enter our door / Went down to Cuba, he's not American anymore." Ochs was arguably the singer of the sixties most fully involved in the movement. Worthy, one of the preeminent journalists of the time, wrote for over twenty-five years for the *Baltimore Afro-American*. He reported

from a number of countries—like Cuba, China, Cambodia, and Iran—which the US State department had forbidden Americans to visit.

16. Leake County, Mississippi. See Winson Hudson and Constance Curry, *Mississippi Harmony: Memoirs of a Freedom Fighter* (New York: Palgrave McMillan, 2002).

17. One of the ways in which that worked is wonderfully illustrated in the 2016 film *Two Trains Runnin'*, which is about the movement in the summer of 1964 juxtaposed with the search for forgotten Mississippi country blues singers like Son House and Skip James.

18. Bernice Johnson Reagon, organizer and lead singer of Sweet Honey in the Rock, made the remark at a conference on SNCC, organized by Cheryl Greenberg and held at Trinity College in Spring 1988.

19. I have been quoting from my letter to *Harvard Educational Review*, Summer 1965, 367–68. I continued: "And here they probably differed most profoundly from colleges, in which the whole approach to knowledge, emphasizing as it does objective, permanent 'truth' and seeking to eliminate subjective, emotional responses, effectually denies—especially in the central intellectual experience of the classroom—the importance of the student himself."

20. "Declaration of Independence by the Freedom School Students of St. John's Methodist Church, Palmer's Crossing, Hattiesburg, Miss." Mimeographed sheet in possession of author, now at Watkinson Library, Trinity College, sixties collection. This declaration of independence, which is about six paragraphs long, was discussed and, with some changes, adopted at the convention.   .

21. KIPP is the name of the Knowledge is Power Program charter school network.

Consider the following set of instructions I found on the wall of a school in working-class Berlin and the relationship of such a pedagogy to the rise of national socialism some twenty years later:

Die Schüler sitzen gerade.

Die Hände liegen geschlossen auf dem Tisch.

Die Füsse stehen nebeneinander auf dem Boden.

Die Schüler schauen dem Lehrer in die Augen.

Lachen, Flüsteren, Sprechen, Herumrücken and Herumgucken sind verboten.

Die Schüler melden sich mit dem Ziegerfinger der rechten Hand. Die Linke Hand stützt den Ellebogen.

(1908, Berlin)

Students must sit up straight.

Hands must be kept together on the desk (table).

Feet must be placed side by side on the floor.

Students must keep their eyes on the teacher.

Laughing, whispering, talking, moving, or looking around are forbidden.

Students must announce themselves with the pointer finger of the right hand, the left hand supporting the elbow.

[My translations.]

22. Paulo Freire, "The Banking Model of Education," from *Pedagogy of the Oppressed*, in Eugene F. Provenzo, ed., *Critical Issues in Education: An Anthology of Readings* (Thousand Oaks, CA: Sage Publications, 2006), 106–19.

23. Jules Henry, *Culture Against Man* (New York: Random House, 1963). The literature on this subject is immense and I do not wish to begin recapitulating it here. Actually, the Wikipedia entry on "learning theory (education)" has a quite useful summary of various theories and a helpful set of references. The section on "transfer of learning" is particularly worthwhile.

24. A number of which we collected for a small volume entitled *Freedom School Poetry* that SNCC later published (1965), with a brief forward by Langston Hughes and a dedication to Emmett Till. The poems were subsequently reprinted in *Letters from Mississippi: Reports from Civil Rights Volunteers & Poetry of the 1964 Freedom Summer*, ed. Elizabeth Martinez (Brookline, MA: Zephyr Press, 2007), 279–315.

25. *Letters from Mississippi*, 295.

26. *Letters from Mississippi*, 311.

27. The version of the poem we initially collected from a freedom school newsletter was called "The Negro Soldier."

28. See my "Caste and Race in the Shaping of the American Literary Canon: A Case Study from the Twenties," *Feminist Studies* 9 (Fall 1983): 435–63. Reprinted in *Feminist Criticism and Social Change*, Judith Newton and Deborah Rosenfelt, eds. (London: Methuen, 1985), 19–44.

29. For example, John Guillory, *Cultural Capital: The Problem of Literary Canon Formation* (Chicago: University of Chicago Press, 1993).

30. Paul Lauter, "Canon Formation," in David Wyatt, ed., *American Literature in Transition, 1960–1970.* (Cambridge: Cambridge University Press, 2018), 352–65.

31. Rev. Charles Sherrod, "Notes on the Democratic National Convention Challenge," in *Risking Everything*, 184.

32. But see Kali Akuno and Ajamu Nangwaya, with Cooperation Jackson, *Jackson Rising: The Struggle for Economic Democracy and Black Self-Determination in Jackson, Mississippi* (Jackson: Daraja Press, 2017). The book may, or may not, speak to that question.

33. *Letters from Mississippi*, ed. Martinez: 347–71.

Chapter Four

1. Flyer dated October 7, 1964, in possession of author, now at Watkinson Library, Trinity College, sixties collection.

2. Flyer in possession of the author, now at Watkinson Library, Trinity College, sixties collection.

3. A detailed account of the events over a number of days can be found in the *The Amherst Student*, XCIX, no. 41 (April 1, 1965): 1–3.

4. Junius Williams, "Selma Marchers Jailed, Segregated in Alabama Prison," *The Amherst Student*, XCIX, no. 41 (April 1, 1965): 5.

5. Flacks and Flacks, *Making History*, 208.

6. His pamphlet, "How the US Got Involved in Vietnam" (Santa Barbara: Center for the Study of Democratic Institutions, 1965), was a particular favorite. An excellent current equivalent that helps to explain the depth and passion of the antiwar movement is the opening chapter, "Moral Imperatives: The Reasons for Radicals," in William H. Tucker, *Princeton Radicals of the 1960s, Then and Now* (Jefferson, NC: McFarland & Company, Inc., 2015), 19–54.

7. Marvin E. Gettleman, *Vietnam: History, Documents, and Opinions on a Major World Crisis* (New York: Fawcett Publications, 1965). Todd Gitlin had assembled a brief bibliography of works about Vietnam in connection with the April 17 March on Washington. It featured work by Bernard Fall, and a number of pamphlets distributed by the SDS Peace Research and Education Project. Flyer in possession of the author, now at Watkinson Library, Trinity College, sixties collection.

8. "Transcript of original 1965 speech by Paul Potter," https://www.marktribe.net/port-huron-project/we-must-name-the-system-paul-potter-1965-2007. Accessed 4/10/2017.

9. The novelist Viet Thanh Nguyen recently commented in "The Great Vietnam War Novel Was Not Written by an American," *New York Times*, May 2, 2017: "Immersed in the stories, feelings and memories of the Vietnamese refugee community in which I grew up, I was determined to tell some of those stories, for I knew that Americans as a whole knew very little about them. Only a small cadre of Americans believed that it was necessary and urgent to learn more about Vietnamese voices and experiences, without which a more complete American understanding of the Vietnam War would never happen. American ignorance of Vietnamese history, culture and politics helped draw the United States into a war and a country that it did not comprehend. This pattern of ignorance arguably continues today, both in terms of what Americans continue to ignore about Vietnam and what Americans refuse to know about the Middle East. Literature plays an important role as a corrective to this ignorance." https://www.nytimes.com/2017/05/02/opinion/vietnam-war-novel-was-not-written-by-an-american.html. Accessed May 5, 2017.

Chapter Five

1. Like other NDEA seminars, this one was addressed to inner-city teachers. It may have been unique, however, in bringing a group of students to participate in the work of the institute. Our plan was to try illustrating the kind of teaching we wished to promote by having one of the institute staff, Florence

Howe, teaching the students and encouraging the students to participate in a variety of opportunities to reflect on what the seminar was accomplishing.

2. Allan R. Brick, "Final Report on the National Defense Education Act Institute for Teachers of Disadvantaged Youth," Code GE-7441, Goucher College, 1965, 7.

3. Brick, "Final Report," 5.

4. Brick, "Final Report," 31.

5. See Jay Gillen, *Educating for Insurgency.*

6. As a teacher, dean, and Democratic Party activist, Lowenstein played a significant role in recruiting young, mainly white, liberal students to join in civil rights work. Sweeney had been one of his recruits at Stanford but had become a paranoid schizophrenic, possibly from the stress of Mississippi activism. See Richard Cummings, *The Pied Piper: Allard K. Lowenstein and the Liberal Dream* (New York: Grove/Atlantic, 1985).

7. Mimeographed leaflet in possession of author, now in the sixties collection at the Watkinson Library, Trinity College.

8. Unpublished manuscript in possession of author, now in the sixties collection at the Watkinson Library, Trinity College.

9. Unpublished manuscript in possession of author, now in the sixties collection at the Watkinson Library, Trinity College. It is worth pointing out that even later, when Martin Luther King Jr. came out against the war (April 4, 1967), he was condemned for precisely the same reasons: Both the *Washington Post* and *New York Times* published editorials criticizing the speech, with the *Post* noting that King's speech had "diminished his usefulness to his cause, to his country, and to his people" through a simplistic and flawed view of the situation ("A Tragedy," April 6, 1967). Similarly, both the National Association for the Advancement of Colored People and Ralph Bunche accused King of linking two disparate issues, Vietnam and civil rights. https://kinginstitute.stanford.edu/encyclopedia/bunche-ralph-johnson. Accessed March 4, 2016.

10. One of the favorite inside jokes among some SNCC activists was calling it the "Student Non-Coordinated Violence Committee."

11. Annelieke Dirks, "Between Threat and Reality: The National Association for the Advancement of Colored People and the Emergence of Armed Self-Defense in Clarksdale and Natchez, Mississippi, 1960–1965," *Journal for the Study of Radicalism* 1, no. 1 (2007): 71–93.

12. See Allan Brick, *Up From Chester,* 117–24, for a particularly insightful discussion.

Chapter Six

1. Most Americans were just beginning to identify the "NLF" as the National Liberation Front, the primary protagonist of guerilla action against the Saigon government.

2. Larry Rottmann, Jan Barry, Basil T. Paquet, eds., *Winning Hearts and Minds* (Brooklyn, NY, First Casualty Press, 1972), 101.

3. Carl Oglesby, "Let Us Shape the Future," in Mitchell Cohen and Dennis Hale, eds., *The New Student Left* (Boston: Beacon Press, 1967), 316; also http://www.studentsforademocraticsociety.org/documents/oglesby_future.html.

4. The main SDS flyer announcing the march argued that the war was not aggression from the North but a civil war, that it was a "losing war," a "self-defeating war," a "dangerous war," and one not declared by Congress. And, finally, that "it is a hideously *immoral* war. America is committing pointless murder." "A CALL TO ALL STUDENTS TO March on Washington to end the war in Vietnam." Flyer in possession of the author, now at Watkinson Library, Trinity College, sixties collection.

5. http://www.studentsforademocraticsociety.org/documents/paul_potter.html.

6. Oglesby, "Let Us Shape the Future," 318; also http://www.studentsforademocraticsociety.org/documents/oglesby_future.html.

7. W. S. Gilbert, "When All Night Long a Chap Remains," *Iolanthe*, Act II.

8. For a somewhat different take on the relationship between liberalism and the radicalism of the New Left, see Steve Max and Doug Ireland, "As the New Left Views Liberalism," May 5, 1967. Article available in Watkinson Library, Trinity College, sixties collection.

9. James Russell Lowell, *The Biglow Papers*, Series I (1848), no. 1, "A Letter From Mr. Ezekiel Biglow of Jaalam to the Hon. Joseph T. Buckingham, Editor of the Boston Courier, Inclosing a Poem of His Son, Mr. Hosea Biglow," Stanza 5.

10. Speech of January 12, 1848, in the US House of Representatives. See https://teachingamericanhistory.org/library/document/the-war-with-mexico-speech-in-the-united-states-house-of-representatives/.

11. Bernard DeVoto had put it this way in 1952: "One of the facts which define the United States is that its national and its imperial boundaries are the same"; from *The Course of Empire* (Boston: Houghton Mifflin, 1952), xiii. Even in 1968, Oscar Handlin in his important classroom text argued that "the experiment in imperialism at the turn of the century had been confusing, because it made the United States party to a kind of domination most Americans did not wish to exercise. After 1900, therefore, they had attempted to withdraw from colonialism, but they still hoped to play an important role in world affairs"; from *The History of the United States* (New York: Holt, Rinehart and Winston, 1967–68, II), 353. As late as 1973, Ernest N. Paolino in his book on William Henry Seward felt constrained to argue against Samuel Flagg Bemis's contention that the Spanish-American War was a "Great Aberration" in American politics; from *The Foundations of the American Empire: William Henry Seward and U.S. Foreign Policy* (Ithaca, NY: Cornell University Press, 1973).

12. American studies gave concrete expression to such exceptionalism by designating particular myths or symbols to explain the uniqueness of the United States. The best known myths and symbols scholars focused upon differed, to be sure: an "Errand into the Wilderness" (Perry Miller), "Virgin Land" (Henry Nash Smith), "the Machine in the Garden" (Leo Marx), the "American Adam" (R. W. B. Lewis). I came to see that what these works had in common—in addition to the idea that something remained exceptional about American culture and society—was their focus on the experiences and perspectives of white, Protestant men. These theories tended to focus on religious communities in New England or on pioneering into the vast midlands of the continent. But none looked at slavery and racism as central to the emergence of American society and its economic structure, nor did they consider how different might the experiences of women be from those of American men.

13. Gary North, *The Libertarian Roots of the All-Volunteer Military*, https://www.lewrockwell.com/2003/12/gary-north/the-libertarian-roots-of-the-volunteer-military/. Accessed March 1, 2016.

14. Kyle Longley "The Grunt's War," *New York Times*, Feb. 17, 2017.

15. One version, an improvement on the long-time CCCO "Men of Draft Age" poster, read: "The U.S. draft law provides alternatives to service in the armed forces for men whose conscience is opposed to war. You should know what your rights and opportunities are. You may be a 'conscientious objector' to war.

If you are against war and want more information about the draft and constructive non-military ways to serve and to help remove the causes of war . . . ." This version ended, all in caps, "KNOW YOUR ALTERNATIVES." Another version said: "The U.S. draft law provides for noncombat and non-military service. There are other ways to serve your country. If you are against war and killing, and want more information about constructive ways to serve . . . ." This version ended, also in caps, "CHOOSE BEFORE YOU ENLIST."

16. http://www.sds-1960s.org/Guide-to-CO.pdf. Accessed April 16, 2016.

17. These flyers and pamphlets are all available in the sixties archive located at the Watkinson Library of Trinity College.

18. Longley, "The Grunt's War," Feb. 17, 2017.

19. Sol Tax, *The Draft: A Handbook of Facts and Alternatives* (Chicago: University of Chicago Press, 1967).

20. My own attack on proponents of versions of national service, including Margaret Mead, Morris Janowitz, and Terrence Cullinan—all of whom prepared papers for the conference—is contained in "Toward Democratic Service," a paper circulated with a number of others during the meetings. I argued that voluntary service, administered by elected boards, might provide for the common good without the authoritarian goals and totalitarian apparatus of what I called "universal servitude."

The paper is available in the sixties archive located at the Watkinson Library of Trinity College.

21. See Paul Lauter, Richard Flacks, and Florence Howe, "The Draft: Reform or Resistance," *Liberation* (January 1967): 34–39.

22. North, *Libertarian Roots.*

23. Kyle Longley "The Grunt's War," Feb. 17, 2017.

24. Peter Henig, "Selective Service System Or, the Manpower Channelers" (Boston: New England Free Press, [1967]). A reprint from New Left Notes of January 20, 1967.

25. Cathy Wilkerson, *Flying Close to the Sun: My Life and Times as a Weatherman* (NY: Seven Stories Press, 2007), 106–7.

26. In 1967 alone, 1,648 men were prosecuted for variously violating Selective Service statutes, most for refusing the draft. Of those, 952 were convicted.

27. New York: Oliver Layton Press (and also Birth Press), 1966. Some examples: 10) Invent a time machine and go back to the 19th century. 11) Start to menstruate. (Better red than dead.) 13) Advocate sexual freedom for children. 14) Shoot up for a day. 37) Proclaim that Mao Tse-tung is the Living God. 50) Ride naked through the streets on white horse. 101) Grow a long straggly black beard with maggots crawling all over it.

28. DCAS Vietnam Conflict Extract File record counts by INCIDENT OR DEATH DATE (Year) (as of April 29, 2008), http://www.archives.gov/research/military/vietnam-war/casualty-statistics.html#date.   Accessed August 3, 2016.

29. For a striking instance, see Hillary Clinton: "I still believe in American exceptionalism," http://www.cbsnews.com/videos/hillary-clinton-i-still-believe-in-american-exceptionalism. Accessed August 6, 2016.

30. http://leavesofgrass.org/vos/. Accessed March 1, 2016.

31. "Draft Reform and Draft Resistance," 34–39.

32. Richard Flacks, Florence Howe, and Paul Lauter, "The Draft: Dodging the Issues," *New York Review of Books* 5 (April 6, 1967): 3–5.

33. Paul Lauter and Florence Howe, *The Conspiracy of the Young* (Cleveland: World, 1970).

34. The most useful account of NCNP I have found is Simon Hall, "'On the Tail of the Panther': Black Power and the 1967 Convention of the National Conference for New Politics," *Journal of American Studies* 37, no. 1 (Apr. 2003): 59–78. Renata Adler had a comical but vicious takedown of the actual Chicago convention in the *New Yorker*, "Letter from the Palmer House," September 23, 1967, https://www.newyorker.com/magazine/1967/09/23/letter-from-the-palmer-house.

35. Martin Peretz, "The American Left & Israel," *Commentary*, Nov. 1, 1967, 28, https://www.commentarymagazine.com/articles/the-american-left-israel/.

36. There are slightly different accounts of this event in different sources—e.g., Jo Freeman, http://www.jofreeman.com/socialmovements/

origins.htm, accessed March 4, 2016; and Alice Echols, "Daring to Be Bad": *Radical Feminism in America, 1967–1975* (Minneapolis: University of Minnesota Press, 1989). But in all cases it has been seen as an iconic moment in the development of the women's liberation movement.

Chapter Seven

1. A. Harry Passow et al., *Toward Creating A Model Urban School System: A Study of the Washington, D.C. Public Schools* (New York: Columbia Univ., Teachers College, 1967), 276. http://files.eric.ed.gov/fulltext/ ED013288.pdf. Accessed April 13, 2016. We had access to some of the material in the Passow report before the term at Morgan began. A couple of additional comments from the report might be useful: "In the three grades visited the children were told what to do, how to do it, and were expected to unquestioningly follow the teachers' directions. The children sang when instructed to do so, chorused responses when given recognized signals, and worked on written assignments, copying exercises from the chalkboard. The children spent most of the day writing at their desks, rarely speaking except in chorus. No one argued, disagreed, or questioned anything. At no time when I was in the room did any child ask a question" (277).

"The many observations that made this same point lead to the conclusion that children in the elementary schools visited by this task force were having *abundant opportunities to overlearn passive conformity*. When the teacher has all the ideas, gives all the directions, handles all the materials, and admonishes the children to sit still and not talk—if they do not rebel or withdraw completely—most children respond with an unquestioning acceptance of the teacher's rulings on all matters. For instance, 'a child was not allowed to color his Hallowe'en pumpkin green, even though the teacher had just read a poem referring to the green of a pumpkin when it was small'" (277—my italics).

2. https://bit.ly/39DoBDI.

3. Manuscript in Morgan Community School file, Watkinson Library, Trinity College, Hartford, CT.

4. Some statistics, mainly gathered from the lawsuit of Julius Hobson against the Washington, DC, school system (Hobson v. Hansen) are relevant here. In areas in which the median income was $3,999 or less, the average per-pupil expenditure was $309, and 46% of the teachers were temporary (i.e., inexperienced). In areas (predominantly white) in which the median income was $11,000–$12,000, the average per-pupil expenditure was $438, and 23% or under of the teachers were temporary. In areas of $3,872 median income, 85% of the students were in the basic or general tracks, which did not lead on to college. In areas

of $10,364 median income, 8% were in the general track, there being no basic track at all. 74% of the students in basic or general tracks were placed there without examinations; about two-thirds of the students in basic track were found to be misplaced when they were tested after Hobson's suit was filed. Painfully low expectations, rotten schools, nonexistent facilities such as libraries, inexperienced and constantly changing teachers condemned students, mainly African American, to an "education" in Washington as seriously defective as that provided to black students in Mississippi.

5. I wrote about these problems in "The Short Happy Life of the Adams-Morgan Community School Project," *Harvard Educational Review* 38 (Spring 1968): 235–62. That article provides a much more detailed analysis of the project, including the differentiated staffing policy, relations to the community, our pre-service institute, and the like.

6. The unit continued: "Pretend you are on welfare. You have five children. You owe twenty-five for rent. One of your children needs special shoes and they cost twenty-five dollars. Would you pay the rent or buy the shoes? Is it right that you should have to make such a decision? What happens if you can't pay the rent? Read 'The Ballad of the Landlord' by Langston Hughes. Who is Langston Hughes? Why didn't the man pay his rent? Why was the man arrested? Read a story by Langston Hughes and share it with the class."

7. One of the Antioch interns, John E. Cawthorne, who happened to be black, created a wonderful unit on "hipness" for seven eight-to-ten-year-olds who were "slow readers." The unit involved using language the students knew but were heavily discouraged from using in school, in order to extend their vocabularies, to write and talk about stories they rendered in "hip" language, and generally to find out more about school and "outside" talk. The unit is available in the Morgan Community School file, Watkinson Library, Trinity College, Hartford, CT.

8. Flyer in Morgan Community School file, Watkinson Library, Trinity College, Hartford, CT.

9. David L. Kirp, "Who Needs Charters When You Have Public Schools Like These?" *New York Times Sunday Review*, April 2, 2017, 2.

10. Paul Lauter and Florence Howe, "Urban Schools: The School Mess in Washington," *New York Review of Books* 10 (Feb. 1, 1968): 16–21.

11. Report of October 11, 1967. In possession of the author, and now in the sixties archive at the Watkinson Library of Trinity College.

12. David L. Kirp, "Who Needs Charters," 2.

· 13. In the battle over the Ocean Hill–Brownsville schools between the teachers' union and advocates of community control, the UFT had quoted my *Harvard Educational Review* article to support its case against school decentralization. The *New York Times* agreed to publish my long letter disputing the UFT's conclusions and reasserting my support for community control, Sept. 11, 1968.

14. "Draft Reform and Draft Resistance," 34–39; "The American Draft and Its Opponents," *La democracie nouvelle* (Spring 1967), 116–20; "The Draft: Dodging the Issues, 3–5; "Rising Opposition to the Draft," 25–31.

15. Gillen, *Educating for Insurgency.*

16. The preference for charter schools on the part of educational "reformers" is hard to understand apart from the ideological belief that privatization, and the profit-making it makes possible, is desirable. Research on charters is far too conflicted to begin citing here, so I will restrain myself to one reference. In 2013 the Center for Research on Education Outcomes at Stanford University, which favors educational "reform," published a major study. It concluded that about 27 percent of charters performed better than district schools serving equivalent student populations; about 25 percent performed worse; the rest were about the same. CREDO (Center for Research on Education Outcomes), National Charter School Study, Executive Summary 2013 (Stanford, CA: Center for Research on Education Outcomes, 2013), 23. See also Julian Vasquez Heilig, "National and Urban NAEP Results: Neighborhood Public Schools 23, Charters 4," *Cloaking Inequity,* May 16, 2017, https://cloakinginequity.com/2017/05/16/national-and-urban-naep-results-neighborhood-public-schools-23-charters-4/. Accessed May 19, 2017. The literature on charter schools is too vast to begin suggesting more references here, but the index to Diane Ravitch's blog is one helpful starting place. For a particularly egregious instance of charter profiteering, see http://www.dispatch.com/news/20170730/how-ecot-founder-william-lager-cooked-up-lucrative-charter-school. Accessed August 1, 2017. See also, "Ohio: Close Down This Phony 'School'!" on Diane Ravitch's blog for August 1, 2017.

17. E.g., "FOR-PROFIT COLLEGES: Undercover Testing Finds Colleges Encouraged Fraud and Engaged in Deceptive and Questionable Marketing Practices," GAO-10-948T, August 4, 2010, http://www.gao.gov/new.items/d10948t.pdf. Accessed April 10, 2016. Also, A.J. Angulo, *Diploma Mills: How For-Profit Colleges Stiffed Students, Taxpayers, and the American Dream* (Baltimore: Johns Hopkins Press, 2016).

18. "Test scores are collected and then marketed by greatschools.org. This nonprofit is a sophisticated and well-funded system for gathering test scores and other information about students and parents, then selling that information. The website literally sells ads and licenses for access to test scores and other data on schools—public, private, and charter—with expansions planned for pre-school and day-care centers.

"This national data hog is funded by billionaire foundations unfriendly to public schools. The logos of the Gates, Walton, Robertson, and Arnold Foundations are prominently displayed. A list of 19 other supporters includes the Friedman Foundation for Educational Choice, Bradley Foundation, Goldman Sachs Gives, and New Schools Venture Fund among others. All of these supporters want to make public schools an artifact from the past." Laura Chapman on Diane Ravitch's blog, April 10, 2016, accessed April 10, 2016. See also David Rosen and Aaron Santesso, "Surveillance and Education," *Birkbeck Law Review* 2, 2 (December 2014): 229–44, accessed April 11, 2016.

19. Florence Howe and Paul Lauter, "How the School System Is Rigged for Failure," *The New York Review of Books* XIV (June 18, 1970): 14–21.

20. See, for example, P. L. Thomas, "The Self-Fulfilling Prophesy: Failing Public Schools," https://radicalscholarship.wordpress.com/2017/03/06/the-self-fulfilling-prophesy-failing-public-schools/. Accessed July 25, 2017.

21. Interestingly analyzed in what is not a very good movie, *Killing Ed*, and also in a series of posts on Diane Ravitch's blog.

22. See Tanya Clay House, *Grading the States June 2018: A Report Card on Our Nation's Commitment to Public Schools* (New York: Network for Public Education and the Schott Foundation for Public Education, 2018), accessed June 21, 2018.

23. Rann Miller, "Why the NAACP Said 'Enough' to School Privatization," *AlterNet*, July 27, 2017, http://www.alternet.org/print/naacp-school-privatization. Accessed August 13, 2017. Miller provides a useful summary of the arguments "reformers" are making: "Here is what the abandonment of the public responsibility for educating all kids looks like. State policymakers declare themselves fed up with overseeing underperforming public schools in poor Black and Brown neighborhoods. Some policymakers, at the behest of their constituents, rather than seeking solutions to improve these schools, tell families that the schools are so bad that they can't be improved. Families are then told that 'experts' will be invited to improve the education of their children. This 'strategy' takes the burden of educating poor children of color off of the state, which many believe is a waste of tax money considering the continuous underperformance of city schools. This strategy also paints education policymakers in an innovative light; they look as though they are thinking outside the box to attack a problem largely created as a result of the state's own negligence."

Chapter Eight

1. The text of the "Call to Resist Illegitimate Authority" can be found in appendix A.

2. Edward C. Burke, "320 Vow to Help Draft Resisters, Some Plan Disobedience to Challenge Government," *New York Times*, Sept. 27, 1967.

3. See Michael S. Foley, *Confronting the War Machine: Draft Resistance during the Vietnam War* (Chapel Hill: University of North Carolina Press, 2003).

4. Norman Mailer, *The Armies of the Night: History as a Novel/The Novel as History* (New York: New American Library, 1968).

5. Robert Bly, *The Teeth Mother Naked at Last* (San Francisco: City Lights, 1970), II, 28–29, 31.

6. For a glimpse of the demonstration from the other side, see Sherwood Rudin, "I Defended the Pentagon in 1967, but I Was Torn Between Duty and Conscience," https://nyti.ms/39Hv54s. Accessed Oct. 26, 2018.

7. New York and Cleveland: World, 1970.

8. Signers, apart from Chomsky, included Robert McAfee Brown, the Rev. Dr. Martin Luther King Jr., Dwight Macdonald, and Howard Zinn.

9. Details about the activities of Resist are drawn from two sources in the archives at the Watkinson Library at Trinity College: First, the Resist papers, which contain board minutes, fundraising appeals, materials from a large variety of applicants for Resist funding. Second, the sixties archive I established at the Watkinson Library, which contains much personal correspondence, as well as early Resist minutes and the like.

10. The most comprehensive account of the Catonsville Nine is Shawn Francis Peters, *The Catonsville Nine: A Story of Faith and Resistance in the Vietnam Era* (New York: Oxford, 2012).

11. Letter to the SDS newspaper, *New Left Notes*.

12. The most devastating account of the war from a civilian perspective is provided by Martha Hess, *Then The Americans Came* (New Brunswick: Rutgers University Press, 1993). A useful brief summary is offered by Mike Hastie in "The Purposeful Killing of Civilians in War: Voices From Vietnam," *Counterpunch*, Sept. 29, 2017, https://www.counterpunch.org/2017/09/29/the-purposeful-killing-of-civilians-in-war-voices-from-vietnam/. Accessed October 2, 2017.

13. *Ramparts*, February 1966.

14. My view of the Burns and Novick film is contained in "Ten Questions to Help View the Burns & Novick PBS Vietnam War Series with a Critical Eye," prepared by Paul Lauter, professor emeritus, Trinity College (with help from his friends), http://www.vietnampeace.org/blog/10-questions.

15. One of the fullest accounts of the problems in the leadership of the North is that of Max Hastings in *Vietnam: An Epic Tragedy, 1945–75* (New York: HarperCollins Publishers, 2018).

Chapter Nine

1. Louis Kampf and I wrote about that event in the introduction to *The Politics of Literature* (New York: Pantheon, 1970), 34–40.

2. Flacks and Flacks, 266–68.

3. Fred L. Pincus and Howard J. Ehrlich, "The New University Conference: A Study of Former Members," *Critical Sociology* 15, no. 2 (summer 1988): 145–47.

4. Agnes Smedley, *Battle Hymn of China* (New York: Victor Gollancz, 1943).

5. By way of a number of issues of a *Newsletter of the Radical Caucus in English and the Modern Languages*, edited by Elaine Reuben and Frank Battaglia.

Chapter Ten

1. *Ramparts*, February 1966. The following year Duncan published *The New Legions* (New York: Random House, 1967), which provided even more detail about the brutal and failing regime in the South and the ruthless policies being taught and implemented by US soldiers like those Duncan had himself trained.

2. He is featured in David Zeiger's film about the GI antiwar movement, *Sir, No Sir.*

3. Generally taken to mean "Fuck the Army," the acronym provided GI wits with many other naming opportunities.

4. James Lewes has located and scanned some 864 separate titles of these newspapers. The number of individual issues of newspapers, newsletters, and related mailings as Lewes has counted them comes to 7,520 items. These are now available through the Wisconsin Historical Society and the Swarthmore Peace Collection.

5. See Heonik Kwon, *After the Massacre: Commemoration and Consolation in Ha My and My Lai* (Berkeley: University of California Press, 2006). Also, Lady Borton, "Overlooking My Lai," http://vietnamfulldisclosure.org/index.php/overlooking-my-lai/. Accessed Oct. 1, 2017. "In Quang Ngai Province, massacres large and small were SOP—standard operating procedure. If there is to be blame, the responsibility rests on all adult Americans from that time. Through our taxes, we paid the sergeants and the GIs; we bought the cluster bombs, the M-16 rifles, that helicopter, those grenades . . . . Moreover, the *Newsweek* reporter had missed this deeper, devastating fact: In Quang Ngai Province, as Nick Turse has documented in *Kill Anything That Moves*, massacres by Americans happened all the time."

See also the following sites:

https://en.wikipedia.org/wiki/B%C3%ACnh_H%C3%B2a_massacre
https://en.wikipedia.org/wiki/Binh_Tai_Massacre
https://en.wikipedia.org/wiki/B%C3%ACnh_An/T%C3%A2y_Vinh_massacre
https://en.wikipedia.org/wiki/H%C3%A0_My_massacre
https://en.wikipedia.org/wiki/Son_Thang_massacre

6. See Col. Robert D. Heinl Jr., "The Collapse of the Armed Forces," *Armed Forces Journal*, June 7, 1971. It needs to be pointed out that Heinl is using this "collapse" to criticize the antiwar movement.

7. "Between 1 July 1966 and 31 December 1973, there had been 503,926 incidents of desertion in all services during the Vietnam War," according to

a 1974 Defense Department report, http://www.encyclopedia.com/social-sciences-and-law/law/crime-and-law-enforcement/desertion. Accessed May 4, 2017. Source: *The Oxford Companion to American Military History*, ed. John Whiteclay Chambers (New York: Oxford University Press, 2000).

8. The Pentagon reported that in 1970 killings by fragging had more than doubled from the previous year (209, up from 96). In one particularly notorious instance a GI underground newspaper, *GI Says*, offered a bounty of $10,000 on the officer, Lieutenant Colonel Weldon Hunnicutt, who decided to carry out the bloody and useless repeat attack on "Hamburger Hill" in 1969. By 1971, estimates were that in the famed Americal Division fraggings occurred about once a week. https://libcom.org/history/1961-1973-gi-resistance-in-the-vietnam-war.

9. The fullest analysis of the class dimensions of the military is Christian G. Appy, *Working-Class War: American Combat Soldiers and Vietnam* (Chapel Hill: University of North Carolina Press, 1993).

10. Fred Gardner has said that the direct inspiration was initially The Committee cabaret in San Francisco, more like a theater than a coffeehouse. See his comment to David Parsons, "How Coffeehouses Fueled the Vietnam Peace Movement," *New York Times*, Jan. 9, 2018.

11. https://www.counterpunch.org/2018/01/16/gi-coffeehouses-recalled-a-compliment-from-general-westmoreland/. Accessed May 4, 2017.

12. The best summary of the work of the GI antiwar movement is contained in Ron Carver, David Cortright, and Barbara Doherty, ed., *Waging Peace in Vietnam: U.S. Soldiers and Veterans Who Opposed the War* (New York: New Village Press, 2019).

13. What he actually said in his powerful testimony to the Senate Foreign Relations Committee was: "How do you ask a man to be the last man to die for a mistake?" Many now would quarrel that the war could not be characterized as a "mistake."

14. See, for example, Stephen B. Young, "The Birth of 'Vietnamization,'" *New York Times*, April 28, 2017, https://www.nytimes.com/2017/04/28/opinion/the-birth-of-vietnamization.html. Accessed May 1, 2017: "On Oct. 14, 1966, Secretary of Defense Robert McNamara, who had been principally responsible for waging war against the Communists in South Vietnam, threw in the towel. A little over a year before he officially resigned as secretary, he sent a long memorandum to President Lyndon Johnson, artfully admitting that he and his Pentagon had no strategy to end the war on favorable terms for the South Vietnamese. . . . It was [Ellsworth] Bunker whose role Johnson considered most pivotal. It was about more than being America's top diplomat in South Vietnam. It was about getting America out of the war. 'I had gotten him out of the Dominican Republic and accomplished his political objective there,' he told me in an interview. 'He wanted me to do the same in South Vietnam.'"

15. By the time the United States ended its Southeast Asian bombing campaigns, experts now approximate, the total tonnage of ordnance dropped approximately tripled the totals for World War II. The Indochinese bombings amounted to 7,662,000 tons of explosives, compared to 2,150,000 tons in the world conflict. Cf. R. B. Frankum, *Like Rolling Thunder: The Air War in Vietnam, 1964–1975* (Lanham, MD: Rowman & Littlefield Publishers, 2005).

16. In "How US Aerial Bombing During the Vietnam War Backfired," Robert Farley argues that a "new survey on the use of aerial bombing during the Vietnam War has seemingly confirmed what many suspected: the systematic bombing of South Vietnam detracted from, rather than furthered, U.S. war aims." http://thediplomat.com/2016/08/how-us-aerial-bombing-during-the-vietnam-war-backfired/. Accessed May 4, 2017.

17. "From 1964 to 1973, as part of the Secret War operation conducted during the Vietnam War, the US military dropped 260 million cluster bombs—about 2.5 million tons of munitions—on Laos over the course of 580,000 bombing missions. This is equivalent to a planeload of bombs being unloaded every eight minutes, 24 hours a day, for nine years—nearly seven bombs for every man, woman and child living in Laos. It is more than all the bombs dropped on Europe throughout World War II, leaving Laos, a country approximately the size of Utah, with the unfortunate distinction of being the most heavily bombed country in history." Santi Suthinithet, "Land of a Million Bombs." *Hyphen* Issue 21 (2010)https://hyphen magazine.com/magazine/issue-21-new-legacy-fall-2010/land-million-bombs. Accessed Jan. 26, 2020.

18. L. A. Kauffman, *Direct Action: Protest and the Reinvention of American Radicalism* (Brooklyn: Verso Books, 2017). Excerpted on *Longreads*, https://longreads.com/2017/01/20/in-1971-the-people-didnt-just-march-on-washington-they-shut-it-down/. Accessed May 24, 2017.

19. Chuck O'Connell, "Ideology as History: A Critical Commentary on Burns and Novick's 'The Vietnam War,'" *Counterpunch*, September 21, 2017, https://www.counterpunch.org/2017/09/21/ideology-as-history-a-critical-commentary-on-burns-and-novicks-the-vietnam-war/. Accessed Sept. 25, 2017.

20. That is the argument, with most of which I agree, made by Tom Hayden in *Hell No: The Forgotten Power of the Vietnam Peace Movement* (New Haven: Yale University Press, 2017).

Chapter Eleven

1. *The Dream of a Common Language* (New York: W. W. Norton, 1978), 73.

2. Adrienne Rich, *Diving into the Wreck*. (New York: W. W. Norton, 1973), 23.

3. For a description of a horrible instance, see Susan Faludi, "Death of a Revolutionary: Shulamith Firestone helped to create a new society. But she couldn't live in it," *New Yorker*, April 15, 2013, http://www.newyorker.com/magazine/2013/04/15/death-of-a-revolutionary. Accessed April 11, 2017. See also, Joreen [Jo Freeman], "Trashing: The Dark Side of Sisterhood," *Ms. Magazine* (April 1976): 49–51, 92–98.

4. The work would not be completed until late in the 1970s when I had access to the library at the Ohio State University, and to its international data base, OCLC; my bibliography was not published in final form until early in the 1980s, though typed or mimeographed drafts circulated earlier, sometimes with related works like Elaine Reuben and Deborah Rosenfelt, "Affirmative Interactions in Literature and Criticism: Some Suggestions for Reading and Research" (Mimeographed). MLA Commission on the Status of Women in the Profession, Dec. 1974. Among other items, this contained Tillie Olsen's invaluable reading lists from the *Women's Studies Newsletter* (vol. 1, no. 1 [1972], nos. 3, 4 [1973]; vol. 2, no. 1 [1974]); and Sonny San Juan's "Provisional Listing for Third-World Literature/Culture Courses," a bibliography from the *Radical Caucus Newsletter* 10 (July–August 1973).

5. "Mr. Eliot Meet Miss Lowell and, ah, Mr. Brown," *Critical Theory and the Teaching of Literature*, James Slevin and Art Young, eds. (Urbana, IL: NCTE, 1996), 258–69; and "Amy Lowell and Cultural Borders," *Speaking the Other Self: New Essays on American Literature*, Jeanne Campbell Reesman, ed. (Athens: University of Georgia Press, 1997), 288–96.

6. E.g., "Teaching Lydia Sigourney," *Teaching Nineteenth-Century American Poetry*, eds. Paula Bennett, Karen Kilcup, and Philipp Schweighauser (New York: Modern Language Association, 2007), 109–24.

7. My essay "Sigourney's Poetry of Death" is included in *Lydia Sigourney: Critical Essays and Cultural Views*, Mary Louise Kete and Elizabeth Petrino, eds. (Amherst and Boston: University of Massachusetts Press, 2018), 195–209.

8. The Reprints Advisory Board, as it was formally called, included Mari Jo Buhle, Ellen Cantarow, Blanche Wiesen Cook, Marsha Darling, Ellen DuBois, Moira Ferguson, Elaine Hedges, Florence Howe, Louis Kampf, Alice Kessler-Harris, Paul Lauter, Dora Odarenko, Marilyn Richardson, Catharine Stimpson, Amy Swerdlow, Rosalyn Terborg-Penn, Mary Helen Washington, Marilyn Young.

9. Janice MacKinnon and Stephen R. MacKinnon, *Agnes Smedley: The Life and Times of an American Radical* (Berkeley: University of California Press, 1988).

10. "Society and the Profession, 1958–1983," *Publications of the Modern Language Association* (centennial issue), 99 (May 1984): 414–26.

11. "Caste and Race in the Shaping of the American Literary Canon: A Case Study from the Twenties," *Feminist Studies* 9 (Fall 1983): 435–63.

Chapter Twelve

1. "Retrenchment—What the Managers Are Doing," no. 1 (1975): 27–35; "Notes on Strategies: A Summation," no. 5 (July 1977): 23–25; "The Assault on the Public Sector in New York," no. 11 (March 1979): 8–9.

2. Staughton Lynd and Daniel Gross, *Labor Law for the Rank and Filer: Building Solidarity While Staying Clear of the Law*, 2nd Edition (Oakland, CA: PM Press, 2011).

3. See my "The Scandalous Misuse of Faculty—Adjuncts," *Canons and Contexts* (New York: Oxford University Press, 1991): 198–209. Much of the article was first published in the UUP magazine, *Universitas*, in December 1978, and in somewhat different form in *The Chronicle of Higher Education*, May 14, 1979.

4. For a quick summary of some of the statistics, see Jordan Weissmann, "The Ever-Shrinking Role of Tenured College Professors (in 1 Chart)," *The Atlantic*, Apr 10, 2013, https://www.theatlantic.com/business/archive/2013/04/the-ever-shrinking-role-of-tenured-college-professors-in-1-chart/274849/. Accessed May 26, 2019. Weissmann's chart was developed by the American Association of University Professors (AAUP). The *Wikipedia* entry for "adjunct professors in North America" provides as useful a summary of the situation as I have encountered.

5. Barbara Ehrenreich, *Nickel and Dimed* (New York: Metropolitan Books, 2001).

6. "Campus Missionaries—The Laying on of Culture" (Chicago: New University Conference, 1971).

7. E.g., in *Canons and Contexts*. I was encouraged recently by some comments about identity politics, the impact of culture, and university education by Marc Lilla in a *New Yorker* interview, August 25, 2017, https://www.newyorker.com/news/news-desk/a-conversation-with-mark-lilla-on-his-critique-of-identity-politics. Accessed August 25, 2017: "There's got to be some way within the Democratic Party to accept that some people are going to have different views while still standing by the majority view. But when you're involved in identity politics, you don't see that. Your mind is not tuned. And nothing that you learn in the university prepares you to reach out and to speak thematically in this way.

Now, we not only have to speak about identity when it comes to understanding our social problems but we also want to change people's hearts and minds. And that doesn't happen through electoral politics. It happens through our churches, education, it happens through television—'Sesame Street,' 'Murphy Brown,' all these shows sort of made this country a more tolerant place."

8. In fact, the Nazis held a "Degenerate Music" ("Entartete Musik") exhibition in Dusseldorf in 1938; the poster for it contained virtually every racial stereotype they could conjure up: a big-lipped black saxophone player wearing a top hat, a red tuxedo, and a "Jewish" star.

9. The list is that of W. D. Ehrhart, a Vietnam vet and an excellent poet, in "Viet Nam: Lessons Learned and Not Learned," *Full Disclosure: Truth About America's War in Viet Nam,* Summer 2017: 1, 12–15.

10. From H. H. Lewis's book *Thinking of Russia* (1932). Thanks to Cary Nelson for resurrecting Lewis's poem in *Repression and Recovery: Modern American Poetry and the Politics of Cultural Memory, 1910–1945* (Madison: University of Wisconsin Press, 1989), 49.

11. *New York Times,* Metropolitan Section, June 23, 2019, p. 5.

12. Harold Bloom, *The Western Canon: The Books and School of the Ages* (New York: Harcourt Brace, 1994).

13. E.g., "On the Implications of the Heath Anthology: Response to Ruland," *American Literary History* 4 (summer 1992): 329–33. "The Heath Anthology and Cultural Boundaries," *English Studies/Culture Studies: Institutionalizing Change,* Isaiah Smithson and Nancy Ruff, eds. (Urbana: University of Illinois Press, 1994), 180–90.

14. In fact, it was a huge group since we solicited and received proposals from hundreds of colleagues.

15. The members of that initial editorial board were, in addition to myself, Juan Bruce-Novoa, Jackson Bryer, Elaine Hedges, Amy Ling, Daniel Littlefield, Wendy Martin, Charles Molesworth, Carla Mulford, Raymund Paredes, Hortense Spillers, Linda Wagner-Martin, Andrew Wiget, and Richard Yarborough.

16. See, for one example of the process of recovery still underway, Mary Chapman, "Finding Edith Eaton," *Legacy* 29, no. 2 (2012): 263–69. Another instance is provided by Robert Dale Parker in recovering the work of Jane Johnston Schoolcraft, *The Sound the Stars Make Rushing Through the Sky: The Writings of Jane Johnston Schoolcraft* (Philadelphia: University of Pennsylvania Press, 2007). See also my "Looking a Gift Horse in the Mouth," *Canons and Contexts* (New York: Oxford University Press, 1991), 243–55.

17. See Dan Tannacito, "Poetry of the Colorado Miners: 1903–1906." *Radical Teacher,* no. 15 (March, 1980), 1–8.

18. Consider the story told by Noam N. Levey, "Soaring Insurance Deductibles and High Drug Prices Hit Sick Americans with a 'Double Whammy,'" *Los Angeles Times,* June 6, 2019, PORTSIDE@LISTS.PORTSIDE.ORG. Accessed June 25, 2019.

19. For a useful argument about this issue, see Paul Krugman, "Notes on Excessive Wealth Disorder," *New York Times,* June 25, 2019, https://nyti.ms/2MWxLBQ. Accessed June 25, 2019.

20. *Clovernook Sketches and Other Stories,* Judith Fetterley, ed. (New Brunswick: Rutgers University Press, 1987).

21. See my "Mr. Eliot Meet Miss Lowell and, ah, Mr. Brown." Brown's speaker presents Ma Rainey's singing about a Mississippi River flood as a transformative experience for her listeners. The impact and the subject matter of her art differ strikingly from that of Eliot in "Prufrock."

22. Toni Morrison, *Playing in the Dark: Whiteness and the Literary Imagination* (Cambridge: Harvard University Press, 1992), 5. It seems to me of interest that Morrison uses four lines from Eliot's *Preludes IV* as the epigraph for chapter one.

23. *Literature, Class, and Culture: An Anthology*, edited with an introduction (with Ann Fitzgerald) (New York: Addison, Wesley, Longman, 2001); *A History of American Working-Class Literature*, edited with introduction (with Nicholas Coles) (New York and Cambridge: Cambridge University Press, 2017).

24. William Andrews has recently published a study of the ways in which class differences affected the lives and writings of slaves. See William L. Andrews, *Slavery and Class in the American South: A Generation of Slave Narrative Testimony, 1840–1865* (New York: Oxford University Press, 2019).

25. For the syllabus, see appendix B.

Chapter Thirteen

1. A Gallup poll of Aug. 13, 2018, finds that "47% of Democrats view capitalism positively, down from 56% in 2016." https://news.gallup.com/poll/240725/democrats-positive-socialism-capitalism.aspx. Accessed 25 October, 2018. The Gallup poll also indicates that about 58 percent of Democrats have a positive view of socialism, however it might be defined. Gallup also remarks that "the drop in Democrats' positive views of capitalism this year has for the first time left Democrats more positive about socialism as a concept than about capitalism."

2. Binyamin Appelbaum and Jim Tankersley, "What Could Kill Booming U.S. Economy? 'Socialists,' White House Warns," https://www.nytimes.com/2018/10/23/us/politics/socialist-democrats-trump-elections.html. Accessed Oct. 26, 2018.

3. Euell Theophilus Gibbons, *Stalking the Wild Asparagus* (Chambersburg, PA: Alan C Hood & Company, 1962).

SELECTED BIBLIOGRAPHY

Most bibliographies use either an author-date system, which is designed to support in-text notes, or list all items to which notes refer. This bibliography is, rather, selective. I omit books and articles recorded in the notes but which really do not bear on the subject of *Our Sixties*. I've also omitted from the bibliography references to individual items or folders in the archival collections I have set up at Trinity College's Watkinson Library, though their locations are in the notes. I have, by contrast, included in the bibliography some books and articles that I have not cited in the notes because they significantly influenced my thinking about the sixties. But this bibliography is by no means a comprehensive listing of significant work about the sixties; that would entail a volume by itself.

I have listed at the end of the bibliography items of which I was author or coauthor, editor or coeditor, and which are relevant to *Our Sixties*.

Adler, Renata. "Letter from the Palmer House." *New Yorker* (Sept. 23, 1967). https://www.newyorker.com/magazine/1967/09/23/letter-from-the-palmer-house.

Akuno, Kali, and Ajamu Nangwaya, with Cooperation Jackson. *Jackson Rising: The Struggle for Economic Democracy and Black Self-Determination in Jackson, Mississippi*. Jackson: Daraja Press, 2017.

Andrews, William L. *Slavery and Class in the American South: A Generation of Slave Narrative Testimony, 1840–1865*. New York: Oxford, 2019.

Angulo, A.J. *Diploma Mills: How For-Profit Colleges Stiffed Students, Taxpayers, and the American Dream*. Baltimore: Johns Hopkins Press, 2016.

Appelbaum, Binyamin, and Jim Tankersley. "What Could Kill Booming U.S. Economy? 'Socialists,' White House Warns." https://www.nytimes.com/2018/10/23/us/politics/socialist-democrats-trump-elections.html.

Appy, Christian G. *Working-Class War: American Combat Soldiers and Vietnam*. Chapel Hill: University of North Carolina Press, 1993.

Borton, Lady. "Overlooking My Lai." http://vietnamfulldisclosure.org/index.php/overlooking-my-lai/.

Bouie, Jamelle. "Why Bernie Sanders Isn't Afraid of 'Socialism.'" *New York Times*, June 17, 2019. https://www.nytimes.com/2019/06/17/opinion/bernie-sanders-socialism.html.

Branch, Taylor. *Pillar of Fire: America in the King Years, 1963–1964.* New York: Simon & Schuster, 1998.

Brick, Allan R. "Final Report on the National Defense Education Act Institute for Teachers of Disadvantaged Youth." Code GE-7441. Goucher College, 1965, p. 7.

———. *Up From Chester: Hiroshima, Haverford and Beyond.* Bloomington, IN: XLibris, 2009.

Burke, Edward C. "320 Vow to Help Draft Resisters, Some Plan Disobedience to Challenge Government." *New York Times*, Sept. 27, 1967.

Carver, Ron, David Cortright, and Barbara Doherty, eds. *Waging Peace in Vietnam; U.S. Soldiers and Veterans Who Opposed the War.* New York: New Village Press, 2019.

Cary, Alice. *Clovernook Sketches and Other Stories.* Judith Fetterley, ed. New Brunswick: Rutgers University Press, 1987.

Catsam, Derek Charles. *Freedom's Main Line: The Journey of Reconciliation and the Freedom Rides.* Lexington, Kentucky: University of Kentucky Press, 2009.

Chambers, John Whiteclay, ed. *The Oxford Companion to American Military History.* New York: Oxford University Press, 2000.

Chapman, Mary. "Finding Edith Eaton." *Legacy* 29, 2 (2012): 263–69.

Clinton, Hillary. "I still believe in American exceptionalism." http://www.cbsnews.com/videos/hillary-clinton-i-still-believe-in-american-exceptionalism.

CNN Library. "Vietnam War Fast Facts." http://www.cnn.com/2013/07/01/world/vietnam-war-fast-facts.

Cobb, Charles E. Jr., *On the Road to Freedom: A Guided Tour of the Civil Rights Train.* Chapel Hill: Algonquin Books, 2008.

Conroy, F. Hilary. "The Conference on Peace Research in History: A Memoir." *Journal of Peace Research* (Special Issue on Peace Research in History) 6, no. 4 (1969): 385–88.

CREDO (Center for Research on Education Outcomes). *National Charter School Study,* Executive Summary 2013. Stanford, CA: Center for Research on Education Outcomes, 2013.

Davidson, Cathy N. *The New Education: How to Revolutionize the University to Prepare Students for a World In Flux.* New York: Basic Books, 2017.

DeVoto, Bernard. *The History of the United States*. New York: Holt, Rinehart and Winston, 1967–68, II, 353.

Dirks, Annelieke. "Between Threat and Reality: The National Association for the Advancement of Colored People and the Emergence of Armed Self-Defense in Clarksdale and Natchez, Mississippi, 1960–1965." *Journal for the Study of Radicalism* 1, no. 1 (2007): 71–93.

Dittmer, John. *Local People: The Struggle for Civil Rights in Mississippi*. Urbana: University of Illinois Press, 1994.

Duncan, Donald. *The New Legions*. New York: Random House, 1967.

Echols, Alice. *"Daring to Be Bad": Radical Feminism in America, 1967–1975*. Minneapolis: University of Minnesota Press, 1989.

Eckstein, Arthur M. *Bad Moon Rising: How the Weather Underground Beat the FBI and Lost the Revolution*. New Haven: Yale, 2016.

Edmonds, Michael, ed. *Risking Everything: A Freedom Summer Reader*. Madison: Wisconsin Historical Society, 2014.

Ehrhart, W. D. "Viet Nam: Lessons Learned and Not Learned." *Full Disclosure: Truth About America's War in Viet Nam*. Summer 2017: 1, 12–15.

Faludi, Susan. "Death of a Revolutionary: Shulamith Firestone helped to create a new society. But she couldn't live in it." *New Yorker*, April 15, 2013. http://www.newyorker.com/magazine/2013/04/15/death-of-a-revolutionary.

Farley, Robert. "How US Aerial Bombing During the Vietnam War Backfired." http://thediplomat.com/2016/08/how-us-aerial-bombing-during-the-vietnam-war-backfired/.

Flacks, Mickey, and Dick Flacks. *Making History / Making Blintzes: How Two Red Diaper Babies Found Each Other and Discovered America*. New Brunswick: Rutgers University Press, 2018.

Foley, Michael S. *Confronting the War Machine: Draft Resistance During the Vietnam War*. Chapel Hill: University of North Carolina Press, 2003.

Frankum, R. B. *Like Rolling Thunder: The Air War in Vietnam, 1964–1975*. Lanham, MD: Rowman & Littlefield Publishers, 2005.

Gardner, Fred. [On GI coffeehouses.] https://www.counterpunch.org/2018/01/16/gi-coffeehouses-recalled-a-compliment-from-general-westmoreland/.

Gettleman, Marvin E. *Vietnam: History, Documents, and Opinions on a Major World Crisis*. New York: Fawcett Publications, 1965.

Gillen, Jay. *Educating for Insurgency: The Roles of Young People in Schools of Poverty*. Oakland: AK Press, 2014.

Guillory, John. *Cultural Capital: The Problem of Literary Canon Formation*. Chicago: University of Chicago Press, 1993.

Hall, Simon. "On the Tail of the Panther: Black Power and the 1967 Convention of the National Conference for New Politics." *Journal of American Studies.* 37, no. 1 (April 2003): 59–78.

Hastie, Mike. "The Purposeful Killing of Civilians in War: Voices From Vietnam." *Counterpunch,* Sept. 29, 2017. https://www.counterpunch.org/2017/09/29/the-purposeful-killing-of-civilians-in-war-voices-from-vietnam/.

Hastings, Max. *Vietnam: An Epic Tragedy, 1945–75.* New York: HarperCollins, 2018.

Hayden, Tom. *Hell No: The Forgotten Power of the Vietnam Peace Movement.* New Haven: Yale University Press, 2017.

Heilig, Julian Vasquez. "National and Urban NAEP Results: Neighborhood Public Schools 23, Charters 4." *Cloaking Inequity,* May 16, 2017. https://cloakinginequity.com/2017/05/16/national-and-urban-naep-results-neighborhood-public-schools-23-charters-4/.

Henig. Peter. "Selective Service System Or, the Manpower Channelers." Boston: New England Free Press, [1967]. A reprint from *New Left Notes,* January 20, 1967.

Henry, Jules. *Culture Against Man.* New York: Random House, 1963.

Hess, Martha. *Then the Americans Came.* New Brunswick: Rutgers University Press, 1993.

Heinl, Robert D. Jr. "The Collapse of the Armed Forces." *Armed Forces Journal,* June 7, 1971.

House, Tanya Clay. *Grading the States June 2018: A Report Card on Our Nation's Commitment to Public Schools.* New York: Network for Public Education and the Schott Foundation for Public Education, 2018. http://schottfoundation.org/sites/default/files/grading-the-states.pdf.

Hudson, Winson, and Constance Curry. *Mississippi Harmony: Memoirs of a Freedom Fighter.* New York: Palgrave McMillan, 2002.

Joreen [Jo Freeman]. "Trashing: The Dark Side of Sisterhood." *Ms. Magazine* 5 (April 1976): 49–51, 92–98.

Kampf, Louis, and Paul Lauter. "Introduction" to *The Politics of Literature.* New York: Pantheon, 1970, pp. 34–40.

Kauffman, L. A. *Direct Action: Protest and the Reinvention of American Radicalism.* Brooklyn: Verso Books, 2017. Excerpted on *Longreads,* https://longreads.com/2017/01/20/in-1971-the-people-didnt-just-march-on-washington-they-shut-it-down/.

Kelley, Robin D. G. "Black Study, Black Struggle." *Boston Review,* March 7, 2016. Portside: https://portside.org/2016-03-16/black-study-black-struggle.

King, Gilbert. *Devil in the Grove: Thurgood Marshall, the Groveland Boys, and the Dawn of a New America.* New York: Harper Collins, 2012.

Kirp, David L. "Who Needs Charters When You Have Public Schools Like These?" *New York Times Sunday Review,* April 2, 2017, p. 2.

Krugman, Paul. "Notes on Excessive Wealth Disorder." *New York Times,* June 25, 2019. https://nyti.ms/2rTwUKP.

Kupferberg, Tuli, and Robert Bashlow. *1001 Ways to Beat the Draft.* New York: Oliver Layton Press—and also Birth Press, 1966.

Kwon, Heonik. *After the Massacre: Commemoration and Consolation in Ha My and My-Lai.* Berkeley: University of California Press, 2006.

Letters from Mississippi: Reports from Civil Rights Volunteers & Poetry of the 1964 Freedom Summer. Elizabeth Martinez, ed. Brookline, MA: Zephyr Press, 2007, pp. 279–315.

Levey, Noam N. "Soaring Insurance Deductibles and High Drug Prices Hit Sick Americans with a 'Double Whammy.'" *Los Angeles Times,* June 6, 2019.

Lewis, R. W. B. *The American Adam.* Chicago: University of Chicago Press, 1955.

Lincoln, Abraham. "Speech of 12 January, 1848, in U.S. House of Representatives." https://teachingamericanhistory.org/library/document/the-war-with-mexico-speech-in-the-united-states-house-of-representatives/

Longley, Kyle. "The Grunt's War." *New York Times,* Feb. 17, 2017.

MacKinnon, Janice, and Stephen R. MacKinnon. *Agnes Smedley: The Life and Times of an American Radical.* Berkeley: University of California Press, 1988.

Marx, Leo. *The Machine in the Garden: Technology and the Pastoral Ideal in America.* New York: Oxford, 1964.

Medsger, Betty. *The Burglary: The Discovery of J. Edgar Hoover's Secret FBI.* New York: Vintage, 2014.

Miller, Perry. *Errand into the Wilderness.* Cambridge: Belknap Press, 1956.

Miller, Rann. "Why the NAACP Said 'Enough' to School Privatization." *AlterNet* [2], July 27, 2017. http://www.alternet.org/print/naacp-school-privatization.

Moody, Anne. *Coming of Age in Mississippi.* New York: Dell, 1972 (1968).

Morrison, Toni. *Playing in the Dark: Whiteness and the Literary Imagination.* Cambridge: Harvard University Press, 1992.

Nelson, Cary. *Repression and Recovery: Modern American Poetry and the Politics of Cultural Memory, 1910–1945.* Madison: University of Wisconsin Press, 1989.

Nguyen, Viet Thanh. "The Great Vietnam War Novel Was Not Written by an American." *New York Times,* May 2, 2017. https://www.nytimes.

com/2017/05/02/opinion/vietnam-war-novel-was-not-written-by-an-american.html?_r=0.

North, Gary. "The Libertarian Roots of the All-Volunteer Military." https://www.lewrockwell.com/2003/12/gary-north/the-libertarian-roots-of-the-volunteer-military/.

O'Connell, Chuck. "Ideology as History: a Critical Commentary on Burns and Novick's 'The Vietnam War.'" *Counterpunch*, September 21, 2017. https://www.counterpunch.org/2017/09/21/ideology-as-history-a-critical-commentary-on-burns-and-novicks-the-vietnam-war/.

Oglesby, Carl. "Let Us Shape the Future," in Mitchell Cohen and Dennis Hale, eds. *The New Student Left*. Boston: Beacon Press, 1967; also http://www.studentsforademocraticsociety.org/documents/oglesby_future.html.

Oppenheimer, Martin. "Pages from a Journal of the Middle Left." *Radical Sociologists and the Movement: Experiences, Lessons, and Legacies*. Ed. Martin Oppenheimer, Martin J. Murray, Rhonda F. Levine. Philadelphia: Temple University Press, 1991, pp. 113–27.

Paolino, Ernest N. *The Foundations of the American Empire: William Henry Seward and U.S. Foreign Policy*. Ithaca, NY: Cornell University Press, 1973.

Parker, Robert Dale. *The Sound the Stars Make Rushing Through the Sky: The Writings of Jane Johnston Schoolcraft*. Philadelphia: University of Pennsylvania Press, 2007.

Parsons, David. "How Coffeehouses Fueled the Vietnam Peace Movement." *New York Times*, Jan. 9, 2018.

Passow, A. Harry, et al. *Toward Creating A Model Urban School System—A Study of the Washington, D.C. Public Schools*. Columbia Univ., New York: Teachers College, 1967.

Payne, Charles M. *I've Got the Light of Freedom: The Organizing Tradition and the Mississippi Freedom Struggle*. Berkeley: University of California Press, 1995.

Peretz, Martin. "The American Left & Israel." *Commentary* (Nov. 1, 1967). https://www.*commentarymagazine.com/articles/the-american-left-israel/*.

Peters, Shawn Francis. *The Catonsville Nine: A Story of Faith and Resistance in the Vietnam Era*. NY: Oxford, 2012.

Pincus, Fred L., and Howard J. Ehrlich. "The New University Conference: A Study of Former Members." *Critical Sociology* 15, no. 2 (Summer 1988): 145–47.

Potter, Paul. "We Must Name the System." https://www.marktribe.net/port-huron-project/we-must-name-the-system-paul-potter-1965-2007.

Putnam, Lara, and Theda Skocpol. "Middle America Reboots Democracy." *Democracy, A Journal of Ideas,* February 20, 2018. https://democracy-journal.org/arguments/middle-america-reboots-democracy/.

Radical Teacher 40 (Fall 1991). Issue containing Freedom School curriculum.

Redding, J. Saunders. *Lonesome Road: The Story of the Negro's Part in America.* New York: Doubleday, 1958.

Reuben, Elaine, and Deborah Rosenfelt. "Affirmative Interactions in Literature and Criticism: Some Suggestions for Reading and Research" (Mimeographed). MLA Commission on the Status of Women in the Profession, Dec. 1974.

Rich, Adrienne. *Diving into the Wreck.* New York: Norton, 1973.

———. *The Dream of a Common Language.* New York, Norton, 1978.

Rothstein, Richard. "A Short History of ERAP." http://content.cdlib.org/view?docId=kt4k4003k7.

Rottmann, Larry, Jan Barry, Basil T. Paquet, eds. *Winning Hearts and Minds.* Brooklyn, NY: First Casualty Press, 1972.

Rudin, Sherwood. "I Defended the Pentagon in 1967, But I Was Torn between Duty and Conscience." https://nyti.ms/2Fjb32q.

Scheer, Robert. *How the US Got Involved in Vietnam.* Santa Barbara: Center for the Study of Democratic Institutions, 1965.

Sherrod, Charles. "Notes on the Democratic National Convention Challeng." In Edmonds, *Risking Everything,* pp. 180–86.

Smith, Henry Nash. *Virgin Land: The American West as Symbol and Myth.* Cambridge: Harvard University Press, 1950.

Stand, Kurt. "The Election Within the Election." *The Stansbury Forum,* November 13, 2018. https://stansburyforum.com/2018/11/13/the-election-within-the-election.

Students for a Democratic Society. "Chester Report, Submitted by the Swarthmore College Chapter of Students for a Democratic Society." http://www.educationanddemocracy.org/FSCfiles/C_CC2b_ChesterPA.htm.

Suthinithet, Santi. "Land of a Million Bombs." *Hyphen,* issue 21 (2010). https://hyphenmagazine.com/magazine/issue-21-new-legacy-fall-2010/land-million-bombs.

Tannacito, Dan. "Poetry of the Colorado Miners: 1903–1906." *Radical Teacher* 15 (March 1980): 1–8.

Tax, Sol. *The Draft: A Handbook of Facts and Alternatives.* Chicago: University of Chicago Press, 1967.

Thomas, P. L. "The Self-Fulfilling Prophesy: Failing Public Schools." https:// radicalscholarship.wordpress.com/2017/03/06/the-self-fulfilling-prophesy-failing-public-schools/.

Tucker, William H. "Moral Imperatives: The Reasons for Radicals." *Princeton Radicals of the 1960s, Then and Now.* Jefferson, NC: McFarland & Company, Inc., 2015, pp. 19–54.

Turse, Nick. *Kill Anything That Moves: The Real American War in Vietnam.* New York: Henry Holt, 2013.

Umoja, Akinyele K. "1964: The Beginning of the End of Nonviolence in the Mississippi Freedom Movement." *Radical History Review* 85 (Winter 2003): 201–26.

United States Government Accountability Office. "For-Profit Colleges: Undercover Testing Finds Colleges Encouraged Fraud and Engaged in Deceptive and Questionable Marketing Practices," GAO-10-948T, August 4, 2010. http://www.gao.gov/new.items/d10948t.pdf.

Watson, Bruce. *Freedom Summer: The Savage Season That Made Mississippi Burn and Made America a Democracy.* New York: Viking, 2010.

Weissmann, Jordan. "The Ever-Shrinking Role of Tenured College Professors (in 1 Chart)." *The Atlantic,* Apr 10, 2013. https://www.theatlantic.com/business/archive/2013/04/the-ever-shrinking-role-of-tenured-college-professors-in-1-chart/274849/.

Wilkerson. Cathy. *Flying Close to the Sun: My Life and Times as a Weatherman.* NY: Seven Stories Press, 2007.

Williams, Junius. "Selma Marchers Jailed, Segregated in Alabama Prison." *The Amherst Student* XCIX, no. 41 (April 1, 1965): 5.

Young, Stephen B. "The Birth of 'Vietnamization.'" *New York Times,* April 28, 2017, https://www.nytimes.com/2017/04/28/opinion/the-birth-of-vietnamization.html.

Zinn, Howard. *The Indispensable Zinn: The Essential Writings of the "People's Historian."* Ed. Timothy Patrick McCarthy. New York: New Press, 2012.

———. *A People's History of the United States.* New York: Harper & Row, 1980.

———. *You Can't Be Neutral on a Moving Train—A Personal History of Our Times.* Boston: Beacon, 1994.

Relevant Articles and Books by Paul Lauter

"The American Draft and Its Opponents." *La democracie nouvelle* (Spring 1967): 116–20.

"Amy Lowell and Cultural Borders." *Speaking the Other Self: New Essays on American Literature,* Jeanne Campbell Reesman, ed. Athens: University of Georgia Press, 1997, 288–96.

"The Assault on the Public Sector in New York." *Radical Teacher* 11 (March 1979): 8–9.

"Canon Formation." In David Wyatt, ed., *American Literature in Transition, 1960–1970.* Cambridge: Cambridge University Press, 2018, 352–65.

Canons and Contexts. New York: Oxford, 1991.

"Caste and Race in the Shaping of the American Literary Canon: A Case Study from the Twenties." *Feminist Studies* 9 (Fall 1983): 435–63.

With Florence Howe. *The Conspiracy of the Young.* New York & Cleveland: World, 1970.

With Richard Flacks and Florence Howe. "The Draft: Dodging the Issues." *New York Review of Books* 5 (April 6, 1967): 3–5.

With Richard Flacks and Florence Howe. "The Draft: Reform or Resistance." *Liberation* (January 1967): 34–39.

"The Heath Anthology and Cultural Boundaries," *English Studies/ Culture Studies: Institutionalizing Change*, Isaiah Smithson and Nancy Ruff, eds. Urbana: University of Illinois Press, 1994, 180–90.

With Nicholas Coles. *A History of American Working-Class Literature*, edited with Introduction. New York and Cambridge: Cambridge University Press, 2017.

With Florence Howe. "How the School System Is Rigged for Failure." *The New York Review of Books* 14 (June 18, 1970): 14–21.

With Ann Fitzgerald. *Literature, Class, and Culture: An Anthology*, edited with an introduction. New York: Addison, Wesley, Longman, 2001.

"Mr. Eliot Meet Miss Lowell and, ah, Mr. Brown." *Critical Theory and the Teaching of Literature.* James Slevin and Art Young, eds. Urbana, IL: NCTE, 1996, 258–69.

"Notes on Strategies: A Summation." *Radical Teacher* 5 (July 1977): 23–25.

"Retrenchment—What the Managers Are Doing." *Radical Teacher* 1 (1975): 27–35.

"The Short Happy Life of the Adams-Morgan Community School Project." *Harvard Educational Review* 38 (Spring 1968): 235–62.

"Sigourney's Poetry of Death." *Lydia Sigourney: Critical Essays and Cultural Views.* Mary Louise Kete and Elizabeth Petrino, eds. Amherst and Boston: University of Massachusetts Press, 2018, 195–209.

"Teaching Lydia Sigourney." *Teaching Nineteenth-Century American Poetry*, Paula Bennett, Karen Kilcup, and Philipp Schweighauser eds. New York: Modern Language Association, 2007, 109–24.

With Florence Howe. "Urban Schools: The School Mess in Washington." *New York Review of Books* 10 (Feb. 1, 1968): 16–21.

INDEX